Brigham Young

AND THE EXPANDING AMERICAN FRONTIER

Newell G. Bringhurst

Brigham Young

AND THE EXPANDING AMERICAN FRONTIER

Edited by Oscar Handlin

LITTLE, BROWN AND COMPANY • BOSTON • TORONTO

Library of Congress Cataloging-in-Publication Data

Bringhurst, Newell G.
  Brigham Young and the expanding American frontier.

  (The Library of American biography)
  Bibliography: p.
  Includes index.
  1. Young, Brigham, 1801–1877. 2. Mormon Church—
Presidents—Biography. 3. Church of Jesus Christ of
Latter-Day Saints—Presidents—Biography. 4. Utah—
History. 5. Frontier and pioneer life—Utah. I. Handlin,
Oscar, 1915–   . II. Title. III. Series.
BX8695.Y7B7 1986   289.3'32'0924 [B]   85-19796
ISBN 0-673-39322-4

Library of Congress Catalog Card no. 85-19796

ISBN 0-673-39322-4

9 8 7 6 5 4 3 2

Published simultaneously in Canada
by Little, Brown & Company (Canada) Limited

Printed in the United States of America

Produced by Newcomer/Muncil Associates

to my father
George Smith Bringhurst
and to the memory of my mother
Alice Cooper Bringhurst

both of whom taught me the value of hard work,
perseverance, and striving for success

Editor's Preface

THE HILL COUNTRY of northern New England, in the early nineteenth century, drove its sons and daughters away. Their parents had come north, up the river valleys, in the search for opportunity, attracted by the promise of available land and by the hope of remedying the failures of the places of their birth. By 1800, the inadequacies of Vermont and New Hampshire were apparent, and young people not content to stay where they were looked west. The Mohawk Valley of New York, and beyond that the virgin lands of Ohio, were the magnets that drew them on.

Brigham Young was among those who responded, carrying with him the Yankee heritage that valued hard work, striving for success, and a sense that all experience was part of God's will. He settled for a time near Rochester, a district repeatedly burned over by religious revivals. There he became a member of the Church of Jesus Christ of Latter-day Saints, founded by Joseph Smith, also a migrant from Vermont. With Smith, Young moved to the settlements the Mormons founded in Kirtland, Ohio; Independence, Missouri; and Nauvoo, Illinois.

When a furious mob murdered Smith, Young assumed the leadership of the Mormon survivors and redirected their vision toward new goals. Far beyond the Mississippi, in theretofore unsettled territory, lay the Great Basin to which he led the remnants of the Church and its followers. There Young supervised the building of a new society that soon attracted thousands of newcomers from other parts of the Union and from Europe as well.

The account of his life is thus an American success story, a rise from poor beginnings to power and wealth. But as told in this careful book, it is also a story that illuminates important features of the social history of the United States—religious enthusiasm, the pioneering spirit, and the encounter with the American West.

OSCAR HANDLIN

Author's Preface

MOST AMERICANS KNOW of Brigham Young as the much-married Mormon leader who led his pioneer followers to the far western United States in the midnineteenth century. But in a broader sense, he can be seen as a personification of the expanding American frontier throughout most of the nineteenth century. Born in Vermont in 1801, Young, like many other Americans who reached maturity during this period, possessed a restless desire to escape the confines of life in the settled eastern states. His story of continuous westward migration across the American continent, first into upstate New York, then to the midwest, and finally to the Great Basin, was not unique. His uprootedness paralleled that of countless other nineteenth century Americans, including Andrew Jackson, Sam Houston, and Mark Twain, all of whom migrated west in search of new social, economic, or political opportunities.

Like other frontier Americans, Young and his followers had to deal with a distant federal government that was often represented by less-than-qualified officials insensitive to their needs and problems, with Indians upon whose lands they encroached, and with life in a remote settlement made more difficult because of inadequate transportation and communication.

From another perspective, however, it might be asserted that Brigham Young is not really representative of the expanding American frontier. As a product of the burned-over district of upstate New York, Young reflected a type of religious enthusiasm not always evident along the frontier, where rowdyism rather than religion frequently held sway. Young and his followers, moreover, looked to the frontier, especially its isolation, for the preservation of their unique religious beliefs and practices (particularly polygamy). In this regard, however, Young and the Mormons did not differ much from other Western types, such as fur traders, miners, or cowboys, who often retreated to the remote reaches of the American frontier seeking an isolation in which to preserve distinctive lifestyles.

In the end, of course, these individualists of the frontier were doomed to failure. Improvements in transportation and communication brought in a continuous stream of new settlers and influences from the east. The protective isolation of the frontier was pierced and then ultimately broken down. The year 1890 marked the formal end of the American frontier: the fur trapper had long since disappeared, the independent sourdough miner was replaced by the paid mine laborer, and the cowboy had become a ranchhand. For the Mormons, 1890 also represented an important turning point, because in that year they were forced to give up their distinctive practice of polygamy and to conform to the norm of monogamy. Brigham Young, who had fought so hard to preserve polygamy through frontier isolation, did not witness this defeat, having died in 1877.

Although the abandonment of polygamy was wrenching to the Mormons, their church as an institution adjusted and has become a major American religious denomination in the twentieth century. Its members are assimilated into the mainstream of American political and economic life, but at the same time, they continue to retain certain distinguishing characteristics that mark the Mormons as a unique religious denomination.

NEWELL G. BRINGHURST

Acknowledgments

I am indebted to many people who provided assistance and encouragement in the preparation of this volume. First, I thank the staff of the Archives of Weber State College at Ogden, Utah for allowing me to examine typescript copies of Brigham Young's papers and correspondence. These copies were made from the original Brigham Young papers contained in the Archives of the Church of Jesus Christ of Latter-day Saints (Mormons) in Salt Lake City by the late Donald R. Moorman, professor of history at Weber State College. He collected these materials over a period of twenty years intending to write, before his untimely death, a definitive biography of the early Mormon leader. These materials were made available to me despite their uncatalogued condition thanks to John R. Sillito, Chief Archivist, his assistant James Cartwright, and the family of Donald R. Moorman. I am also grateful to the staff of the Library of the Utah State Historical Society which gave me access to materials on Brigham Young from their collection. Particularly valuable were the Susa Young Gates Papers. These papers compiled by the Mormon leader's most articulate daughter provide an enlightening, often frank view of life within the Young household. Jeffery O. Johnson and Richard Jenson were generous in sharing with me the results of their own research on Brigham Young as a family man and colonizer. Eugene Campbell and Michael Marquardt also provided copies of materials unavailable elsewhere resulting from their own research. I also thank the interlibrary loan staff here at College of the Sequoias, particularly Nancy Finney who secured various primary and secondary materials thus saving me the time and expense of travelling elsewhere to examine these sources.

A number of individuals were particularly helpful as I sought to develop my own biographical portrait of the Mormon leader. Leonard Arrington, Eugene Campbell, Ronald Esplin, Jeffery O. Johnson, and Ronald Walker all shared with me their views and knowledge of Brigham Young and patiently listened as I reflected and tried to get know the Mormon leader.

As I actually wrote my manuscript a number of individuals read all or part of the first two drafts offering valuable suggestions which markedly improved it. These included Susan Collins, Ronald Esplin, Paul Ezelle, Stanford Layton, Michael Marquardt, N.B. (Tad) Martin, Glen Robertson, and Ronald Walker. I am particularly grateful for the assistance of Oscar Handlin, whose incisive, cogent comments on the first draft were invaluable in sharpening its interpretive focus and improving its overall quality.

Also helpful were William Slaughter of the Historical Department-Archives of the Church of Jesus Christ of Latter-day Saints, Susan Whetstone of the Utah State Historical Society, and Thomas G. Alexander, director of the Charles Redd Center for Western Studies at Brigham Young University who provided and gave me permission to use the maps and photographs contained herein. Bradford C. Gray, editor of the College Division of Little, Brown, was extremely helpful in guiding this volume through the peaks and valleys of writing, editing, and production. I also appreciate the help of Newcomer/Muncil and Associates in the production of this volume. Dee Cochran lent her aid in typing the revised draft of the manuscript.

Special thanks go to my immediate family who encouraged me in this project. My father George S. and his wife La

Verne Dalton Bringhurst generously extended to me the hospitality of their home during my stay in Salt Lake City in 1983 while I did the bulk of my primary research. My wife Mary Ann, like Brigham's Mary Ann, made frequent sacrifices in the interest of Brigham Young. She moreover acted as an initial sounding board for my ideas, offered valuable suggestions, typed the first complete draft of the manuscript, and compiled the index. I also appreciate the patient forbearance of my daughter Laura who also helped with the index and tolerated the continuing presence of Brigham Young as a houseguest during the four years that he remained in our midst. All this help notwithstanding, I alone assume full responsibility for this work.

Contents

Brigham Young

AND THE EXPANDING AMERICAN FRONTIER

I

Unsettled Times

BRIGHAM YOUNG, from the moment of his birth on June 1, 1801, was exposed to the uprooted conditions of life along the American frontier. The place of his birth, Whitingham, Vermont, was a frontier community recently opened to settlement following the resolution of a long-standing land patent controversy. Brigham's father, John Young, had settled here in January of 1801, hoping to gain from the region's rocky, hilly soil the means to support his large family of nine children.

Despite their frontier unsettledness, Brigham Young's family roots were actually deep in the soil of eighteenth century New England, where his ancestors had achieved prominence and respectability. His great-grandfather, William Young, was a shoemaker who lived first in New Hampshire and then Hopkinton, Massachusetts, where he prospered and left ten thousand dollars when he died in 1747. Another great-grandfather, Ebenezer Goddard, was a respected land-owner and sheriff of Middlesex County, Massachusetts. On his mother's side, a third great-grandfather, John Howe, served as Hopkinton's first town councilman when that community was chartered in the 1730s. The Howes achieved later prominence through Elias Howe, Jr., the inventor of the sewing machine, and Samuel Gridley Howe, a prominent nineteenth century reformer. Brigham's maternal grandfather, Phinehas Howe, was a respected farmer in Hopkinton. His daughter, Abigail (or Nabby), Brigham's mother,

1

Earliest known photograph of Brigham Young taken in Nauvoo, Illinois during the early 1840s. (Courtesy of the LDS Church Library-Archives. Printed with permission.)

was a beautiful, blue-eyed woman with ash blond hair who had a sprightly sense of humor and was an excellent singer.

The Youngs, Howes, and Goddards were all swept up in the events surrounding the Great Awakening of the 1740s. This religious outpouring, which split New England Congregationalists, also divided Brigham's ancestors. William Young supported those Scotch Presbyterians who had broken away from churches in Boston and believed that Bostonians had watered down the criteria for church participation through the Half-Way Covenant, whereby church membership was extended even to those individuals who had not undergone spiritual conversion. By contrast, John Howe believed that all persons of good intentions should be permitted communion in the Hopkinton congregation to which he belonged, even though they might be unable to meet rigid membership standards. A third Young ancestor, Ebenezer Goddard, accepted the beliefs of John Wesley, the founder of Methodism. Goddard's daughter (Brigham's grandmother) felt that local residents of Hopkinton had not paid sufficient attention to religion. She hoped for a powerful revival to restore people's faith.

However, Joseph Young, Brigham's paternal grandfather, did not concern himself with religious matters and ultimately lost the family's respectability. Trained as a physician, he served in the French and Indian War and later settled in Hopkinton, where he practiced medicine. Here he met and married Betsy Hayden Treadway, an attractive widow with four children. He also fathered six children of his own, including John (Brigham's father), born in 1763. But he was less than successful in his medical practice because of his addiction to alcohol and fondness for gambling.

Tragedy struck in 1769 when Joseph died and left behind not only a widow and ten children but a stack of unpaid bills. Joseph's farm was sold to pay these debts, and every possession covered by law was confiscated. The family was scattered and the children were placed in various homes. John, then six years old, and his four-year-old brother were bound as servants to a wealthy Hopkinton landowner, Colonel John Jones, who held a number of white as well as black servants. Jones, described as a wicked man, routinely whipped his servants, including young John, for the slightest infraction. John endured this situation over the next eleven years.

Finally, in 1780, during the War for American Independence, John Young asserted his personal independence. The small and wiry seventeen-year-old youth left Colonel Jones' farm and enlisted in the Fourth Massachusetts Brigade of Musketry, which came under the regular Continental line army command of General George Washington. Upon his return to Hopkinton, John met and courted Nabby Howe. Her parents strenuously objected to the match, considering John beneath their beloved Nabby. But Nabby and John were married in 1785 in the Congregationalist Church at Hopkinton. The newlyweds established a home in nearby Ashland, near where John worked as a craftsman and millworker. A year later their first child, Nancy, was born, and in 1787 Nabby gave birth to a second daughter, Fanny.

John, however, found life in Hopkinton less than satisfactory and looked for a new place to settle. Like other post-Revolutionary War Americans, he suffered from economic hard times and wanted to get away from his watchful, critical in-laws. John packed up his wife and two young daughters in 1788 or 1789 and moved to Durham, in the Platauva District, on the eastern side of the Catskills in New York. The Youngs, like other restless, hard-pressed New Englanders, looked to this frontier region for a new beginning. Shortly after they arrived there, their third daughter, Rhoda, was born.

Here, John and Nabby shifted their religious affiliation from Puritan Congregationalism to Methodism. They responded to the teachings of a group of Methodist itinerants frequenting the New York frontier. These itinerants, who, for the most part, were as uneducated and rough-mannered as the people to whom they preached, emphasized inner conversion and Christian perfectionism. They appealed to uprooted New Englanders like John Young who were dissatisfied with the harsh, punitive, exclusionist doctrines of Puritanism. A strong commitment to Methodism on the part of John Young and his family would wax strong until their ultimate conversion to Mormonism.

John found farming much more difficult in this wild New York frontier region than he had anticipated. In 1790 he returned to Hopkinton, where he remained for the next ten years. John settled on the south side of Sadler's Hill, where he apparently farmed. The family increased in size, with the three oldest girls being joined by five siblings—John Jr., Nabby, Susannah, Joseph, and Phinehas.

In January of 1801, John Young made another effort to strike out on his own. He moved his wife and eight children one hundred miles north to Whitingham, Vermont, where Brigham, named for his great-grandmother, Sybil Brigham, was born six months later. Brigham's first years were spent in a frontier environment marked by uncertainty. John could not achieve economic security because his farm land was too steep and rocky. Looking for ways to supplement their meager income, John and his elder sons hired themselves out to other farmers, while Brigham's older sisters wove and sold straw hats to earn grocery money.

Additional misfortune affected the family. Nabby's health began to deteriorate after she contracted consumption, or tuberculosis. She suffered her first serious sick spell about the time of Brigham's birth and was unable to nurse or care for the infant. Fourteen-year-old Fanny stepped in and cared for him, nursing him from the bottle. Gentle and dexterous, Fanny became a substitute mother figure to whom Brigham clung. Within two years, however, Brigham lost the comfort of Fanny's companionship when she met and married Robert Carr.

Life for the Young family in Vermont proved too difficult.

In 1804 John moved 130 miles southwest to Chenango County and the community of Smyrna, located in upstate New York. This isolated frontier region lacked good roads until the completion of the Albany-Ithaca Turnpike a year after the Youngs' arrival. John found the land relatively expensive—three dollars an acre—in contrast to the one dollar an acre he paid back in Vermont. But he probably found such obstacles less objectionable than the prospect of returning to Hopkinton and being consigned to survival on a scrubby farm near his critical, condescending in-laws. The Youngs' westward move was part of a mass migration of New Englanders who were attracted to the region by the rich soil that contrasted sharply with the rocky soil in New England. Smyrna was situated among small, wooded hills, with a lively brook traversing the town. The soil and improved roads facilitated the rapid growth of the entire region during the early nineteenth century.

The family lived in at least two different homes—the first at Smyrna, and the second a log house near Cold Brook, located about three miles southwest of Smyrna; here, Brigham grew from childhood to adolescence during the years 1804 to 1813. John, in farming, utilized the services of his sons, including Brigham. Subjected to hard, backbreaking work year-round in the woods, logging and driving a team of horses, Brigham later recalled being not half-clad: "If I had on a pair of pants that would cover me I did pretty well." Brigham and his older brothers were also hired out to supplement the family's meager income, with Brigham working for Judge Isaac Foote, a prominent member of the community. The extra income came in handy, for Nabby gave birth to Louisa in 1804 and Lorenzo three years later in 1807.

Brigham was influenced by religion both within the home and in the larger community. A wave of extreme religious enthusiasm repeatedly burned over the region of upstate New York where the Youngs lived. Throughout the so-called "burned over district," recently arrived farmers including the Youngs were drawn to religion. Brigham described his family as some of "the most strict religionists that lived upon the earth." He was brought up a Christian and taught to live a strict, moral life. His father subscribed to an austere, ascetic Methodism. He opposed dancing and would not even permit his children to listen to a fiddle—activities that, Brigham was taught, would put him on the highway to hell. Brigham was not allowed to walk more than a half an hour on Sunday for exercise and prohibited from using such expressions as "the devil" and "I vow." Nabby, while not as heavy-handed as John, was every bit as religious, admonishing her children to pray so that God would send His guardian angel to watch over them.

Brigham and his brothers and sisters were also taught not to steal—not even so much as a pin from the dooryard of a neighbor. To wrong a fellow human being, even if injured by them, was forbidden. Brigham's father, probably recalling the hardships that alcohol had placed on his own early life, enthusiastically supported the burgeoning temperance movement and attempted to recruit Brigham into the ranks of the "Cold Water Army" and to sign a temperance pledge. Brigham later recalled the influence of his parents' training on his youthful behavior, noting that he "never stole, lied, gambled, got drunk, or disobeyed my parents." Brigham's brother Lorenzo agreed, describing the future Mormon leader as "a boy of strictly moral habits [never] known to drink or use profane language."

Outside the family, Brigham also found encouragement for religious, upright behavior. At that time revivalism affected Smyrna and the Chenango region, with competing denominations vying for the allegiance of the Youngs. Brigham's family attended numerous meetings, becoming acquainted with the Episcopalians, Presbyterians, New Lights, Baptists, Freewill Baptists, Wesleyan and Reformed Methodists, and almost every other kind of religion.

Local camp meetings conducted by the Methodist itinerant Lorenzo Dow caused the greatest stir within the Young family. Brigham had high expectations concerning Dow, looking forward to his teachings about Jesus Christ, the will of God, and what the prophets did and received, saw and heard, and knew about God and heaven. Various family members were inspired, with Brigham's father coming "into perfect light," and so impressed that he named his son, born in 1807, Lorenzo Dow Young. Brigham's two older brothers, swept up by Dow's brand of revivalism, joined the Methodist Church.

But Brigham was not similarly affected and held back from joining the Methodists or any other church. He rejected these preachers and their teachings. He later claimed that he made up his own little prayer: "Lord, preserve me until I am old enough to have sound judgment, and a discreet mind ripened on a good, solid foundation of common sense." Brigham's independent, deliberate personality would not permit him to embrace any set of religious beliefs under pressure. He was, moreover, repulsed by the revival meetings, finding them loud, crowded, and hyperactive. The sight of grown men crying and of persons lying on the floor of the meeting houses for many long minutes disgusted him. Such behavior ran counter to Brigham's desire for neatness and order.

Lorenzo Dow's specific religious teachings, moreover, did not appeal to young Brigham because Dow merely told the people that they should not work on the Sabbath, lie, swear, steal, or commit adultery, offenses he had already been warned against. He found Dow's attempts to discuss matters of God unenlightening. Even though Brigham's religious views differed sharply with those of other family members, his parents left him alone and did not impose their beliefs upon him.

By the time Brigham turned thirteen, the Young family moved to a new frontier region, Genoa, New York, located

fifty miles west of Smyrna on the shores of Cayuga Lake.
The move to Genoa, a region of extraordinary beauty on the
Salmon River amidst vistas of far-reaching hills, was apparently motivated by John Young's failure to gain long-sought
but elusive economic security in Smyrna. Or he may have
been drawn to Genoa by the presence of some of Nabby's
relatives in the community.

But from the beginning, conditions within the new community were not promising. John, unable to purchase property, was forced to make a living hired out as a farmer or
working at some other menial trade. Brigham helped out
the best he could, devoting most of his time to hunting and
fishing in order to put food on the family table and was
apparently also hired out. But he did find time to gain some
rudiments of formal education, attending the Drake School
House, located on the shore of Cayuga Lake. And he was
apparently taught some additional reading and writing by
his mother.

Brigham was also affected by several changes within the
family. His older brother, John Jr., and two older sisters,
Rhoda and Susannah, all married and left home, all at about
the same time in 1813–14. A third sister, Nabby, had contracted consumption and died in 1807, and his mother continued to suffer from this same affliction. Growing weaker,
she finally died on June 11, 1815, just ten days after Brigham's fourteenth birthday. Brigham was deeply affected by
the loss of his mother, who had stood as an ameliorating
contrast to his strict, devout, and rather dour father, whose
discipline involved "a word and a blow," with the blow usually
coming first. In retrospect, Brigham summed up his own
feelings: "Of my mother—she that bore me—I can say no
better woman ever lived in the world." The impact of Nabby's
death was softened somewhat by the return of Brigham's
favorite sister, Fanny, to the Young household. Having left
her unfaithful and profligate husband, she served as a temporary stabilizing influence within the family.

In 1815, Brigham found himself uprooted once more when the family moved to the Sugar Hill district of Steuben (now Schuyler) County, near Tyrone, thirty-five miles southwest of Genoa. Brigham's father purchased one hundred acres of land fifteen miles from the nearest trading community. On this land, thick with maple trees, the family produced maple sugar. John and his sons would gather and process the sap into sugar and then put it into a fifty- or sixty-pound pack, which Brigham, or some other family member, would transport to the nearest settlement, exchanging it for flour and other supplies. But success continued to elude the Youngs and they remained poor. They hired themselves out to clear and work the land of others, and John bottomed chairs while the sons did odd jobs for neighboring farmers. Brigham, the youngest able-bodied son, was left with the household chores, since there were no women left at home. He learned to bake bread, wash the dishes, milk the cows, and churn butter.

This routine of hard work and strict discipline took a psychological as well as a physical toll on Brigham. Isolated, deprived of a loving mother, he described his bouts with frontier depression: "I was troubled with . . . feeling cast down, gloomy, and desponding with everything wearing to me, at times a dreary aspect. . . I felt lonesome and bad." Other family members, including his older brother Joseph, to whom Brigham felt particularly close, experienced similar moods. According to Brigham, "For many years no person saw a smile on [Joseph's] countenance."

Brigham's dreary, frontier existence was tempered somewhat by the relatively favorable relationship that he now enjoyed with his father. John apparently treated Brigham less severely than the older sons, and he was, according to one of his brothers, a favorite. This enabled Brigham to develop a deliberative manner and independence of spirit, as reflected in his refusal to sign a temperance pledge urged upon him by his father. Although he disliked hard liquor,

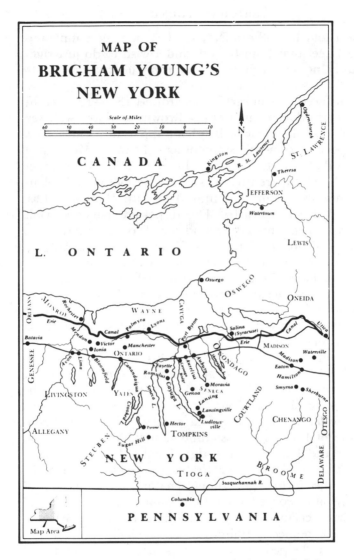

Map showing area of upstate New York that was Brigham Young's territory. (Courtesy of Charles Redd Center for Western Studies, Brigham Young University.)

Brigham told his father: "No, sir. If I sign the temperance pledge I feel that I am bound, and I wish to do just right, without being bound to do it; I want my liberty."

Brigham faced new uncertainties around 1816–17 when his father married Hannah Dennis Brown, a widow with several children of her own. Brigham apparently did not live with or get to know his stepmother. He was driven out of the crowded quarters caused by the suddenly enlarged family. John apparently broke up the household, abandoned his own farm, and moved in with Hannah, whose own residence was nearby. The displaced sixteen-year-old lad took to heart his father's advice: "You now have your time; go and provide for yourself," and set out for Auburn, located about forty miles north of Sugar Hill on an outlet of Owasco Lake along the well-traveled Seneca Turnpike. In Auburn, a bustling, frontier town, Brigham stayed briefly with his sister Susannah and her husband, James Little. He initially worked as a hired hand for farm families in and around Auburn.

But farming did not appeal to this son of a less-than-successful farmer. So Brigham left the countryside to see what he could do in the village. In Auburn, he found the woodworking shop of John C. Jefferies and apprenticed himself to learn the trades of carpentry, painting, and glazing. One of his earliest assignments involved painting and finishing the home of a Judge Elijah Miller, who later turned this residence over to his son-in-law, William H. Seward, the future governor, senator, and secretary of state. He also worked on other Auburn homes, many of which later claimed the distinction of having a Brigham Young mantelpiece, staircase, or semielliptical fanlight doorway. He helped build Auburn's first meat market, and he worked on the Auburn Theological Seminary. Following the completion of his apprenticeship, he worked for Colonel John Richardson in a cabinet shop, a water-powered facility located on the bank of Crane Brook.

Young, however, could not establish roots in Auburn, despite his skills and training. Like other Auburn residents, he was adversely affected by a general decline of economic activity resulting, in part, from the Panic of 1819. Auburn and other frontier communities felt the impact of the decision by the Second Bank of the United States to curb land speculation by recalling its loans. Also hurting the community were changing transportation patterns—in particular, the loss of traffic and commerce through Auburn via the Seneca Turnpike to the Erie Canal ten miles to the north.

In 1823, Young moved north to Port Byron, an emerging port town located on the Erie Canal. Here he worked for at least four different employers over the next five years. His first employer, a repairer of old chairs, paid him seven dollars a month and gave him an antique vehicle to collect the furniture for repairs. He then labored in a carding mill owned by William Hayden and shortly thereafter found employment in a pail factory at Haydenville, just south of Port Byron. While employed there, he developed a water-powered device that ground more efficiently the oil and lead used in the manufacture of the paint. He left the pail factory to accept employment in a local boatyard that built boats used on the Erie Canal. Starting as a painter, he soon became involved in other aspects of boat building and was put in charge of supervising the selection of timber to be used for boat construction. He developed a reputation as a hard worker who "would do more work in a given time and secure more and better work from his help without trouble than any man . . . ever employed."

While living in the Auburn–Port Byron area, Young manifested a strong interest in religion and moral self-improvement. Like many other Americans during the economically depressed years of the early 1820s, he was swept up by religious enthusiasm, and in 1824 he joined the Methodist Church. Young hoped that embracing the faith he had rejected as a child would alleviate his sense of weakness and ignorance. Methodism would, in his own words, help "break off my sins and lead a better life and be as moral as I possibly could." Young's increased sense of religiosity was like that of other family members. His older brother Phinehas converted to Methodism about the same time as Brigham in 1823, and a year later he was licensed as a Methodist minister. In 1825, his oldest brother, John Jr., also received his license as a Methodist minister, and by 1830 a third brother, Joseph, along with a brother-in-law, John P. Greene, were both active, practicing Methodist ministers. In addition, a friend, Moses Lyon, a trustee of the local Methodist Church near Port Byron, may have influenced Young. Young later recalled: "I got religion in order to prevent my being any more pestered about" it. He did not like being called an infidel by his more religiously inclined friends.

Brigham Young's conversion to Methodism was, moreover, part of a more general program of self-improvement. He said that he "sought to use language on all occasions, that would be commendable and to carry myself in society in a way to gain for myself the respect of the moral and good among my neighbors." Confessing to being addicted to swearing, despite his strict upbringing, he claimed he thought it was easily overcome when his judgment and will decided to overcome it. He also worked to become an effective public speaker, attempting to overcome his shyness before groups of people. He participated in the activities of at least one schoolhouse debating society while living in the Port Byron area. He also sought to improve his eating habits through his brief experimentation with vegetarianism. Young's quest for self-improvement in an environment of religious enthusiasm was not unique. Self-improvement, as part of a more general trend toward moral perfectionism, was common in American society at large. The dual tendencies of moral perfectionism and religious revivalism were impulses that fed off of and reinforced each other.

Brigham Young's life changed in another important way.

He met and courted Miriam Angeline Works from nearby Aurelius, a beautiful blond girl with blue eyes and wavy hair. She was the daughter of Asa Works, who, like Brigham's father, was a native of Massachusetts and a Revolutionary War veteran. During their courtship, Young took Miriam dancing, a pasttime that he enjoyed despite his father's earlier stricture against it. On October 5, 1824, Brigham and Miriam were married in a civil ceremony performed by Gilbert Weed, a town trustee. They established their first home at Haydenville, near the pail factory where Young worked. By 1825 the Youngs had moved to Port Byron, where their first child, Elizabeth, was born.

Although Brigham Young was primarily a creature of an unsettled, upstate New York frontier environment, two events made it clear that he, along with his Port Byron-Auburn neighbors, was also part of the larger American society of the 1820s. The first involved a visit to Auburn in 1825 by the Marquis de Lafayette, the Frenchman who had aided the Americans in their revolutionary cause fifty years earlier. His arrival was described as one of the grandest spectacles that residents of this region had ever seen. Large crowds from the village and adjacent counties came to greet him. He rode in a barouche drawn by six chestnut horses, accompanied by a display of military companies, Revolutionary War soldiers, and Freemasons.

A second event of greater significance involved completion of the Erie Canal in October of 1825. At the celebration in Port Byron, the canal was characterized as "the most splendid work of internal improvement undertaken in any country." For Young and other local residents, the completion of the canal meant new employment opportunities. Also, the canal made it easier for Young to visit his father and other family members in Mendon, forty miles west of Port Byron. For countless numbers of upstate New York residents all along the canal's route, from Utica to Buffalo, life would never be the same. Fortunes were made by merchants involved in canal trade, cities grew up overnight along its route, and agricultural growth took place.

But for Brigham Young, such economic opportunities did not materialize. By 1828 he was uprooted once more, forced to move his family from Port Byron to Oswego, New York, on the shore of Lake Ontario, twenty-eight miles to the north. Here he helped build a large tannery. At the same time Young expressed a deep interest in religion by joining a number of other individuals in the formation of a religious study group. Young, according to the recollections of Hiram McKee, a close friend, affirmed a "deep piety and faith in God."

Less than a year later, Young and his wife moved their family once more, this time west to Mendon, where most of his family were now living. At Mendon, Young went into business for himself, manufacturing furniture. As his own man, he would no longer be at the mercy of employers who could fire or lay him off at will. Mendon seemed ideal due to its location along the Genesee Turnpike, only four miles from the nearest shipping point on the Erie Canal. Indeed, this bustling frontier town had already started to show great commercial and agricultural prosperity since the opening of the Erie Canal.

On land given to him by his father, Young constructed a two-story building designed to serve both as a place of business and family residence. The first floor served as Young's shop and contained machinery—saws, grindstones, and lathes—powered by water diverted from a nearby stream. The shop also contained a forge for blacksmith-type work. This enabled Young to manufacture various types of furniture, including chairs, tables, blanket chests, chests of drawers, spinning wheels, and bedsteads. The family residence on the second floor was rather modest, combining a large, single room with a bed in one corner, a cupboard for dishes in another, and also a table, a few splint-bottom chairs, and a fireplace.

Brigham Young, however, never got the chance to de-velop his potential as a successful furniture maker. His wife, Miriam, like his mother before, contracted consump-tion. Her health had been slow to return following the birth of their first child, and she was further incapacitated following the birth of a second child, Vilate, in June of 1830. As a result, Young was forced to divert more and more of his time from furniture making to take care of those household tasks normally performed by his sickly wife. At first he tried to juggle both his furniture making and household responsibilities. Each morning he would arise early to fix breakfast and perform other household chores while Miriam remained bedridden. He would then turn to his furniture-making until evening, when he would return to care for the household. He would carry Miriam to the fireplace, prepare the evening meal, clean up, and carry her back to bed.

But Young soon found that he could not care for the household and continue his furniture manufacturing. He turned to part-time work as a common-day laborer for local farmers, and when he had time he did some work as a car-penter. This change in employment meant still another move for the unsettled family, this time to Number Nine, a rural community a few miles west of Canandaigua, New York. Here they remained for the next two years.

By 1832, for some unknown reason, the family returned to Mendon. But poverty continued to stalk Brigham Young. He had left a trail of creditors all the way back to Port Byron and continued to incur debts in both Mendon and Canan-daigua. Young's desperate economic circumstances were re-flected in one incident at Mendon. A creditor called on the family to collect a debt, and not finding Brigham at home, he confronted Miriam "in feeble health . . . poorly and thinly-clad, having an old black shawl thrown around her shoulders, endeavoring to keep warm over a single stick of wood on the fire in the fireplace." When pressed for payment, Miriam replied, "I do not know how or when Mr. Young can pay." The family, she explained, had "no flour or meat nor anything else in the house to eat" and Brigham would have to "first . . . provide fuel and provision for the family."

In the face of this grinding frontier poverty, Brigham Young sought comfort and satisfaction where he could find it. He maintained close ties with his father and other family members and developed a very close friendship with Heber C. Kimball, a neighbor, who turned out and sold pottery. Kimball, a six-foot tall, barrel-chested, slightly balding man with dark, piercing eyes, was the same age as Young, and also a native New Englander. His parents, like Young's, had migrated to the New York frontier in search of greater economic opportunity. The friendship between Young and Kimball was further strengthened by Brigham's older sister, Fanny, who had lived in the Kimball household and cared for Heber's sickly wife, Vilate.

Young also renewed his interest in religion, embracing a type of reformed Methodism by 1830. He became an exhorter, frequently leading the meetings of the neighborhood at the Number Nine meeting house, and also joined a group of independent seekers led by his brother Phinehas. This group opened a house for preaching in Mendon, "and commenced teaching the people according to the light [they] had." They found a receptive audience and a kind of reformation started. The local Baptist church and its minister all seemed to have a great interest in their work. This reformation spread, with hundreds of individuals taking an interest in it. The Mendon group was similar to the group to which Brigham had belonged in Oswego. These groups were common on the American frontier, with many being restorationist in character, seeking through close study of the New Testament to return to the forms and practices of the original Christian Church as it existed during the time of Jesus Christ.

In this environment of renewed religious awareness, Young first came into contact with Mormonism. Joseph Smith, the founder of the Mormon Church (or the Church of Jesus Christ of Latter-day Saints, as it came to be known officially), had a background in many ways remarkably similar to Young's. Smith was born of Puritan stock on the Vermont frontier of New England. His parents, like Young's, were uprooted by economic misfortune and moved around a great deal, unable to establish firm, permanent roots in the rocky soil of New England. By 1816, the Smiths ended up in Palmyra, New York, a bustling frontier community close to the Erie Canal, about fifteen miles from Mendon. In this religiously charged environment fourteen-year-old Smith, in 1820, had his first religious experience.

Concerned about the salvation of his soul, and confused concerning the correct source of religious authority, he retired to pray in a grove behind the family house and received a vision of Jesus Christ. He learned he was destined for great and divine things and was told to await further instructions. Later, around the same time that Young embraced Methodism at Port Byron, Smith received another divine visitation. This time he saw an angel, Moroni, who revealed the existence of a set of gold plates located in a hillside near the Smith home. These plates, which contained the sacred writings of an ancient American civilization—the ancestors of the American Indians—were given to Smith with orders to translate them into English. This he proceeded to do; the finished product was completed and published at Palmyra in 1830 as the *Book of Mormon*. In that same year, this work was accepted as holy scripture on a par with the Bible by Smith's followers, following the formation of the Mormon Church.

Young's first direct contact with Mormonism did not come until the summer of 1830, although he had heard of Joseph Smith and his teachings prior to this time. In Port Byron, Young heard "rumors of a new revelation, to the effect of a new Bible written upon golden plates . . . at Palmyra," and later recalled, "I was somewhat acquainted with the coming forth of the *Book of Mormon* . . . through . . . the newspapers [and] many stories and reports . . . circulated . . . as the *Book of Mormon* was printed and . . . scattered abroad." Finally, in June of 1830, Young actually saw a copy of the so-called "golden Bible" when Samuel Smith, a younger brother of Joseph, arrived in Mendon on a mission to preach Mormonism and sell copies of the *Book of Mormon.* Smith gave John P. Greene and Phinehas Young a copy of this book. Phinehas read it, and convinced of its truthfulness, passed it around to other members of the Young family, including Brigham's father and sister, both of whom praised it.

But Brigham was more cautious, declaring his desire to wait and apply his heart to it. He wanted enough time to "see whether good common sense was manifest." Brigham was not alone in holding back from joining the Mormons. So were John Sr., Phinehas, and Fanny, despite their initial enthusiasm.

A year and a half later, in the fall of 1831, Young and his family again came into contact with the Mormons when a group of missionaries visited and preached in Mendon. The Youngs, despite their continuing interest in Mormonism, still held back from joining.

In January of 1832, Brigham Young, his brother Phinehas, and Heber C. Kimball wanted to observe first-hand a Mormon congregation in action. In the middle of the winter they traveled 130 miles south to Columbia, Pennsylvania, where the nearest Mormon branch was located. Here, they observed the Mormons speaking in tongues, interpreting, and prophesying. To Brigham's relief, they did not indulge in the wild animated behavior he found so disgusting in the camp meetings of his youth. At the end of six days, Young was convinced Mormonism was "the Gospel in its purity."

Brigham Young returned to Mendon, ready to cast his lot with the new sect. But before doing so, he sought the counsel of Joseph, his older brother. Joseph, however, was in Canada fulfilling his duties as a Methodist minister. So Brigham, despite the severe winter weather, traveled to Canada and consulted with him. Finally, in early April, 1832, the Young family cast its lot with the Mormons. John Sr., Phinehas, and Joseph were the first to be baptized, and later that month, on April 14, Brigham was baptized in the stream behind his Mendon workshop and home. Immediately thereafter, before Brigham's clothes "were dry on my back [the Mormon Elder] laid his hands on me and ordained me an Elder, at which I marveled." This ordination into the Mormon priesthood gave Young authority to preach the gospel.

Other members of the Young family living in and around Mendon followed Brigham into the Mormon faith in quick succession, including his ailing wife, Miriam, his sisters and brothers-in-law, his stepmother Hannah, and her son Edward. Outside the Mendon area, other Young family members accepted the new faith, including brothers Lorenzo, John Jr., and sister Nancy. Thus, for Young, entry into the Mormon Church was clearly a family affair, undertaken only after careful consultation, study, and deliberation among family members over a period of two years.

Joseph Smith, the founder of Mormonism to whom Brigham Young remained steadfastly loyal and whom Young continued to idealize and try to emulate following the Mormon Prophet's death in June 1844. (Courtesy LDS Church Library-Archives. Printed with permission.)

I I

Status and
Recognition

ALTHOUGH FAMILY CONSIDERATIONS figured prominently in Brigham Young's decision to join the Mormon movement, he was attracted as much if not more by certain beliefs and practices inherent in the religion. One of these was "Christian primitivism," a belief that the Mormons were restoring Christianity exactly as it had existed when first established by Jesus Christ. This primitivism hearkened back to that of the religious seekers with whom Young had associated in both Oswego and Mendon. Young was also attracted by Mormonism's millennialistic orientation or belief that mankind was living in the "latter days" and that the second coming of Christ and his thousand-year reign of peace were imminent.

Brigham Young also found Mormonism appealing because of its Puritan-like tendencies, similar to those in his New England heritage. These included an emphasis on common sense which encouraged members to reason out their relationship with God in a practical manner. Like Puritanism, moreover, Mormonism emphasized the need to be always engaged in a good cause or performing good works. Mormon good works involved the restoration of the church as a total institution regulating all aspects of social activity—political, economic, and religious. Although the Mormons encouraged good works in all aspects of human activity, they, like their Puritan forebears, assigned an important place to the concept of salvation through "divine grace." Like that of Puritanism, Mormon divine grace avoided the wild, animated emotional demonstrations of piety that had repulsed Young as a child. Young was also drawn by Mormonism's emphasis on perfectionism, that is, the need to perfect both oneself and the larger society.

Mormonism's emphasis on authoritarianism, or its basic belief that the Church and its leaders were the only true source of divine authority, also appealed to Young. Mormon authoritarianism—which demanded unswerving loyalty to Joseph Smith, the Mormon prophet—struck a responsive chord in Young, who had grown up in a strict home. Mormon authoritarianism, moreover, offered order and stability to Young, which contrasted with his heretofore disordered frontier existence. Finally, Young was drawn to Mormonism by its lay priesthood, which provided followers an avenue to status and recognition. Through this priesthood, an organization open to virtually all adult male members, any ambitious, devout Mormon could rise to a position of power and influence. This aspect of Mormonism was tailor-made for Young, a frustrated individual whom misfortune had repeatedly robbed of economic and social success. He had failed to achieve social status in a Jacksonian frontier society, which emphasized success through competitive individual enterprise. For Young, therefore, it was logical to drop out of this competitive environment and embrace Mormonism— a communitarian institution that provided not only for his religious needs but his economic and social needs as well. Young's Mormon conversion represented a withdrawal from the freedom of Jacksonian individualism and free competition. But it did provide a means to gain power and long-sought status and recognition.

Almost from the moment of his conversion, Young threw himself wholeheartedly into the task of preaching the gospel, baptizing, and raising up churches in the regions around Mendon. He soon enjoyed a local reputation as a man of action who was hard at work building up the Mormon kingdom. Young's increased commitment came at a time of great personal loss, for his wife, ravaged by consumption, finally died on September 8, 1832. Brigham and his two young daughters moved in with his friend, Heber C. Kimball. But Young did not spend much time in the Kimball household. In October of 1832, Young, along with Kimball, who had converted to Mormonism at the same time as Young, traveled to Kirtland, Ohio, the principal Mormon settlement located near Cleveland. Young made the 325-mile trek west to meet Joseph Smith—the founder and leader of the Church of Jesus Christ of Latter-day Saints. When he encountered Smith, Young found the Mormon leader in the woods with his brothers chopping and hauling lumber. Young was impressed, despite this unreligious setting. His sheer physical presence commanded respect. The twenty-six-year-old Mormon leader stood 6'2", weighed 212 pounds, and took pride in his physical strength. Smith's face radiated a youthful appearance with his large head, fair complexion, peaked nose, and agile blue eyes set deep behind high cheekbones.

Thus, Young, like other faithful Mormons, was in awe of Smith's imposing physical presence and charismatic personality. But another of Smith's qualities appealed to the deferential, enthusiastic Young. This was Smith's behavior as a self-proclaimed prophet, by which he projected a certain mysticism. Young later recalled: "my joy was full at the privilege of shaking the hand of the Prophet of God." All of these qualities in Smith made Young a loyal disciple from that moment on.

At the same time, Young manifested strong support for Smith; he sought to impress the Mormon leader with his own religiosity. When Young, Smith, and a number of other Mormons gathered at Smith's home to talk, Smith called on Young to pray. Young spoke in tongues, or in garbled utterances, previously unwitnessed by the Mormon leader. When others present asked Smith his opinion of Young's behavior, Smith proclaimed Young's utterances as a gift of tongues manifested in "the pure Adamic language." Young interpreted his own behavior like unto the "day of Pentecost, when the Apostles were clothed with cloven tongues of fire;" a manifestation of Christian primitivism.

Following his return to Mendon, Young sought to back his religious mysticism with specific actions. In December of 1832 he undertook a mission to Kingston, Canada, in company with his older brother Joseph, who had labored there as a Methodist minister. The Youngs exploited Joseph's earlier contacts, baptizing about forty-five souls and organized a branch (congregation) at West Loughborough, along with other branches, and returned to Mendon in February of 1833. Two months later, Brigham left on a second mission, visiting various communities in upstate New York and Canada, where he was again successful in baptizing new members and organizing several Mormon branches. In July of 1833, Young traveled to Kirtland to escort a number of Canadian converts who wished to settle in this Mormon community. This second Kirtland visit gave Young the opportunity to visit once more with Joseph Smith.

Following his return to Mendon, Young decided in September of 1833 to move to Kirtland, wanting to be near Joseph Smith and the center of Mormon activity. This move also came in response to Smith's instructions that all his followers gather either to Kirtland or to a second Mormon population center—Independence, Missouri—designated by Smith as Mormonism's Zion, or main gathering place. At Kirtland, Smith established a Mormon stake (or diocese) and unveiled plans for a Mormon temple.

Kirtland itself was a small trading and milling center of about 1,300, nested in gentle rolling hills along the Chagrin River near Lake Erie. In Kirtland, Young found work as a carpenter. He finished a house for a fellow Mormon, did work for Father John Smith (an uncle of Joseph Smith's) and others, built a house for Heber C. Kimball out of gratitude for the aid Kimball had provided during earlier difficult times, and worked on the Kirtland Temple.

During his first winter in Kirtland, Young courted Mary Ann Angell. A matronly, thirty-year-old woman, Mary Ann had never married. Born in Seneca, New York, and a former Free Will Baptist, she was a student of the Bible. A devoutly religious person who had resolved never to marry until she met a man of God, she felt Young to be such a man. Young saw in Mary Ann a woman who could take charge of his children, keep his house in order, and bear the sacrifices of being married to an extremely busy Mormon minister. In February, 1834, Brigham and Mary Ann were married by Sidney Rigdon, an important Mormon leader.

As for Rigdon, he was Joseph Smith's most influential follower. Distinguished looking but grim and emotional, Rigdon had a reputation as a charismatic public speaker who could move audiences with his fluent, articulate delivery. A successful Ohio Campbellite preacher prior to becoming a Mormon, he had brought many of his Campbellite followers into the Church and had urged Smith to move from New York to Kirtland in 1831. Rigdon therefore stood in contrast to Young, who struggled to distinguish himself.

In May of 1834, Young was presented with an opportunity to distinguish himself when Smith asked him to join an expedition to Missouri, known as Zion's Camp, in an effort to aid besieged Mormons in that state who had clashed with their non-Mormon neighbors. Missouri non-Mormons, generally rough, frontier types from the South, disliked the Mormons, who were primarily from the North, and took particular offense at Mormon claims that Independence was their Zion. In response to the large influx of Mormons into this region, the Missourians took vigilante action. Alleging the Mormons to be anti-slavery and pro-black, they brutally attacked and expelled at gunpoint some 1,200 Mormons from their homes in Jackson County in late 1833 and early 1834. The uprooted Mormons found temporary refuge north of Jackson in neighboring Clay County. But Smith wanted to redeem Zion in Jackson County and thus formed Zion's Camp, a Mormon armed force of about 200 men. He hoped for a negotiated settlement and intended to use Zion's Camp as leverage to improve his bargaining position.

Brigham Young joined Zion's Camp, making the 900-mile trek to Missouri, taking with him a gun and bayonet, plenty of ammunition, and some tools. The army was subdivided into companies of twelve men each under an individual commander, with Young appointed to command one of these companies. This represented Young's first position of responsibility within the Church.

From May until early June, Zion's Camp made its way across Ohio, Indiana, Illinois, and then into Missouri, where they encountered difficulties. Officials there were unreceptive to the Mormons' plight, failing to aid them in regaining their lost property. The Mormons, moreover, had to deal with a anti-Mormon vigilante force of 300 poised to launch a full-scale attack on Zion's Camp, then trapped on a flood plain with water on three sides. But a fierce squall of hail and heavy rain broke the momentum of the attack, cooling the enthusiasm of the attacking force to regroup. A few days later, the camp faced greater tragedy—a cholera epidemic left seventy individuals violently ill and thirteen dead. Young himself escaped its ravages and aided in caring for the ill and burying the dead. By late June, the camp recovered and disbanded, with Young and other members returning to Kirtland on their own.

By all accounts, Zion's Camp appeared an unmitigated disaster. But for Young there were personal benefits. Zion's Camp provided him valuable leadership training and gave Young the opportunity to affirm his strong loyalty to Joseph Smith under adverse circumstances. Joseph Smith did not hesitate long in entrusting Young with additional Church duties. In February of 1835, the Mormon leader appointed Young a member of a newly created Council of Twelve Apostles, modeled on the twelve apostles of Jesus in the New Testament. The Twelve were to promote the expansion of Mormon missionary activity both within the United States and abroad and oversee the functioning of Mormon branches throughout the United States and in Canada. Smith was not only impressed by Young's basic loyalty, but also by his earlier missionary successes in the United States and Canada.

Despite Smith's confidence, Young did not at first appear destined for great Mormon prominence. Age was used as the basis for selecting the president of the Twelve, and Young stood third behind Thomas Marsh and David W. Patten. Young was also overshadowed by others both in education and economic achievement. Three Quorum members—John F. Boynton, and two brothers, Luke S. and Lyman Johnson—were successful in farming and business. A fourth, William E. McLellin, a native of Tennessee and the best educated of the Twelve, taught classes that Young and other less-educated Mormons attended. Finally, one other apostle, William Smith, was noteworthy due to his position as the younger brother of the Mormon leader and because of his pugnacious, flamboyant personality. Young, by contrast, seemed to stand in the shadows. Young later recalled that some certain individuals lamented at his appointment and with their looks affirmed, "What a pity!"

Young was anxious to disprove these doubters and demonstrate his abilities. Over the next year and a half, from May of 1835 until September of 1836, Young fulfilled two missions for the Church. Leaving his wife, two daughters, and infant son Joseph Angell, born the previous October, Young departed Kirtland in May of 1835 and traveled to upstate New York, Canada, and New England, where he preached and organized various Mormon branches into conferences. Young was also assigned to preach to the Indians—or "seed of Joseph," as they were labeled by the Mormons, (due to a Mormon belief that the Indians had descended from a portion of one of the Twelve Tribes of Israel). Although he preached to members of the Iroquois tribe at two different New York locations—Big Valley and Cold Spring—he did not gain any new converts. Other Mormon missionaries also found limited interest in Mormonism within the diverse tribes from New York State to the Missouri River.

Mormon concern for the Indian reflected a general American interest during the Jacksonian period. Andrew Jackson's controversial Indian removal policy stimulated widespread debate and discussion among Americans in general, with Joseph Smith himself supporting this program. This Mormon support stemmed from the fact that the Latter-day Saints, like most Americans, did not want to live among a people they considered racially inferior—"a dark and loathsome people" cursed with a dark skin due to their unrighteous behavior during pre-Columbian times, beliefs vividly articulated in the *Book of Mormon*. But at the same time, the Mormons considered the Indians objects for Christian salvation and felt that Jackson's removal policy would make it easier for the Indians to be converted.

After leaving the Indians, Young resumed his duties. Traveling to Boston, he visited various relatives, including his father's and mother's sisters, and in Hopkinton visited more family, including his aged Grandmother Howe, who was overjoyed for the privilege of seeing one of her daughter's children. He returned to Kirtland in late September of 1835.

In Kirtland, Young kept busy, spending time preaching to the neighboring branches. Theological matters also occupied his attention. He, along with the other apostles, affirmed the divine truth of the *Doctrine and Covenants*, a collection of Joseph Smith's revelations. This work was canonized by the Church as holy scripture on a par with the Bible and the

Book of Mormon. Young also had the opportunity to examine a set of Egyptian records that Smith utilized as the inspiration for another set of sacred writings—the Book of Abraham—a supplement to the Old Testament. He also sought to augment his limited formal education by attending a Hebrew school organized by Joseph Smith and conducted by Joseph Seixas, a Jewish scholar from the nearby Hudson Ohio Seminary.

Later, in February, 1836, Young utilized his trade skills as a carpenter and painter, superintending the finishing of the Kirtland Temple. A month later the temple was ready for dedication. Young participated in the dedication ceremony, which was a time of intense religious excitement. He, along with other Latter-day Saints, received washings and annointings, considered by the Mormons as sacred ritual. Also, he and other Mormon apostles received the ordinance of the washing of feet administered to him by Joseph Smith, a ceremony inspired by the ritual performed by Jesus to his twelve apostles. Young gave a short address in tongues, interpreted by Apostle David W. Patten. Many of those present later claimed to have witnessed divine and supernatural manifestations, including the presence of Moses, Abraham, Jesus, and hosts of angels. Young's own recollection, however, was more circumspect, simply noting, "the power of God was displayed."

Shortly thereafter, Young left for a second Church mission to the east coast. His family suffered from his five-month absence; only letters bridged the gap between them. In one letter, Young tried to comfort Mary Ann and admonished his oldest daughter Elizabeth to "be a good girl and mind your mother . . . studdy your book . . . and be good to Vilate and letle Joseph." Following his return, Mary Ann gave birth to twins—a boy and a girl they named Brigham Young, Jr., and Mary Ann. Young, however, devoted only a limited amount of time to his family because economic problems and internal divisions within the Church drew him away.

These difficulties stemmed in large measure from Joseph Smith's direct involvement in economic and political activities, in particular, his banking activities. Smith tried to establish Kirtland Bank in response to the rapid economic growth of that community and the accompanying need for banking services, money, and credit. Smith's own heavy indebtedness, moreover, added a personal motive for such an institution. Through the printing of its own money, a bank would allow Smith to pay off his debts and acquire liquid capital. Young, along with two hundred other Mormons, purchased stock. Apostle Orson Hyde traveled to the state capital at Columbus to secure a banking charter, but state officials rejected the Mormon request. Undaunted, Smith decided to go ahead anyway. He established a financial institution and named it somewhat defiantly the Kirtland Safety Society Anti-Banking Company.

Difficulties developed when this institution started issuing its own bank notes in January, 1837. Smith and other Mormons tried to use these bank notes, which were not recognized as legal tender due to the lack of a charter, to pay off their debts and transact other business. Thus creditors and outsiders in general were reluctant to accept the banknotes. The nationwide Panic of 1837 further aggravated the Kirtland Safety Society's difficulties. Smith's banking practices were not all that unique, since wildcat banking activities undertaken by numerous, unstable financial institutions like the Kirtland Safety Society helped facilitate the panic and subsequent depression.

Joseph Smith tried to save the struggling Society. He borrowed money from at least three banks and enlisted help from Brigham Young and other Church leaders. In March, 1837, and again the following July, Smith dispatched Young on two so-called business missions to the East to try to secure additional capital. Over the next few months Young and his cousin from Massachusetts, Willard Richards, a recent Mormon convert, traveled through various eastern states, including Pennsylvania, New York, Massachusetts, and Connecticut, apparently disposing of $10,000 in Kirtland Safety Society paper.

Despite the efforts of Young and others, the Kirtland Safety Society failed, sending shock waves throughout the entire Mormon movement. Some prominent Latter-day Saints denounced Joseph Smith. They criticized the Mormon leader for being too involved with banking activities and felt he should limit himself to purely religious matters. Although not among the rebellious Mormons, Young later admitted having some momentary doubts about Smith: "I felt a want of confidence in Brother Joseph Smith . . . in relation to his financing—to his managing of the temporal affairs which he undertook." But such doubts did not last and he stood firmly behind Smith. At a meeting in the Kirtland Temple, Young recalled:

> I rose up, and in a plain and forcible manner told them that Joseph was a Prophet, and I knew it, and that they might rail and slander him as much as they pleased, they could not destroy the appointment of the Prophet of God, they could only destroy their own authority, cut the thread that bound them to the Prophet and to God and sink themselves to hell.

Many were enraged at Young's remarks, and one of the dissidents threatened him with physical violence remarking, "how can I keep my hands off that man?" Unafraid, Young defiantly replied, "he might lay them on [me] . . . if he thought it would give him any relief." At a second meeting, Smith's opponents tried to dominate the proceedings, but Young made sure that Smith loyalists maintained control. Young then spoke in an energetic manner against one of the rebellious apostles, John F. Boynton.

Over the next two months, Young continued to be at the center of controversy and turmoil—a time "when earth and hell seemed leagued to overthrow the Prophet [Joseph Smith] and Church of God." By December, 1837, Young found that he could no longer remain in Kirtland. He felt the need to escape his creditors and avoid the wrath of those who had lost their money in the Kirtland Safety Society scheme. On the morning of December 22, Young quickly left Kirtland, escaping the fury of a group that threatened to destroy him. He left behind Mary Ann, his five children, and property valued at $4,000.

Young fled first to Dublin, Indiana, where he joined his brother Lorenzo and other Mormon settlers temporarily encamped there for the winter. Less than a month later, Joseph Smith and Sidney Rigdon arrived in Dublin, fleeing Kirtland for the same reason that had prompted Young's earlier departure. Shortly after his arrival, Smith turned to Young for aid. "Brother Brigham," he said, "I am destitute and without means to pursue my journey, and as you are one of the Twelve Apostles . . . I shall throw myself upon you and look to you for counsel in this case." Young assured Smith that he would have plenty of money to pursue his journey. He then approached a well-fixed fellow Mormon living in Dublin and persuaded him to donate $300 to Smith. Young thus affirmed once more his support for the Mormon leader.

In February of 1838, Young, Smith, and the others left Indiana for their ultimate destination, Far West, Missouri, a major Mormon settlement. Arriving there the following month, Young found it bustling with activity. Between eight to ten thousand Latter-day Saints lived in this Missouri frontier region located in the northwestern part of the state near the Missouri and Grand Rivers. Although this region's soil was less fertile than in Ohio and the land less valuable than in Independence, this region held great promise. It was a beautiful, rolling country and, best of all, distant from non-Mormon settlements. The Mormons gained political control of one county, Caldwell, location of Far West, where they elected their own political officials and organized the local militia.

This frontier region, therefore, represented a new beginning for Brigham Young and his fellow Mormons. Young put his earlier difficulties behind him and looked toward the future with hope. He bought some land at Mill Creek, a small settlement eight miles northeast of Far West, and proceeded to fence in a farm. Mary Ann and the children arrived from Kirtland in what was an extremely difficult journey, for she was very ill. Young concentrated on family matters during the spring and early summer of 1838, since Joseph Smith admonished him through revelation to provide for his family.

However, by March of 1838, Young found himself increasingly occupied with Church affairs due to continuing dissension from individuals who opposed Joseph Smith and his policies. Smith purged such individuals from the Church, a move that involved reorganizing the High Council of Zion—the principal Church governing body in Missouri. Smith removed its three presidents—David Whitmer, John Whitmer, and William W. Phelps—and replaced them on an interim basis with the three senior members of the Council of the Twelve Apostles: Thomas Marsh, David W. Patten, and Brigham Young. This gave Young both the title and responsibilities as assistant president pro tempore of the Church in Zion, in addition to his duties as an apostle.

By the summer of 1838, Young found himself drawn even closer to the center of Mormon power and influence as the result of conflict between the Mormons and Missouri non-Mormons. The Missourians viewed with alarm the gathering of the thousands of Latter-day Saints to Far West and northwestern Missouri, fearing Mormon political and economic domination of this region. Tensions further increased in the wake of provocative actions and statements by certain Latter-day Saints.

Young himself avoided those activities that might unduly provoke local non-Mormons, maintaining a low profile and concerning himself with his family and farm. But certain of his brethren were not so cautious, particularly Sidney Rigdon, who in two public speeches got carried away by his own rhetoric, threatening to use violence to deal with opponents both within and outside of the church. In his June 17 speech, known as the Salt Sermon, he thundered at the Mormons, "Ye are the salt of the earth . . . but if the salt hath lost its savor . . . [it] is henceforth good for nothing but to be cast out and trodden under the foot of man." He warned Mormon dissidents that they "would eventually be trodden under foot until their bowels gushed out." In a second speech, his Fourth of July oration, Rigdon proclaimed that outside agitators would face a war of extermination in which avenging Mormons would

> follow them till the last drop of their blood is spilled, or else they will have to exterminate us, for we will carry the seat of War to their own houses and their own families, and one part or the other shall be utterly destroyed.

Such talk encouraged the formation of a secret paramilitary organization—the Danites, or Sons of Dan—composed of some young, militant Mormons under the leadership of Sampson Avard, a recent convert. In carrying out vigilante justice, individual Danites would respond to the command of their particular group leader and at a moment's notice effect immediate revenge for any act of violence committed against the Mormons. Rigdon's rhetoric, plus the formation of the Danites, alarmed moderate Latter-day Saint leaders like Brigham Young, who denounced the tactics of Avard and his followers. Eventually Avard was excommunicated and an effort was made to halt Danite activity. In viewing this entire situation, Young later noted that Rigdon was the chief cause of their trouble in Missouri through his Fourth of July oration.

Trouble was not long in coming. Missouri frontiersmen, Young observed, rode "from neighborhood to neighborhood making inflammatory speeches, stirring up one another against us." In August, armed conflict commenced at Gallatin, Daviess County, after non-Mormons tried to prevent local Mormons from voting in a local election. No lives were lost in the scuffle, but the incident set the stage for a series of more violent clashes. Armed Missouri mobs and militia men attacked outlying Mormon settlements, burning homes and haystacks. In late October a major conflict, the Battle of Crooked River, took place in Ray County, south of Far West, resulting in the deaths of one Missourian and three Mormons, including one of Brigham's fellow apostles, David W. Patten. Just five days later, on October 30, the bloodiest incident of the entire Missouri Mormon War took place at an isolated Mormon settlement in eastern Caldwell County, seventeen miles from Far West—the notorious Haun's Mill Massacre. Seventeen Mormons, including women and children, were killed and fifteen seriously wounded by an armed mob of around 200 men.

Brigham Young responded to these developments by moving his still ailing wife and children from Mill Creek into the Mormon stronghold of Far West. Soon after Young's arrival, word came that anti-Mormon Missourians were preparing to attack Far West itself. Smith bolstered Far West's defenses. He appointed Brigham Young and other Mormon leaders as captains of fifty. They were then ordered to build temporary fortifications on the city's outskirts. But the Mormons soon found themselves surrounded by a hostile military force much larger than one they had anticipated.

The governor of the state, Lilburn Boggs, an avowed anti-Mormon, had called up the entire Missouri militia and issued an extermination order, declaring that the Mormons "must be exterminated or driven from Missouri, if necessary for the public good." Joseph Smith quickly realized that further resistance was futile, and in return for the safety of Far West and its settlers, turned himself over to Missouri authorities for trial on charges of treason. Smith's brother Hyrum and Sidney Rigdon were also arrested.

The Latter-day Saints were thus at the mercy of a hostile occupying force that "commenced their ravages by plundering the citizens of their bedding, clothing, wearing apparel; and everything of value" and violated "the chastity of the women in sight of their husbands and friends." "The soldiers," noted Young, also "shot down our oxen, cows, hogs and fowls . . . taking part away and leaving the rest to rot in the streets."

Brigham Young and his fellow Latter-day Saints were in a most desperate situation. Their three principal leaders—Joseph Smith, Hyrum Smith, and Sidney Rigdon—were in jail. Five of Young's fellow apostles had apostatized, including Thomas Marsh, the Quorum's president and senior member. A sixth apostle, David Patten, was dead, and a seventh, Parley P. Pratt, was in jail with the Smiths and Rigdon. The Saints had been disarmed and ordered to leave the state immediately under the threat of extermination. Young could at least console himself that he and his family were safe and had not fallen victim to the ravages of the mob force. He had managed to elude Missouri authorities and avoid arrest due to his recent arrival in the state, which made him unknown to outsiders.

The defection of Thomas Marsh and death of David Patten made Young the most important Church leader not in captivity. Young received written instructions from the imprisoned Smith outlining his leadership role, along with that of the other apostles: "On you that is the twelve . . . devolves . . . management of the affairs of the Church." Smith also instructed that Young, as the oldest of the Twelve, be appointed president of the Quorum. Thus, Young assumed primary responsibility in looking out for the destitute Saints and evacuating them from Missouri.

Young moved quickly to assert this role as de facto Mormon leader. To aid the task of Mormon removal, Young addressed a memorial to the Missouri State Legislature, requesting an appropriation for property seized. The legislature appropriated a token amount of $2,ooo, far from adequate. So the Mormons fell back on their own resources. Young and six other Mormon leaders formed a committee of seven in charge of securing the means to migrate. Although some Mormons had adequate financial means, many did not. So Young persuaded 380 of his fellow Mormons to pool their available property to be disposed of for the purpose of providing means for the poor to migrate. A second committee of seven oversaw the removal of these destitute Saints. In all, Young supervised the removal of twelve to fifteen thousand individuals from Missouri to Illinois.

In mid-February, 1839, Young himself was forced to leave Missouri due to threats on his life. Young's position as acting Church leader made him a target for anti-Mormon Missourians. By the time he left, heading east to Illinois, Mary Ann had recovered from her long illness. They left behind their property and joined a seemingly endless stream of Mormon refugees making their way across the Missouri prairie.

Upon their arrival in Illinois, the Youngs took up residence in Atlas, a small town in Pike County, and then moved to Quincy, a larger community along the Mississippi River. From Quincy, Young continued to supervise the Missouri exodus and direct the general affairs of the Church, including the settlement of the hundreds of Mormon refugees who were pouring into Illinois.

In mid-April, Young decided to briefly return to Far West to literally fulfill an earlier revelation given by Joseph Smith. This revelation, actually a set of instructions, told Young and his fellow apostles to be in Far West on April 26, 1839, to do three things: first, to ordain two new members to the Twelve to replace those who had fallen; second, to lay the cornerstone and dedicate a temple site at Far West; and finally the Twelve were to take leave of Far West and travel abroad in missionary service for the Church. Young acted against the advice of some Saints who argued that the deteriorating Mormon situation in Missouri since the previous summer nullified the need to fulfill these instructions.

Young rounded up five of his fellow apostles and returned to Far West, arriving there on the morning of April 26. Finding the city nearly deserted, Young and his companions tried to carry out Smith's instructions precisely. First, they ordained two new members to the Twelve, Wilford Woodruff and George A. Smith (a cousin to Joseph Smith), and then offered a dedicatory prayer at the proposed temple site, symbolically laying the cornerstone by rolling up a large stone. Finally, they left Far West and returned to Illinois.

Upon his return, Young discovered that Joseph Smith had escaped from his six-month captivity and had taken up temporary residence in Quincy. Young met Smith on May 3 in what he described as one of the most joyful scenes of his life. Smith's safe return ended Young's temporary tenure as Latter-day Saint leader.

Young demonstrated once more his strong, unswerving loyalty to Joseph Smith and thus enhanced his own status. Young's dramatic and risky return to Missouri, literally fulfilling the Prophet's revelation/commandment, underscored this fact. But Young affirmed his loyalty in a more subtle way by *not* challenging Smith's leadership or even questioning his authority, a position of restraint that stood in contrast to the behavior of other ambitious Mormons. The temptation to seize control was certainly there, for Young wielded great power during Smith's imprisonment. But with Smith's return, Young quickly relinquished power and, moreover, accepted Smith's commandment to travel to England to direct Mormon missionary activity there, thus removing himself from the very center of Mormon power and influence.

Before leaving for England, Young faced the task of settling his family. He was not alone in this—an undertaking facing thousands of refugee Mormons. Joseph Smith tried to solve this problem by selecting a place to settle the Mormons fifty miles up the Mississippi River from Quincy, where he purchased two large parcels of land—one on the Illinois side of the river at Commerce, a small village, and the second just across the river in Iowa on what was known as the "Half-breed tract." In May, Young moved his family to Montrose on the Iowa side of the river, locating them in one room of an abandoned military barracks that they shared with Apostle Wilford Woodruff and his family. From this modest residence, Young could gaze across the Mississippi River to Commerce on the Illinois side, which Joseph Smith renamed Nauvoo—from a Hebrew word meaning "beautiful place." Nauvoo, destined to be the Mormons' most important city, was indeed beautifully situated on the bend of the Mississippi River, its land sloping gradually from the river bank to a height of about 500 feet. But the land itself was marshy and its climate unhealthy, which explains the region's unsettled, frontier condition when the Mormons first arrived.

Young and his entire family suffered from ill health. Along with countless numbers of recently arrived Mormons, the Youngs felt the ravages of cholera and the ague, most likely malaria, a debilitating disease of alternating chills and fever. The means of treating this illness were limited in this age of primitive medicine and the persistent recurrence of the disease itself. On occasion, Young and other Mormons relied on the power of faith healing. Joseph Smith cured Young in this way in July of 1839 as he lay sick in his cabin. Young recalled that Smith entered "and commanded me, in the name of Jesus Christ, to arise and be made whole. I arose and was healed." Young also administered to the sick when well himself and tended to other Church responsibilities, including the inspection of new sites on which to settle the multitude of Mormons that continued to stream into Nauvoo.

By September, 1839, Brigham Young was ready to depart for his English mission. However, the time could not have been worse. Mary Ann had just given birth to the Young's sixth child, a daughter they named Emma Alice (after the wife of Joseph Smith), which left her weak, a condition further complicated by the ague. Young himself was suffering from this same sickness and was unable to "go thirty rods to the river without assistance." Somehow he made it across the river to Nauvoo and the cabin of Heber C. Kimball. Finding Kimball suffering from the same affliction, both men remained in Nauvoo for a few days to regain their strength. Finally, they left, making their way to Quincy, where Brigham's ailing father was living after his own expulsion from Missouri. He saw his father one last time before his father's death one month later. Young later reflected on his father's unfulfilled ambitions, noting, "to the day of his death he wanted to command worlds, but the Lord would never permit him to get rich."

Young and Kimball then moved on to Kirtland, the former center of Mormon activity, where Young visited with his brother John and sister Nancy Kent and preached in the Kirtland Temple. Young and Kimball were joined by Apostles John Taylor and George A. Smith, also en route to England. From Kirtland, Young and his fellow apostles crossed the Erie Canal, made their way through upstate New York, into Massachusetts, Connecticut, and, finally, on February 6 arrived in New York City, their final destination before embarking for England. Another five weeks passed before Young and the others managed to book passage on the *Patrick Henry*, a packet ship of the Black Ball Line, paying $18 for steerage passage, plus $1 for a cook, who would prepare whatever food they brought along.

Departing on March 9, Young found the twenty-eight-day voyage pure misery. He was sick nearly all the way and confined to his berth. Upon his arrival in Liverpool on April 16, 1840, Young expressed relief in touching land by giving "a loud shout of hosannah." He was so debilitated from both the voyage and his recent bout with the ague that his cousin, Willard Richards, already in England, did not at first recognize him.

Young arrived in England at an opportune time in order to promote the growth of Mormonism. His arrival, however, did not represent the first Mormon effort in England. Three years earlier, Heber C. Kimball, accompanied by Willard Richards, had with moderate success opened England up to the new faith, scoring his greatest successes in the industrial northwest, particularly in and around Preston, managing to gain 1,300 converts. This figure increased slightly to 1,670 by the time of Young's arrival in 1840. The earlier efforts of Kimball and Richards were soon eclipsed as Mormon conversions reached 5,817—a more than threefold increase in just one year.

Several factors contributed to this phenomenal growth. First, English socioeconomic conditions aided the Mormon cause. By the early 1840s, England was suffering from a severe economic depression; part of the same worldwide economic crisis that affected America following the Panic of 1837. Unemployed English workers and destitute farmers looked for relief and comfort in religion, but major religious denominations failed to attract working-class converts. Methodism, which in the past had scored its greatest successes among the English working classes, now shunned these groups as it gained middle-class "respectability." Mormonism benefited from this negligence. Also, certain Mormon teachings and practices appealed to distressed Englishmen— including Mormon primitivism, millennialism, and utilization of a lay ministry—the same qualities that attracted Brigham Young ten years earlier.

In addition, the collective socioeconomic backgrounds of Young and his fellow apostles contributed to Mormon success. Several of the Twelve, like the people among whom they worked, came from an artisan, working-class background and thus could identify with their potential converts. Both Young and Kimball were in this category. Wilford Woodruff, another apostle who succeeded in converting some 1,800 people, had been a farmer and owner of a sawmill prior to his own Mormon conversion. Other apostles could claim similar agrarian/artisan roots, including John Taylor and George A. Smith. Taylor, in addition, was a native-born Englishman. Even the more educated and professionally trained apostles, including Parley and Orson Pratt, and Young's cousin, Willard Richards, were not far removed from their working-class roots.

Besides bonds of socioeconomic identification, Young's own extraordinary abilities as an organizer and administrator contributed to the Church's success. He kept close track of affairs in the various small, scattered, Mormon branches throughout the English Midlands, regularly visiting these branches and maintaining constant communications with local Mormon leaders. As he visited various Midland cities—including Preston, Liverpool, Manchester, Strafford, and Birmingham—he frequently preached to Mormon and non-Mormon audiences, delivering a total of over 400 sermons within a one-year period!

Young also strengthened the Church's missionary force. Until Young's arrival, most Mormon missionaries came from America. But more missionaries were needed to keep up with the needs of the rapidly expanding Church. Thus, Young decided to recruit more local English Mormon missionaries who could be pressed into service quickly. He also improved the efficiency of these missionaries by having the Church provide them food and clothing so that they would not be distracted from their primary task of preaching. In addition, he encouraged open-air meetings to publicize Mormonism when the missionaries were denied access to churches and other meeting halls.

Young also supervised the emigration of English Mormons to America, realizing that one of Mormonism's greatest appeals was its concept of the Gathering. Large numbers of English Saints clamored to leave their depression-ridden country for a better life in Nauvoo. Starting in June of 1840, with the departure of the first English Mormons to America,

Young oversaw the emigration of about 1,000 individuals. He arranged the booking of ship passages, provisioning, and tried to regulate the type of Mormon emigrant leaving England. He sought, under direction from Joseph Smith, to have men with capital migrate first so that they could purchase land and build mills and factories and thus establish an adequate economic base for the poorer Mormons to follow later. Young also suggested that the English Mormons live apart from the rest of the Nauvoo Saints since they had different customs. "My counsel," he said, "is that they go to the western states."

But Young's recommendation was not followed. The more than 4,000 English Mormons who migrated over the next six years settled in and around Nauvoo itself, mingling freely with American-born Mormons. These new immigrants provided an essential infusion of new blood, replacing the many individuals who had earlier left the Mormon faith. This English Mormon migration was part of the great Atlantic migration from Europe to America, which gathered steam by the 1840s as millions of uprooted English, Irish, and German immigrants—fleeing economic difficulties or political oppression—made their way to the New World.

Young attended to matters affecting those Mormons who remained behind. He sought to tie them closer together through the printed word, establishing an official periodical, the *Latter-day Saints Millennial Star,* which commenced publication in May of 1840. He also secured the copyright and had printed the *Book of Mormon,* making this work available for the first time to the English Saints, and supervised the composition and printing of a Mormon hymn book.

Brigham Young clearly demonstrated his abilities as an organizer and administrator. But at the same time he took care to defer to Joseph Smith on all important questions of policy. In one letter, he outlined his proposed actions and then carefully added, "If you see anything in or about the whole affair that is not right I ask . . . that you would make

[it] known to us." However, he did not let deference get in the way of acting on his own when necessary. Thus, he told Smith on another occasion:

> We want council and wisdom and anything that is good. Our motto is *go ahead*. Go ahead—and *ahead*. We are determined to go—until we have conquered every foe. So come life or come death we'll go ahead, but tell us if we are going wrong and we will right it.

Despite his extremely busy schedule, Young found time for sightseeing and diversion. In late November and early December of 1840, he traveled to London and visited such famous sights as the Tower of London, Buckingham Palace, and Westminster Abbey. He also attended services at St. Paul's Cathedral and visited the British Museum. In Manchester, where he was headquartered and spent most of his time, he also found things to see and do. On one occasion he attended a street fair, where he "saw a great variety of curiosities," including "a man nearly eight feet high, weighing 450 lbs, and a pig 1,200 lbs, a living skeleton [and] an elephant said to be the largest in Europe."

Young also observed the less entertaining, grim side of English life during the "Hungry 40s," noting that "Hunger & Rags are no curiosity here." England was filled with beggers. He found them present at the doors of his Manchester headquarters, he said, at the rate of from half a dozen to a dozen a day. He tried to help in his own small way by filling his pockets with coppers to give to them whenever he left the office. The corrosive effects of this poverty were everywhere. "Theft, robbery, murder . . . now fill the land," he said, and "drunkenness & gambling, sweering & debauching . . . are common on every hand." Those Englishmen lucky enough to be employed were not much better off. Predatory employers cared "little for their manufacturers & have reduced the workmen's wages to almost the lowest extremity." Workers labored all day for almost nothing. Young also noted with alarm that children as young as eight were working in the factories.

This general economic distress undoubtedly caused Young to worry about his wife and six children, whom he had left in an almost destitute state back in Nauvoo. This concern played on his subconscious. In a dream just two months after his arrival, Mary Ann told her absent husband, "we [the family] feele well but you must provide for your own families for the church are not able to doe [it] for them." That same month Young articulated his worries in a letter to Mary Ann, confessing "I think much about you having the c[are o]f such a large famely upon your hands and no one to see to or doe enything for them but yourself. Your task must be grate." He promised to send assistance as often as possible, and apparently provided funds on a regular basis.

Young also worried about the family's health, particularly when Mary Ann revealed the debilitating effects of living in Nauvoo's unhealthy environment. "The girls did not recover from their sickness until January. There was four or five months my family was helpless." Concerning her own health, Mary Ann noted that she was constantly fatigued. Deciding she had had enough, she asked for permission to move herself and the children from Nauvoo to a healthier climate east, but Young advised against this. Such a move, Young implied, could be interpreted as an act of disloyalty to Joseph Smith or at least inconsistent, in light of Young's concurrent efforts at gathering English Saints to Nauvoo. A desire to be close to the center of Mormon power and influence also dictated Young's position. He explained, "I . . . want to be with the Brotherin [of] the first Presidency . . . when I com home."

Young's basic attitude toward his prolonged, two-year separation from his family can be best described as ambivalent. He told Mary Ann, "I am as happy in this country as I could be in enny place in the world where I had got to be deprived of the sociity of my famely." Despite being away,

Young was enhancing his reputation as the most important Mormon leader in England, directing a rapidly growing Church. His ambivalence was summed up in the following to Mary Ann: "You might think that I am verry anxious to get home, but it [is] not so . . . but when the time has fully com, and the Lord says goe home my hart then will leap for joy."

In the spring of 1841, Joseph Smith ordered Young and his colleagues to return to America, noting satisfaction with their work. "The leaven" he pointed out, "can now spread without your being obliged to stay." Worsening international relations between the United States and Great Britain apparently also influenced Smith's decision. There were persistent rumors of possible war between the two countries, resulting from Canadian-American border skirmishes around New York, as well as a longstanding controversy over the boundary between Canada and Maine. This war scare served to feed basic Mormon millennialistic expectations that the entire world would soon be engulfed in a series of bloody conflicts.

Young and the Twelve Apostles, along with 130 British Mormons, boarded the *Rochester* and departed Liverpool on April 21, 1841. Young apparently weathered his return trip somewhat better than his earlier voyage to Britain. While nearly all the passengers were seasick, Young at first was well enough to assist those not so fortunate. But the roughness of the sea eventually got to Young and made him sick. Finally, on May 20, Young reached New York. From here he traveled west by way of Philadelphia to Pittsburg where he boarded a river boat that traveled along the Ohio and Mississippi Rivers. He finally arrived in Nauvoo along with the other Apostles on July 1, 1841.

Even before Young could be reunited with his family, Joseph Smith insisted on meeting with him and the rest of the Twelve Apostles. Young, in reporting to the Mormon leader, could point with pride to his numerous accomplishments. Seven to eight thousand Englishmen had been baptized, branches organized, and a permanent shipping agency established to facilitate the gathering of these new converts to Nauvoo. Also, five thousand copies of the *Book of Mormon,* three thousand hymn books, and an English Mormon periodical, the *Millennial Star,* were made available to local Mormons. Smith, impressed with Young's hard work and personal sacrifices, assured his loyal disciple through revelation, "your offering is acceptable to me." Status and recognition were his. Young had established himself as an important leader and part of Mormonism's ruling elite. But new trials lay ahead that would put Young's Mormon commitment to the ultimate test.

Brigham Young, Mary Ann, and their children, from a painting done in Nauvoo about 1843. From left to right, Brigham, Sr, Luna, Joseph Angell, Brigham, Jr, Mary Ann, Emma Alice, John W. and Mary Ann. (Courtesy of the Utah State Historical Society.)

III

New Trials and Renewed Commitment

UPON HIS RETURN FROM ENGLAND, Brigham Young found that Nauvoo had changed drastically in the twenty-two months he had been gone. No longer a rude frontier village of log dwellings astride a swampy marshland, Nauvoo had become a rapidly growing city of 3,000 and would grow to 10,000 by the end of 1841. An orderly procession of houses, many of them stone and brick, dotted the hillside rising from the Mississippi. At the top of the hill, work had begun on a new temple slated to be larger and more magnificent than the one in Kirtland.

Young also noted the way Nauvoo was governed under the Nauvoo Charter—a liberal document that gave its citizens broad powers of self-government. The mayor and city council could pass any law not directly conflicting with the provisions of the American and Illinois State Constitutions. The mayor and city council also had the power to act as a municipal court and the city was authorized its own armed force—the Nauvoo Legion. Nominally a part of the state militia, the Legion actually functioned as the city's private army, recruiting all able-bodied men over twenty-one into its ranks. The Charter also allowed Nauvoo citizens to organize their own university. The Mormons gained this liberal charter from the Illinois State Legislature, enlisting the support of such diverse Illinois politicians as Abraham Lincoln

51

and Stephen A. Douglas—both serving in the legislature at the time.

Another change evident to Young was the emergence of John C. Bennett as an important political and economic advisor to Joseph Smith. A recent Mormon convert and physician by training, Bennett did not even belong to the Church when Young left for England in late 1839. He had joined in 1840 and his rise to power had been meteoric. In physical appearance, Bennett stood 5'5", with a dark complexion and dark eyes, and seemed a stark contrast to the tall, blond Mormon leader. But he was charming, handsome, and patently ambitious. By 1841, Bennett held several important positions, among them mayor of Nauvoo, major general in the Nauvoo Legion, and assistant counselor in the Church. Thus Bennett was a formidable figure within Mormonism. Bennett gained Smith's confidence because he helped secure legislative approval for the Nauvoo Charter and aided in draining the swamps near Nauvoo, thereby eliminating the cause of that city's earlier health problems. Bennett, therefore, stood as a potential rival to Brigham Young.

Young's immediate concern upon returning to Nauvoo was not the potential rivalry of Bennett but the well-being of his family. During his absence they had moved into a small log cabin situated on a low, swampy lot in Nauvoo. Young concentrated on improving the family's habitat and cultivating the lot into a garden. Improving his property in other ways, he built a temporary shed for his cow and a fruit and produce cellar. Young's improvements accommodated a family that changed in several ways. His oldest daughter, Elizabeth, married Edmund Ellsworth in July of 1842. But her place was taken by Mary Ann's last two children: Luna, born in August, 1842; and John W., born two years later in October, 1844.

Despite the time allocated for family, Young continued to spend most of his time in the service of the Church. Young and the Quorum of the Twelve were assigned an ever-increasing number of duties and responsibilities, including the settling of emigrants in Nauvoo. The Twelve appointed Mormon missionaries working both within the United States and abroad to give advice and direction to those Mormons migrating from England to Nauvoo—a total in excess of 4,700 by 1846. Young and the Twelve also operated the Church's printing facility and assumed editorial responsibility for its official newspaper, *The Times and Seasons*. The Twelve also participated in the development of new ritual within the Church, namely baptism for the dead, which was practiced for the first time in the partially completed Nauvoo Temple in 1841.

Young also assumed a prominent role in other Nauvoo affairs. In September, 1841, he became a member of the Nauvoo city council and three months later became a Mason, joining Joseph Smith and other Latter-day Saint leaders who also embraced Masonry. This Mormon interest resulted because Smith and other Mormon leaders looked toward Masonry as a means to gain social acceptance and protection. On the Illinois frontier, as in other frontier regions, the most successful and powerful men were Masons. Also, the Mormons hoped their association with the Masons would prevent a reoccurrence of the anti-Mormon violence that had led to their expulsion from Missouri, relying on the Masonic promise of protection and assistance in times of distress. Another feature of Masonry that appealed to the Mormons was its use of symbolism, which bore some resemblance to Mormonism, including the utilization of secret oaths, penalties, signs, grips, and secret means of recognition that bound members together.

Indeed, Masonic ritual bore some similarities to the secret temple ordinances that Joseph Smith revealed to Brigham Young and other select Mormons in May of 1842. Through what came to be known as the "endowment ceremony," Young manifested his strong commitment to Mormonism. He gave an oath of loyalty and secrecy along with pledges of chastity and faithfulness. The last part of the ritual involved a special marriage ceremony in which Young was remarried to Mary Ann.

Brigham Young's commitment to Mormonism went through its greatest trial when, in 1841, Joseph Smith unveiled his concept of plural marriage. There are several possible explanations for Smith's decision to introduce this practice. One was the influence of the upstate New York environment of Smith's youth, which produced widespread marital experimentation as evidenced in the practices of the Shakers, Oneida Perfectionists, and others. Also, Smith, through his continuing involvement in translating holy scripture, strongly identified with polygamous Old Testament patriarchs like Abraham as cultural models. Also, it is possible that Smith wanted to give religious sanctification to his own allegedly strong sexual drives, which his wife Emma apparently could not satisfy. Perhaps polygamy was the product of a so-called "middle-age crisis" that Smith, along with other Mormon leaders, experienced by the late 1830s and early 1840s. The taking of plural wives, particularly young, attractive ones, represented an effort to recapture youthful vigor and vitality. Finally, and perhaps most important polygamy may have been the product of Smith's belief that the Mormons had arrived at a critical millennialistic stage, "suspended between two worlds," i.e., an old, decadent order on the verge of dying and a new glorious order on the verge of being born. At this critical time, polygamy would serve as a means to test the loyalties of his followers and thus secure greater social cohesion.

Young's first reaction to polygamy was shock and dread. He later recalled that it "was the first time in my life that I had desired the grave . . . when I saw a funeral, I felt to envy the corpse in its situation and to regret that I was not in the coffin, knowing the toil and labor that my body would have to undergo." He expressed his reservations directly to Joseph Smith, but Smith simply replied, "Brother Brigham, the Lord will reveal it to you." Thus, Young found himself in a dilemma relative to his Mormon commitment with the alternatives less than attractive. He could embrace polygamy, a practice he found morally abhorrent; or he could refuse, which would place him in defiance of Joseph Smith—a move that could lead to his departure from the Church. Young would thus be left to his own devices, perhaps forced to resume his pre-Mormon occupation as an artisan which, in contrast to his achievements while a Mormon leader, had brought him precious little success and less recognition.

In the end, Young overcame his initial reservations and accepted polygamy. He took his first plural wife in June of 1842, marrying 20-year-old Lucy Ann Decker Seeley. The mother of two children, Lucy Ann had previously separated from her first husband, Isaac Seeley, an abusive individual. Young knew Lucy Ann due to the close ties between the Youngs and Deckers. Bonds of friendship going back many years existed between Brigham Young and Lucy Ann's father, Isaac. Also, Lucy Ann's mother, divorced from Isaac, had married Brigham's younger brother, Lorenzo Dow.

How Mary Ann reacted to Young's marriage to Lucy Ann is not known. But any Mormon husband entering polygamy had to secure the consent of the first wife before doing so. But, given the known reaction of the first wives of other Mormon polygamists, she was probably less than enthusiastic. Mary Ann, at least, did not have to tolerate Lucy Ann under the same roof, for Lucy Ann lived away in her own residence or with relatives. Besides Lucy Ann, it appears that Young attempted to induce at least one additional woman into polygamy during the summer of 1842. But Martha Brotherton, an 18-year-old convert from Manchester, England, rejected Young, left Mormonism, and went public, asserting that Young with the help of Joseph Smith and Heber C. Kimball had tried to force her into polygamy. These charges circulated widely in the non-Mormon press in 1842. Young and other Mormons dismissed Brotherton's accusation as "a base falsehood," castigating her as a "mean harlot" or "old Jezebel, whom the dogs eat."

The still secret practice of polygamy sent shockwaves throughout the Mormon community. Two prominent Mormon leaders, Sidney Rigdon and Orson Pratt, a member of the Twelve, bitterly opposed polygamy. Pratt's opposition resulted from his belief that Joseph Smith had tried to induce his wife Sarah into becoming one of his plural wives during Pratt's absence in England. A third Mormon leader, John C. Bennett, went to the other extreme, utilizing polygamy as a means to justify his own profligate behavior. When Smith called him to account, Bennett rebelled and was excommunicated in the spring of 1842. The ex-Mormon then wrote a lurid exposé of polygamy first published in the *Sangamo Journal,* then reprinted in newspapers throughout Illinois, and finally published as a book, *The History of the Saints, or, An Exposé of Joe Smith and Mormonism.*

Brigham Young affirmed his commitment to Mormonism by supporting Joseph Smith in his actions against both Orson Pratt and John C. Bennett. Young tried to get Pratt to cease his "rebellion against" Smith and "obey his counsel" by laboring with him "diligently in a spirit of meekness [and] long-suffering . . . forbearance." But Pratt refused to recant his charge against Smith and was temporarily excommunicated under Young's direction. Young found the John C. Bennett case more complicated due to his widely published exposé. To "show the falsity" of Bennett's charges, Smith asked Young to travel throughout Illinois in company with four other apostles. Over the next three months, Young visited and preached at Lima, Quincy, Jacksonville, and Springfield.

In late November, Young suffered from a severe case of scarlet fever that almost took his life. Joseph Smith intervened and administered to his stricken disciple. But the fever remained and, according to Young, "the skin began to peel from my body, and I was skinned all over." By the eighteenth day he appeared to improve, but then the fever entered a critical phase. His "chin dropped" and "breath stopped." Mary Ann, who was attending him, acted immediately and as Young himself later recalled:

> . . . threw some cold water in my face; that having no effect, she dashed a handful of strong camphor into my face and eyes, which I did not feel in the least, neither did I move a muscle. She then held my nostrils between her thumb and finger, and placing her mouth directly over mine, blew into my lungs until she filled them with air. This set my lungs in motion, and I again began to breathe.

Throughout this ordeal, he was attended not only by Mary Ann but also by Isaac Decker, the father of his plural wife, Lucy Ann. Whether Young saw any connection between his plural marriage to Lucy Ann and his severe illness can only be conjectured. Perhaps there were moments of despair and self-doubt when he felt he was being punished for practicing polygamy while at the same time denying its existence, as he had done the previous summer.

But Young was not one to brood over such possibilities, particularly after he recovered and by January, 1843 resumed his full agenda of Church duties. He continued to supervise the activities of missionaries both within the United States and abroad, dispatching them to the British Isles where Mormonism continued to grow, and to a new arena, the South Pacific. In July of 1843, Young was instructed by Joseph Smith to travel to the eastern United States to collect funds from Church members for the completion of the temple and a guest hotel called the Nauvoo House. Throughout the 3–4 months that he was gone, he exchanged letters with Mary Ann back in Nauvoo. He received distressing news of the family's poor health. Mary

Ann suffered from influenza and cholera morbus, while Brigham Jr. and his daughters were afflicted with scarlet fever. Tragedy struck Young's own household when Young's frail, sickly daughter Mary Ann died of "dropsy and canker," in August. Brigham himself remained weak from his own bout with scarlet fever the previous winter. He revealed his feelings towards home and family, remarking "when I was so sick I thought I could only be at home, I should be thankful. There is no place like home to me." Finally, on October 22, he arrived back in Nauvoo.

Efforts to promote polygamy occupied a significant portion of Brigham Young's time following his return to Nauvoo. He received instructions from Smith on the "many principles . . . of celestial [plural] marriage." Smith had given this practice elaborate scriptural sanctification through a revelation during Young's absence. Immediately after he was briefed by Smith, Young took two additional plural wives, Augusta Adams Cobb and Harriet Cook, marrying both of these women on the same day, November 2, 1843. Young apparently met these women, both from New England, during his missionary activities in the East. Augusta Adams Cobb, at 41 the older of the two, was an educated, Bostonian, married, and the mother of seven children. After converting to Mormonism in Boston, she left her husband and five oldest children, taking her two youngest to Nauvoo and Brigham Young. Harriet Cook, by contrast, was only nineteen, unmarried, less educated and apparently less sophisticated in her language and actions. Six months later, in May of 1844, the 42-year-old Young took a fourth plural wife, 15-year-old Clarissa Decker, sister of Lucy Ann Decker, his first plural wife.

Mary Ann's reaction to the quickening pace of Brigham's marital activity is unknown. But, as with Lucy Ann, Mary Ann had to give her consent. Mary Ann, however, did not have to tolerate these women in the same household. Augusta Adams Cobb returned to New England, taking up residence in Salem, Massachusetts. Harriet Cook and Clarissa

Decker both found accommodations with family or friends in Nauvoo. Mary Ann, moreover, possibly found it easier to accept this situation as her own living condition improved. For in late May, 1843, Young moved her and the children into a large two-story brick house.

Increased difficulties in Nauvoo, stemming in part from the still-secret practice of polygamy, caused Joseph Smith, Brigham Young, and other Mormon leaders to seriously consider a Mormon move from Nauvoo to the Far West. Recurring rumors of polygamy's existence intensified local non-Mormon feelings of jealousy and animosity already strong due to Nauvoo's status as the most prosperous city in Illinois. The Mormons looked to the Far West as "a place of refuge" where "the devil cannot dig us out" and "where we can live as old as we have a mind to." Therefore, in February, 1844, Smith instructed Young and the Twelve "to send out a delegation and investigate the locations of California and Oregon and find a good location where we can move after the Temple is completed. And build a city in a day— and have government of our own." At first they selected eight men for a small, limited expedition, but then Smith pushed for a larger expedition requiring the services of twenty-five men.

Increased Mormon interest in the Far West was part of a general mood of Manifest Destiny that reached a fever pitch by the mid-1840s with large numbers of Americans migrating to the Pacific Northwest and Americans in Texas and California pushing for annexation to the United States. In harmony with this mood of Manifest Destiny, Smith, Young, and other Mormon leaders expanded their own concept of Zion to include "the whole [of] America" both North and South America "where the Mountain of the Lord's house shall be." Mormon leaders anticipated the settlement of Latter-day Saints in California and Oregon plus the possible establishment of extensive Mormon settlements in southwestern Texas.

But the Mormons did not follow through on plans for an immediate western migration. In January, 1844, Joseph Smith decided to run for president of the United States as an independent candidate. The Mormons felt that involvement in presidential politics would publicize their grievances with the federal government after they had tried unsuccessfully to enlist the aid of federal officials to secure compensation for losses suffered during their earlier expulsion from Missouri. Smith had earlier written letters to leading contenders for the presidency in 1844—John C. Calhoun, Henry Clay, Lewis Cass, Richard M. Johnson, and Martin Van Buren—asking each his "rule of action relative to [the Mormons] as a people," but had failed to receive any satisfactory replies. Besides dramatizing Mormon grievances, a presidential campaign would further publicize Mormonism itself, attracting new converts to the faith.

Smith's pursuit of the presidency was also encouraged by a strong sense of Mormon millennialism. He felt that the government of the United States was on the verge of collapse to be replaced by the just rule of the King of Kings. In anticipation of the imminent millennium, Smith established a Council of Fifty to serve as interim government just prior to the millennium. If by some quirk of fate (or act of God) Smith won the presidency, he could step into office and personally hasten the Second Coming and the millennium.

As he undertook his presidential campaign, Smith adopted a presidential platform containing a conglomeration of ideas drawn from others. Echoing Henry Clay and the Whigs, Smith called for a high tariff and a national bank. Like the Democrats and James K. Polk, he called for the annexation of Texas and Oregon. In the spirit of James G. Birney and the Liberty Party, Smith called for the abolition of slavery before 1850 under state initiative and through the payment of federal compensation to the slaveholders. And echoing the social reformer Dorothea Dix, Smith advocated prison reform.

Joseph Smith sought the presidency at a time of increased

internal opposition. A dissident group of influential Mormons opposed polygamy. This group included William Law, a prominent Canadian Mormon recently appointed to the Church First Presidency, his brother Wilson Law, and Austin Cowles of the Nauvoo High Council. Smith excommunicated these dissidents. But, undaunted, they set up their own rival Mormon organization, declaring Joseph Smith a fallen prophet. Brigham Young viewed this development with minimal concern, for Smith had faced similar dissension on earlier occasions. He noted rather nonchalantly, "Tis the same old story over again—'The doctrine is right but Joseph is a fallen prophet.' "

Despite these problems, Smith, Young, and others pushed ahead with the presidential campaign. Smith adhered to the established practice that presidential candidates did not "electioneer" for themselves. Thus, Brigham Young and other church leaders assumed prominent roles in the campaign. Young helped recruit over three hundred Mormon volunteers and sent them to different parts of the United States. On May 21, Young himself left Nauvoo to campaign in the East. He visited Kirtland, Ohio, the former Mormon stronghold where he preached in the Kirtland Temple, but found the Saints there "dead and cold to the things of God." In Kirtland and in the Western Reserve, generally a hotbed of abolitionist sentiment, Young presented Smith's antislavery views. But Young was no abolitionist and, in fact, when confronted by "a large company" of anti-slavery advocates on their way "to an abolitionist convention" in Akron, he criticized them for manifesting a spirit "to put down everybody but themselves." After he left Kirtland and arrived at Fairport, on the shore of Lake Erie, he wrote Mary Ann, confessing: "I feele lonsom. O that I had you with me this somer I think I should be happy . . . [the] older I grow the more I desire to stay at my home instead of traveling." He made his way east, arriving in Boston on June 16. From there he traveled to Salem, visiting his plural wife Augusta

Adams Cobb, and daughter Vilate, who was attending a local girls' school. Attempting to promote closer bonds in his extended family, Young encouraged Vilate to seek council from Augusta. He continued to promote Joseph Smith's candidacy, characterizing the Mormon leader the "smartest man in the Union."

Young's flattering observation, however, was not upheld by Smith's less-than-prudent actions against William Law and other dissidents back in Nauvoo. These opponents had promoted their rival Mormon movement by establishing an opposition newspaper, the *Nauvoo Expositor,* in which they attempted to expose alleged misdeeds of Smith. Smith responded by calling upon the Nauvoo city council to have the *Nauvoo Expositor* declared a public nuisance, ordering the destruction of the press and all available copies of the newspaper.

This action, a clear violation of freedom of the press, stimulated intense anti-Mormon feelings in the communities surrounding Nauvoo, with the most rabid anti-Mormons calling for extermination of all of the Mormons in Nauvoo. In an apparent replay of the situation he faced six years earlier in Missouri, Smith agreed on June 25, to give himself up to county officials in Carthage to face trial on charges of treason. He allowed himself with his brother Hyrum and Apostles John Taylor and Willard Richards to be incarcerated in the jail at Carthage. By this action, Smith sought to guarantee the safety of his Nauvoo followers and hopefully ride out the firestorm of anti-Mormon protest as he had done in Missouri. But this time the outcome was different. Just two days after Smith's arrest on June 27, a well-organized, disciplined mob, aided and abetted by a number of the leading citizens of Carthage and surrounding towns entered the jail killing Joseph, his brother Hyrum, and wounding John Taylor. Willard Richards alone escaped injury.

These traumatic events transpired unknown to Brigham Young in Massachusetts, who continued to campaign for

Nauvoo, Illinois as it appeared from the Iowa side of the Mississippi River in the mid-1840s at the time Brigham Young emerged
as principal Mormon leader. (Courtesy of the LDS Church-
Library-Archives. Printed with permission.)

Smith. On June 27, the day of Smith's assassination, Young
later claimed he "felt a heavy depression of spirit, and so
melancholy I could not converse with any degree of pleasure." Unaware of the tragic events at Carthage, he could not
assign any reason for his peculiar feeling. On July 9, he
heard "for the first time, the rumors concerning the death
of Joseph and Hyrum," and a week later, on July 16, he
received absolute confirmation.

The violent death of Joseph Smith brought Brigham Young
new trials. As a principal Mormon leader and probable successor to Smith, he faced the possible threat of assassination
himself. He was warned by both his wife Mary Ann and
Willard Richards that Smith's assassins were lying in wait for
him as he prepared to leave Boston and return to Nauvoo.
Thus, Young traveled in great haste, avoiding his usual
route along the Ohio and Mississippi Rivers, taking instead

an out-of-the-way route and arrived back in Nauvoo on August 6.

In Nauvoo, Young sought to affirm his claim as Mormon leader, beating back the counterclaims of a series of rivals. The first of these was Sidney Rigdon, who had set out to push his own claim to Mormon leadership, even before Young's return to Nauvoo.

Rigdon seemed a formidable opponent. In the wake of Smith's death and William Law's apostasy, he was the sole remaining member of the Church's First Presidency. But by 1844 he had lost much of his charisma and vigor as a result of his debilitating imprisonment during the Missouri persecutions. Personal and doctrinal differences, including his opposition to polygamy, had alienated Rigdon from Joseph Smith and other Mormon leaders. By the time of Smith's death, he was no longer part of Mormonism's ruling inner circle and had actually left Nauvoo to return to his former home at Pittsburg.

Brigham Young personally confronted Sidney Rigdon when both men presented their rival claims to a special conference of the Church on August 8. Coming before this meeting, Rigdon, a tall man, appeared stout, elderly—much older than his 51 years. Hollow-mouthed, having lost his front teeth, he "harrangued the Saints for about one and a half hours," presenting himself as the "ordained spokesman" for the martyred Joseph Smith, and offered to serve as "guardian for the Church."

Young then addressed the same group. In contrast to Rigdon, Young claimed Mormon leadership *not* just for himself alone, but "in connection with the Quorum of the Twelve," whom he maintained "have the keys of the Kingdom of God." Young's forceful presentation electrified those present, some of whom later claimed that Young, in his speech, mannerisms, and even physical appearance, assumed the characteristics of the martyred Joseph Smith! It seemed to the assembled Saints that the slain Mormon leader had returned to indicate that his mantle had fallen on the shoulders of Young.

When the assembled Saints were asked to vote on whom they wanted to lead the Church, they chose Young and the Twelve. Although Rigdon continued to challenge Young and started his own rival church, he found himself relegated to the fringes of Mormonism, no longer a significant threat to Brigham Young.

Although he brushed aside the challenge of Rigdon with relative ease, Young faced the more formidable task of keeping his followers together in Nauvoo and consolidating his position as Mormon leader. This task was complicated by the violent hostility that the Saints continued to face from their non-Mormon neighbors. Young maintained that while he wanted the Mormons to remain in Nauvoo, he would lead his followers "into the wilderness" if the hostility continued and intensified. Anticipating a general exodus, two of Young's followers promoted their own migrations from Nauvoo. The first was organized by Lyman Wight, one of Young's fellow apostles, who secured permission to take a group of Mormons to Texas—then an independent republic under the leadership of Sam Houston. A second Mormon leader, James Emmett, acting on earlier permission from Joseph Smith, led a company of two hundred Latter-day Saints into a wilderness region along the upper Missouri River.

Young, however, soon had second thoughts. Fearful that Emmett and Wight's activities might precipitate a general exodus, Young urged the faithful to remain in Nauvoo. He withdrew his earlier permission for Wight's Texas migration. As for Emmett, Young urged him to return to Nauvoo. Young, moreover, promoted a general gathering of his Latter-day Saint followers to Nauvoo. Young envisioned Nauvoo as a Temple city, with completion of the Temple a top priority. Here, sacred Temple ordinances essential for Mormon salvation could be performed. Young also hoped to

promote in Nauvoo "every branch of industry and manufacture," and the "purchase of farms in the adjoining country"
so that "our infant city may grow and flourish and be
strengthened a hundred fold." Under Young's direction,
Nauvoo continued to grow, as Mormons from the eastern
states and England continued to migrate there, bringing its
total population to 12,000–15,000, making it one of the largest cities in Illinois.

Meanwhile, Young continued to face opposition. From
within the family of Joseph Smith the Mormon prophet's
younger brother William challenged Young, despite his earlier support at the time of Sidney Rigdon's challenge. By
1845, Smith came to believe that as the sole surviving
brother of Joseph Smith he was entitled to a higher leadership position than that of apostle. Young tried to placate him
by appointing him a "Patriarch to the whole church." At first
Smith appeared satisfied, but soon the erratic Smith turned
against Young, claiming that Young and the rest of the
Twelve were all dependent upon his family for the priesthood. A short time later Smith declared himself president of
the Church.

Despite Smith's provocative actions, Young exhibited extraordinary forebearance due in large part to his respect for
the family of the slain Mormon leader—still considered by
most Saints as the First Family of Mormonism. Various
Smith family members, Lucy Mack Smith, the prophet's
mother, and Emma, his widow, tended to support William.
However, Young's tolerance reached its limits when William
Smith published a pamphlet entitled *A Proclamation and
Faithful Warning to All the Saints,* which attacked Young in
personal terms. Smith assailed Young's tyrannical leadership
and accused him of promoting polygamy and also implicated
him in the murder of dissident Mormons in Nauvoo. Smith
questioned Young's right to wear the mantle of his slain
brother, maintaining that Joseph, just prior to his death, had
characterized Young as "a man whose passions, if unre-

strained, were calculated to make him the most licentious man in the world," and that if Young "should [ever] lead the church, he would certainly lead it to destruction." These attacks caused Young to order Smith's excommunication from the Church.

His punitive actions notwithstanding, Young continued to seek the support of both Lucy Mack and Emma Smith. Young flattered Lucy Mack Smith as the "aged and honored parent of Joseph Smith," proclaiming her "a mother of Israel" and gave her a new carriage, property in Nauvoo, and a promise to "supply all her wants." Soon, Lucy Mack backed away from William and publically endorsed Young as Mormon leader. Young, however, found Emma more difficult to deal with. Emma was important due to her status as Joseph Smith's principal widow, and because she was the mother of Smith's four young adolescent sons, including his namesake, 11-year-old Joseph Smith III. The Mormon prophet had secretly designated "Young Joseph," as he was known, his successor shortly before his death. Young failed to gain Emma's support because differences between these two strong-willed individuals were just too great. Emma clashed with Young over the disposition of the martyred prophet's estate and strenuously opposed Mormonism's still secret practice of plural marriage.

Despite the challenge posed by Emma and ultimately her sons, Young faced a more immediate threat from James J. Strang. A brilliant individual, Strang had been born and educated in upstate New York where he was admitted to the bar. He then migrated to Burlington, Wisconsin, where he practiced law and converted to Mormonism in January of 1844, six months prior to Joseph Smith's death. Strang, an enthusiastic convert, visited the Mormon prophet in Nauvoo and received authorization to establish a stake of Zion in Wisconsin. In the wake of Joseph Smith's death, Strang presented a letter that he claimed Smith had written him shortly before his death, designating Strang his successor with all his spiritual and temporal powers. Young was unimpressed. Proclaiming Strang's letter a forgery, he excommunicated the Mormon upstart delivering him over to "the buffetings of Satan."

Undaunted, Strang set up a rival Mormon organization. Superficially the charismatic Strang appeared a formidable challenger. Strang appeared physically unimpressive, standing five foot nine with a large head, an exceptionally high forehead, florid complexion, small hazel eyes, and black beard. But he possessed a rapid, loud-talking voice and a spellbinding personality. He projected a type of mysticism similar to that of Joseph Smith himself. Like Smith earlier, he claimed supernatural powers translating into holy scripture a set of brass plates which he claimed had been Divinely revealed to him.

Although Young, in his typically earthy language, advised his followers to: "let Strangism alone. It is not worth the skin of a flea," Strang through his ideas, including his initial opposition to polygamy, made serious inroads into the ranks of Young's movement, finding pockets of support in the eastern states and in England. Strang's followers included at one time or another William Smith and John C. Bennett—the ever-opportunistic, former assistant counselor under Joseph Smith. Also joining Strang were two former apostles: William E. McLellin and John E. Page, along with William Marks, a one-time president of the Nauvoo stake.

Despite his direct challenge, Strang faced difficulties of his own. Unlike Young, Strang did not inherit a functioning church organization and did not have a large Mormon population base from which to draw a following. And Strang eventually adopted his own form of plural marriage, which not only blurred the doctrinal differences between himself and Young, but also alienated many followers who had initially favored him over the polygamous Young. Thus, by the late 1840s, Strang was no longer a major threat, having led his small Mormon following to an isolated island settlement on Lake Michigan.

In Nauvoo, Young and his followers continued to face strong opposition from their non-Mormon neighbors. In September, 1844, an anti-Mormon mob appeared to be making preparations for a "wolf hunt" designed to drag "authorities of the Church out to Carthage to murder them." Young strengthened the defenses around Nauvoo and assumed command of the Nauvoo Legion. But the Legion's effectiveness as a defense force was limited after Illinois Governor Thomas Ford ordered it to give up its state-issued weapons in an attempt to restore peace between the Saints and their non-Mormon neighbors.

The anti-Mormon wolf hunt never materialized. But Young and his followers found themselves even more vulnerable when the Illinois state legislature in January of 1845 repealed the Nauvoo Charter, thereby disincorporating the city of Nauvoo and nullifying the authority of both the city police and Nauvoo Legion. Young looked for other ways to maintain order and protect his followers. He organized his own ad hoc police force that consisted of two to three hundred deacons known as the "whittling and whistling society." This organization, under the direct supervision of bishops ordained by Young, assumed responsibliity for safety within particular geographic districts (or wards) of the city. The deacons were stationed within particular wards to "maintain peace and good order." Upon the approach of any suspicious outsider, the deacons would take out their large bowie knives and begin whittling pine shingles, accompanying their action with quiet but suggestive whistling. Following the stranger wherever he went, the deacons' intimidating behavior usually convinced the stranger to leave Nauvoo as soon as possible. One such stranger, a member of the State Legislature that had just repealed the Nauvoo Charter, complained to Young about this inhospitable treatment. Young satirically replied, "I am very sorry you are imposed upon by the people: we used to have laws here, but you have taken them away from us."

Young strengthened his hold over the Mormon movement in other ways. He asserted control over various branches in the eastern states and in Great Britain by utilizing the services of apostles faithful to him. Thus he dispatched Apostle Parley P. Pratt to the East and Apostle Wilford Woodruff to England. The two apostles averted the rival claims to Mormon authority of Sidney Rigdon, James J. Strang, and others, thus holding in line these branches for Young and the Twelve. Mormon activity in Great Britain flourished as more than six thousand Englishmen joined the Church.

Young also asserted authority by pushing construction on the still-unfinished Nauvoo Temple. This activity gave Young's followers a sense of purpose or goal. The Temple itself, moreover, stood as a symbol of continuity between Young and the martyred Joseph Smith. Completion of the Temple was crucial because certain sacred rites were performed exclusively within its walls. By late 1845, both the ground floor, designed for general Church meetings, and the upper sealing rooms—set aside for sacred endowment and marriage ceremonies—were complete and ready for use.

In addition to his demanding role as Church leader, Young had to concern himself with his large, growing family. The frail health of Mary Ann occupied his attention during the late summer of 1844. Pregnant with their sixth child, Mary Ann was very ill and Brigham spent time at home waiting upon her. She recovered sufficiently to give birth on October 1 to a son they named John Willard. In response to his growing family, Young remodeled and enlarged the family residence, adding wings one story high on each side of the existing structure.

Young's domestic responsibilities increased in other ways for during the hectic nine-month period from September of 1844 to May of 1845, he took fifteen additional wives, increasing his total number of plural wives to twenty—a fourfold increase. Five of these women were formerly married to the slain Joseph Smith. Young offered himself to these women with the understanding that they would receive the protection of his name in this life, but were "sealed" to Joseph Smith in the next. Also, any offspring resulting from these marriages while part of Young's household would be considered the posterity of Joseph Smith in the next world. Two of Smith's widows, Emily Dow Partridge and Louisa Beaman, would bear Young a total of eleven children. But Eliza R. Snow, the most prominent of Smith's widows to marry Young, did not bear him any children at all. Instead, it appeared that Snow and Young maintained a strictly platonic relationship. Young, however, looked to Eliza for advice and counsel, respecting her as one of Mormonism's brightest, most articulate women. She was noted for her work in founding the Relief Society in 1842—an important Church women's organization—and her authorship of poetry and church hymns earned her the titles of "Zion's Poetess" and Mormonism's "First Lady of Letters."

It appears that many of Young's wives were like Eliza R. Snow, married in name only. Of the fifteen, only five would bear him children. Others were widows or older women, like forty-eight-year-old Clarissa Blake, or the sickly Olive Frost, who died within a year. To these women, Young gave financial aid or merely the protection of his name.

Since Young's wives did not live in any single residence, Young spent a great deal of time traveling from household to household looking after their needs. Within the year, Young became the father of three sons. These included Brigham Heber, born in June, 1845, the son of Lucy Ann Decker, Young's first plural wife; Edward Partridge, born to Emily Dow Partridge in October, 1845—one of Joseph Smith's widows whom he had recently married; and Oscar Brigham, born in February, 1846, the son of Harriet Cook, the sharp-tongued New Englander whom Young had married in 1843. In summation, the birth of these three children plus his marriages to fifteen women meant additional responsibility, and this in turn reinforced his commitment to Mormonism and its peculiar institution. Young's enlarged family also meant new trials and

difficulties as he tried to conceal the secret practice of polygamy from prying outsiders.

Indeed, Young and his followers found themselves increasingly at odds with these neighbors by the spring of 1845.
Governor Ford pledged to bring the murderers of Joseph
Smith to justice. Although several suspects were arrested and
tried in Carthage, the non-Mormon jury and judge acquitted
them. This angered Young, who denounced not only the
lawyers involved in this case but lawyers in general. "All of the
lawsuits," lamented Young, "that have been got up against the
Saints have been hatched by fee lawyers, tavern keepers, et
cetera." He concluded, "I would rather have a good six-
shooter than all the lawyers in Illinois."

As it turned out, Brigham Young needed more than a
good six-shooter to deal with the increasing violence directed against the Mormons. In September, anti-Mormon
mobs attacked Mormon settlements in the outlying areas
surrounding Nauvoo, burning barns and crops. Young
ordered the harassed Mormons into Nauvoo and seemed
determined to resist these attacks. He issued instructions to
some of his beseiged followers who remained behind: "at the
first sign of aggression . . . give them the cold lead."

This increasingly tense situation meant no letup in the trials
Brigham Young found himself and his followers subjected to.
But at the same time, Young's commitment to Mormonism
itself was absolute, strengthened by his acceptance of polygamy and success in securing primary control of the Mormon
movement following Joseph Smith's death. He had turned
back the challenges of various rivals, including Sidney Rigdon, James J. Strang, and even the slain Mormon leader's
own brother, William Smith. By late 1845, however, as hostilities between the Mormons and their non-Mormon neighbors
reached critical proportions, Young faced a new monumental
trial—the need to migrate with his followers to a new frontier
sanctuary.

I V

A New Frontier Sanctuary

BRIGHAM YOUNG, after consulting with his closest advisers, concluded that the only way to prevent continuing Mormon/non-Mormon violence would be to completely abandon Nauvoo and migrate to a new frontier sanctuary. The idea of a general Mormon migration West did not originate with Young. Joseph Smith in 1842 had considered a possible Mormon migration to some remote frontier region. Following Smith's death, Young, in February of 1845, organized a pilot expedition to travel "West to seek out a location and a home where the Saints can dwell in peace and health," and the following month an expedition of nine left Nauvoo.

As for the exact location of Mormonism's new sanctuary, Young considered several options. One was the Republic of Texas. Still an independent nation, this region was favored by Apostle Lyman Wight, Lucien Woodworth, and several other influential Mormons. Woodworth had traveled to Texas to confer with Sam Houston. The Texan leader was anxious to promote the settlement of additional Americans, particularly along the disputed, uninhabited region between the Nueces and Rio Grande Rivers. Such a settlement would strengthen Texas' claims to this territory. But Young balked at the idea of settling in a disputed region of potential explosiveness between Texas and Mexico.The situation there became even more critical following the American annexation of Texas in March, 1845.

Mormon Pioneers in Echo Canyon from a photograph by Charles Savage taken during the 1850s (Courtesy of the Utah State Historical Society.)

Rejecting Texas, Young sought advice concerning other options from prominent individuals outside the Mormon faith. Illinois Governor Thomas Ford, anxious for the removal of the troublesome Mormons from his state, suggested California, noting that "it is but sparsely inhabited and by none but the Indian or imbecile Mexican Spaniard." Two other Illinois politicians, U.S. Representatives John J. Hardin and Stephen A. Douglas, recommended Vancouver Island. As an alternative, Douglas suggested Oregon, where he saw Mormon migration as a means to strengthen American claims to the entire Pacific Northwest.

California, Oregon, and Vancouver Island all had appeal as potential places of Mormon settlement, in particular geographic remoteness and mild, temperate climates. But all had drawbacks. In both California and Oregon a significant number of white American settlers had already migrated, which could lead to a resumption of Mormon/non-Mormon conflict. Oregon and Vancouver Island, moreover, were disputed regions between the United States and Great Britain and could thus place the Mormons in the middle of another international dispute. Thus, Young's options for a Western sanctuary narrowed, as he focused more and more on the Great Basin—a remote interior region about a thousand miles from the Pacific Coast and completely uninhabited by whites.

This region belonged to Mexico but, unlike Oregon and Texas, was not an area of dispute. Its remoteness and arid climate made it a region shunned by both Mexican and American settlers. As early as March, 1845, Young discussed the possiblity of settling this region. He studied the accounts of John C. Fremont and Lansford Hastings, both of whom had extensively explored the Great Basin. Hastings himself lectured in Nauvoo during the summer of 1845, arguing for a Great Basin Mormon settlement. Young, in addition, was impressed with John C. Fremont's descriptions of the Great Basin's grazing land and excellent soil. Although located in an arid climate, the land could be readily irrigated by the dozens of mountain streams.

As he weighed various options, Young wrote President James K. Polk to ask his help in finding an "asylum where we can enjoy our rights of conscience and religion unmolested." In the prevailing spirit of Manifest Destiny, Young asked Polk to approach Congress and plead their "views concerning what is called the 'Great Western Measure' of colonizing the Latter-day Saints in Oregon, the northwestern territory, or some location remote from the states where the hand of oppression shall not crush [them]." Although President Polk did not follow through on Young's request, the Mormon leader continued to push for federal aid. Young wrote Polk's Secretary of War, William L. Marcy, asking for a contract to build stockades and blockhouses between the western frontier and the Rocky Mountains. Although he argued that the Mormons could handle this task, in light of their impending westward migration he did not secure the contract.

The Mormons prepared for their migration west even though Young had not completely settled on a final destination. Young dispatched a reconnaissance mission in August of 1845 to find the best route across Iowa. The following month he ordered a second Mormon expedition to the Missouri River to confer with representatives of the Seneca and Cherokee tribes. The Cherokees gave the Mormons permission to settle nearby and were willing to lend them any assistance they could. Young also directed Samuel Brannan, a New York-based Mormon leader and newspaperman, to take his "press, paper, and ten thousand of the brethern" and migrate to California. Brannan was to lead his migration by sea around Cape Horn and settle at San Francisco. Here Brannan was apparently to await the arrival of the main Mormon contingent traveling overland under the leadership of Young.

In September, Young announced that the main contingent would leave Nauvoo in the spring of 1846. Young busied himself with every detail of organization and outfitting by establishing twenty-four companies of one hundred—each company under a captain selected by Young. He oversaw the outfitting of these pioneers, recommending certain items for "each family of five across the plains" which included one good strong wagon, well covered, three good yokes of oxen, one thousand pounds of flour, one bushel of beans, two pounds of tea, five pounds of coffee, and one keg of alcohol. To deal with the unexpected, in particular Indians, he recommended "one good musket or rifle to each man." At the same time, however, he advised taking "a few goods to trade with the Indians." Looking toward ultimate settlement, he advised taking farming tools and ten to fifty pounds of seed.

Each pioneer company established its own wagon shop where wheelwrights, carpenters, and cabinetmakers took newly-cut timber, cured it, and then used it to build the finished wagons. Nearly every large dwelling in Nauvoo became a wagon shop and by late November 1,500 vehicles had been built, with an additional 1,900 in the process of construction.

Young also oversaw efforts to sell Nauvoo's buildings, houses, lots, and other property. Apostle Orson Pratt, then in the East, met with the utopian communal leader, Robert Owen, and attempted to interest him in the Mormons' homes and lands. It appears that Owen gave some thought to establishing the Owenites at Nauvoo. At the same time, several Catholic leaders expressed interest in Nauvoo property, particularly the Nauvoo Temple. Two Catholic priests, representing the Catholic Bishop of Chicago, traveled to Nauvoo to inspect the Temple. Unfortunately nothing came of the negotiations with either the Catholics or the Owenites and the bulk of Nauvoo Mormon property remained unsold. Those few Mormons lucky enough to find buyers sold their property for a fraction of its value. Brigham Young himself took enormous losses, selling "four pretty nice brick houses and a nice large barn, [and] timber land" for "one span of little horses" worth about sixty dollars apiece, a harness worth about twenty, and a carriage "worth about a hundred dollars."

As Young made final preparation for the migration West, he found himself harrassed by hostile state and federal officials seeking his arrest and imprisonment throughout the fall and winter. In September of 1845, anti-Mormons in Carthage secured a writ calling for Young's arrest, charging him with treason in "colleaguing with the Indians, building an arsenal, and making cannon." Young escaped arrest, but one month later a deputy United States marshal obtained a second series of writs calling for Young's arrest along with his fellow apostles on charges of counterfeiting. Troops of the Illinois state militia entered Nauvoo to issue these writs, but the militia officer in charge withdrew them after meeting with Young, who convinced him the charges were unjustified. In December federal officers traveled from Springfield to Nauvoo with still another writ calling for Young's arrest on charges of counterfeiting. Young avoided arrest this time by having one of his elders, George Miller, who bore a striking resemblance to Young, pose as the Mormon leader. The officers, mistaking Miller for Young, arrested him, whisked him off to Carthage, and charged and jailed him before they discovered their mistake. Throughout this entire ordeal, Young later recalled carrying a "large bowie knife," maintaining that had he been taken into custody he would not have hesitated using it to send his antagonists "to hell across lots."

Young looked upon all of these attempts at arrest and imprisonment as part of a general effort to prevent the Latter-day Saints from migrating west. Young received word in October of 1845 that William Smith, the still embittered younger brother of the slain Mormon prophet, was trying to get the president of the United States to prevent the Mormons from moving west. Young was told by Samuel Brannan that the secretary of war, William L. Marcy, and other members of President Polk's cabinet were laying plans to prevent the Mormon migration west. According to Brannan, these officials justified this action on the grounds that it was against the law for any large armed group to travel from the United States into any territory belonging to another government. Likewise, Illinois Governor Thomas Ford warned Young: "It is very likely that the government at Washington will interfere to prevent the Mormons from going west of the Rocky Mountains" because many individuals believed that the Mormons would "join with the British . . . and be more trouble than ever." Such fears seemed plausible due to the current strained relations between the United States and Great Britain over the disputed Oregon country. In January, 1846, Samuel Brannan again warned Young of alleged federal government intentions to stop the Mormons. In response to these warnings and the repeated efforts to arrest him, Young moved up the Mormons' departure date to early February of 1846.

In anticipation of this earlier than expected departure date, Young took upon himself added family responsibility in the form of nineteen additional wives, married during the hectic three-week period from January 14 to February 6, 1846. Three of the nineteen new wives were widows of Joseph Smith, to whom Young felt a special obligation. Young married the vast majority of the nineteen women apparently in name only, since just two would bear his children. It appears, moreover, that most of these women approached Young, rather than the other way around, desiring the protection of a husband as they prepared to venture into the unknown Western wilderness. Along with Young, other Mormon leaders took a large number of plural wives just prior to the Mormon exodus. Heber C. Kimball added twenty-two wives to his household. All this marital activity points up to the often overlooked historical fact that Young, by 1846, and *prior* to his departure from Nauvoo, married thirty-nine women—the majority of the fifty-five he would ultimately marry.

At long last, on February 15, 1846, Young departed Nauvoo directing what would become the largest and best organized westward trek of pioneers in American history. Young was deliberately vague concerning the Latter-day Saints' final destination as the first wagons pulled out of Nauvoo and crossed the Mississippi River into Iowa. An official circular indicated Mormon intentions to settle "in some good valley in the neighborhood of the Rocky Mountains," but at the same time, Young indicated to Samuel Brannan that the Mormons were headed for California. Further confusing matters, Young wrote Apostle Wilford Woodruff and Secretary of War William L. Marcy suggesting Vancouver Island as the Mormons' final destination. This confusion notwithstanding, Young pointed out that wherever the Mormons finally settled they would remain loyal to the United States and its Constitution.

Through declarations of Mormon loyalty, Young hoped to allay the fears of Polk and other federal officials that the Mormons did not intend to cast their lot with either Great Britain or Mexico. Indeed, Young offered Mormon help to sustain American claims to the Oregon country in response to the ongoing American-British conflict over that region.

Brigham Young led his pioneer contingent to Sugar Creek, the first Mormon encampment in Iowa, only nine miles from Nauvoo. Young expected an orderly migration to this camp in accordance with the careful way in which he had organized the pioneers back in Nauvoo. But he was appalled to find the first 3,000 pioneers at Sugar Creek in a highly disorganized state, having fled Nauvoo in a pell-mell fashion. Many of these pioneers arrived inadequately outfitted and lacked sufficient provisions. Sugar Creek suffered from a sudden cold snap in late February that sent the temperature plunging to twelve degrees below zero!

Young moved to bring order out of this chaos. First he called the camp together and in a forceful voice admonished those without adequate supplies to "Never borrow without asking leave and return what has been borrowed." Young continued to hold the pioneers together as they inched their way westward through Iowa at the rate of about three miles a day over roads and trails muddied by the spring thaw. In late May, after arriving at Shoal Creek, about one hundred miles west of Nauvoo, Young organized the pioneers into three companies of one hundred each, reinstituting his original plan of organization. He then pushed his followers westward along the nearly impassable roads and after another month of travel arrived at Garden Grove, about 150 miles from Nauvoo and halfway across Iowa. Here Young established the Mormons' first permanent camp with log dwellings. He ordered his followers to plow and plant crops for later pioneers.

Upon completing these tasks, the pioneers departed Garden Grove, traveling at an "exceedingly slow" pace. A month later they arrived at Mount Pisgah. Young blamed the slowness of the Mormons' progress on the nearly impassable roads. Young also noted the "want of teams and wagons" with many Mormon teamsters withdrawing to Nauvoo because they were worried about the safety of their families. Although shorthanded, the pioneers established a second permanent camp at Mount Pisgah, complete with cabins and several thousand acres of cultivated crops. This Mormon willingness to plant crops and make other provisions for subsequent Mormon companies stood in contrast to the prevailing practices of the typical pioneer, who generally exhibited little or no concern for the welfare of later emigrant companies.

Besides his responsibilities for the general Mormon migration, Young had to provide for his own family. A total of fifty-one family members in fifteen wagons, including eleven wives, had joined him when he left Nauvoo the previous February. Other wives that were not a part of this group of eleven traveled with their own parents or friends in other pioneer companies. Some wives remained behind in Nauvoo for the time being.

Young's varied responsibilities made it difficult to provide for his numerous wives. The situation of two wives, Emily Partridge, who accompanied Young through Iowa, and Harriet Cook, who remained temporarily behind in Nauvoo, illustrate these problems. Emily Partridge left Nauvoo shortly after giving birth to a son, Edward. During the confusing first days of the exodus from Nauvoo, Emily found herself separated from the rest of the family. Hungry and dejected, child clasped in her arms, she wandered from one camp to another seeking aid. She found her way to Mount Pisgah, joining another of Young's plural wives, Zina D. Huntington, and together they survived the winter in a crudely constructed hut. In her later recollection, Emily noted: "President Young had to look after the welfare of the whole people [and therefore did not have] much time to devote to his family."

In Nauvoo, Harriet Cook and the other wives who remained behind had difficulty providing for themselves. Young, despite distance, tried to see that Harriet and the others were provided for. Ultimately he wanted all of his family together in one place and was thus apprehensive when Harriet revealed plans to travel east to visit her relatives. Fearing that Harriet would find life in the East more attractive, Young pleaded with her: "I cannot bare the thought of your going East. You will not enjoy yourself if you goe. Come here. Your friends are here." Harriet did heed Young's advice. Along with most of the rest of his Nauvoo-based wives, she eventually migrated west and joined the rest of the family in Iowa. Meanwhile, Young continued to push his followers westward across Iowa, leaving Mount Pisgah in late May, heading toward Council Bluffs on the Missouri River.

This leg of the journey was relatively pleasant as the company traveled over dry roads. On June 14, the group arrived at Council Bluffs, an Indian Agency and an established point of departure for Oregon and California. From this point, Young planned to immediately dispatch a pilot company of 200 to 500 men to the Great Basin.

Young's timetable for westward migration, however, was upset by the outbreak of the Mexican-American War in May of 1846. Word of these hostilities came from Captain James Allen of the United States Army who rode into the Mormons' Council Bluffs camp on June 30. Allen also presented a request for a Mormon battalion to march west to California under the command of General Stephen Watts Kearny. Allen's call surprised Young and appeared one more obstacle for the pioneers. But Young felt that compliance with this request could be turned to the pioneers' advantage. The dispatch of Mormon volunteers would assure the migration west of some Mormons at government expense. Also, the army's willingness to pay the Saints a total of $21,000 would help compensate the soldiers' families and aid the Mormons generally. The government, moreover, offered the Mormons camping rights on Indian lands located on both sides of the Missouri River near Council Bluffs. Most important, Mormon compliance with the government's request gave Young the opportunity to demonstrate support for the United States at a time when President Polk and other federal officials were questioning Mormon loyalty.

Thus, Young told Allen, "You shall have your Battalion, Sir, and if there are not young men enough, we will take old men, and if they are not enough, we will take women." Young personally helped to round up the necessary volunteers by taking his carriage and retracing the route of his recently completed journey all the way back to Mount Pisgah. He admonished the Saints in these scattered camps to volunteer for service and tried to allay fears by telling volunteers that they "would have no fighting to do." At the end of two weeks, Allen had his five hundred volunteers.

As the Mormon Battalion marched away, Young realized that the loss of these men meant a delay in the Saints' westward trek until spring of 1847. In the meantime, Young organized the thousands of pioneers for the winter. The main Mormon site, six miles north of present-day Omaha, was designated Winter Quarters. Here, Young supervised the building of a temporary Mormon community at the edge of the American frontier consisting of 538 log houses, 83 sod houses, and 3,483 people.

Winter Quarters was divided into 22 wards with a bishop over each and each company ordered "to prepare a yard for cattle, build a necessary [outhouse] . . . keep hay in the cattle yard and keep up a nightwatch." Schools were organized "for the education of children during the coming winter." Young clamped down on all forms of disorderly conduct through a vigilante police force. Serious offenses, including adultery, were subject to the corporal punishment of whipping since the Mormons had no jail.

Young also tried to establish good relations with the local

Indians, upon whose lands the Mormons were encamped. His basic creed was that it was "better to feed the Indians than fight them"—a philosophy that would influence all of Young's subsequent behavior. In this spirit, he met with the chief of the local Potawatomi Indians, Pied Riche, who sympathized with the plight of the Mormons, noting "so we have both suffered. We must keep one another." Young was given permission to live on any part of the land not occupied by the Indians. Young also met with Big Elk, Chief of the Omaha Indians, who possessed the lands on the west side of the Missouri and secured his permission for the Mormons to stay on their land.

Young also felt it expedient to affirm Mormon loyalty to the United States. Writing President Polk, Young characterized the "Constitution of the U. States as the most precious among the nations." Despite private doubts about Polk resulting from his belief that the president had a hand in trying to stop the Mormons' earlier departure from Nauvoo, Young declared his "fullest confidence in the friendly protection of Prest, Polk" and promised cooperation in all matters. He also revealed to Polk the Mormons' ultimate destination and expected future relationship with the federal government:

> *Resolved*, That as soon as we are settled in the Great Basin we design to petition the U.S. for a territorial government, bounded on the North by the British and South by the Mexican dominions and East and West by the Summits of the Rocky and Cascade Mountains.

Attempting to promote good Mormon-federal relations, Young enlisted the services of Thomas L. Kane, a supportive non-Mormon lawyer from a prominent Philadelphia family. Kane had first come into contact with the Mormons in that city and sympathized with their cause even though he did not join their movement. After hearing of the Mormon plight following their expulsion from Nauvoo, Kane traveled west to offer his help. But upon his arrival in Winter Quarters, he became sick with fever—so sick that he feared for his life. However, Young's wife Mary Ann nursed him back to health. The grateful Kane then acted as an intermediary to the federal government trying to secure permission for the Mormons to camp on Indian lands once they resumed their westward trek in the spring.

Young also had to worry about those Mormons not in Winter Quarters. He issued instructions to those Saints who had traveled further West beyond the Missouri River into present-day Nebraska. These Saints were advised to winter at Grand Island on the Platt River. Young also told those pioneers behind him scattered all along the Iowa frontier from Council Bluffs to Nauvoo to halt for the winter. In Nauvoo, those Mormons who had remained behind faced new dangers when an anti-Mormon mob of about eight hundred men attacked them. This mob, emboldened by the departure of most Nauvoo Mormons, quickly overran the city's defenders, killing three Mormons and wounding several others. The remaining Nauvoo Mormons—consisting mainly of the poor, sick, and elderly—were forced to leave Nauvoo immediately. Young, hearing of their plight, quickly dispatched teams and wagons to transport them west.

At Winter Quarters, Young also attended to the needs of his own immediate family. He built himself a house and constructed dwellings for some of his wives. Other wives resided separately or with friends. Thus, Young's numerous wives did not live together or dwell in equal comfort.

The less-than-ideal living conditions of Young's wives made for tensions that sometimes exploded into open dissent. One wife, Mary de la Montague, divorced and left the Mormon leader in 1846. But other wives worked together. Eliza R. Snow, who became severely ill, was nursed back to health by Mary Ann Angell. Young's wives sought each other's companionship, particularly on holidays and other festive occasions. Eliza R. Snow described her positive relationship with Young's wives noting, "my love [for them] seems to increase with every day's acquaintance."

At Winter Quarters, Young took three additional wives. Two of these were sisters: sixteen-year-old Lucy Bigelow and her nineteen-year-old sister Mary Jane, both pushed into marriage by their father. Nahum Bigelow, concerned that his two daughters were approaching a marriageable age and anxious to see them married, asked Young's counsel on this matter. Young then approached the two women asking them to marry him. Mary Jane agreed, but Lucy, a strong-willed woman, held back resolving never to marry into a plural relationship with a man old enough to be her father. But she evidently changed her mind and both she and her sister married Young in March. Young also fathered a son and two daughters born at Winter Quarters.

Young also faced family tragedy at Winter Quarters. Numbered among the 600 Mormons who died during the winter of 1846–47 of maladies ranging from malaria to "black leg" scurvy were two wives, Jane Terry and Mary Pierce. In addition, his infant son, Moroni, born that same winter, died the following August. Young himself also suffered from ill health, which, according to one observer, resulted from fatigue and overwork.

Despite his ill health, Young stayed extremely busy preparing for the spring migration. In November he consulted with Father Pierre-Jean de Smet, a Jesuit priest who visited Winter Quarters following a five-year mission to the Flathead Indians in the Oregon country. Young eagerly questioned de Smet on his travels and was particularly interested in his observations concerning the Great Salt Lake Basin.

In January, 1847, Young gave divine sanction for the Mormons' westward trek through his only canonized revelation, "The Word and Will of the Lord." It gave divine approval to Young's efforts to organize his followers into companies of hundreds, further subdivided into fifties and tens, supervised by captains, and it gave practical advice on pre-paring for the journey. The revelation admonished the Saints to avoid drunkenness, stealing, and speaking evil of one's neighbor and encouraged the Saints: "If thou are merry, praise the Lord with singing, with music, with danc-ing, and with a prayer of praise and thanksgiving." In issu-ing these instructions within the context of a revelation, Young sought to avoid a repetition of the confusion that had prevailed in the wake of the Mormon migration from Nau-voo the previous year. This revelation also gave further credibility to Young's status as the Mormons' undisputed leader and clear successor to Joseph Smith.

However, not all Mormon pioneers accepted Brigham Young. Bishop George Miller, who had led a group of Mor-mons to Grand Island (in present-day Nebraska) wanted Texas to be the Mormon gathering place and split with Young rather than go to the Salt Lake Basin. Miller was joined by Apostle Lyman Wight, a stubborn individual dubbed "the Wild Ram of the Mountains," who was dis-satisfied with Young's leadership. Miller and Wight migrated to Texas with their followers and established a small Mor-mon sect with Wight as leader. A second Mormon dissident, Alpheaus Cutler, chose to remain in the Midwest, where he founded his own small Mormon sect known as Cutlerites.

A third challenge, one with long-lasting consequences, came from William McCary, a half-breed black Indian. McCary performed for the Mormons as a musician playing his "flute, fife, saucepan, rattler [and] 36¢ whistle" and, along with his wife, performed as a mimic. Young accepted these forms of entertainment, but became alarmed when McCary turned to certain religious practices that challenged Young's authority. McCary preached transmigration, that is, the passing of the soul at death into some other body. He claimed to be Adam and set up his own rival Mormon sect in opposition to Brigham Young and the Twelve in which he performed his own form of plural marriage. He had several women "sealed" to him by requiring them to go to bed with him. Upset over these activities, Young ordered McCary's expulsion from Winter Quarters.

But McCary left his mark on Mormonism by prompting Young to reassess the role and place of black people generally within Mormonism—an issue that previously received minimal attention since the Church had only a handful of black members. Only two blacks had apparently been ordained to the Mormon priesthood up to this time. Young, in response to McCary, implemented for the first time in 1847 a ban on ordaining blacks to the Mormon priesthood—an organization that remained open to males of every ethnic group, including Indians. This ban would remain in effect for the next 131 years and portended a generally negative relationship with black people.

Brigham Young's main concern in early 1847 was outfitting the pioneers for the long journey "over the mountains." He took personal charge of the pilot company of 159 pioneers traveling with 72 wagons, 66 oxen, and 92 horses. This company's primary responsibility involved charting a road into the Great Salt Lake Valley to be used by subsequent Mormon pioneers. To carry out this task, the company took along various scientific instruments, including sextants, a circle of reflection, artificial horizons, barometers, thermometers, and telescopes.

Young organized the company for speed and mobility, selecting only experienced frontiersmen with particular pioneering skills, intending to include only men. But just prior to the company's departure, Young allowed the inclusion of three women, largely in response to a request by his brother Lorenzo, who wanted to include his asthmatic wife, Harriet Decker, for health reasons. So that Harriet would have female companionship, Young allowed one of his wives, Clara Decker (Harriet's daughter by a previous marriage), along with one of Heber C. Kimball's wives, to join the company.

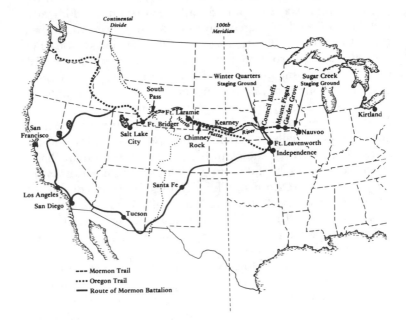

U. S. map showing the Mormon Trail, route of the Mormon Battalion, and the Oregon Trail.

Also in Young's group were three black slaves belonging to some Southern Mormons.

In early April, 1847, this pilot company left Winter Quarters. Unlike most westward-bound emigrants, Young did not utilize professional guides and outfitters. Instead, he relied on maps and other information and his own men to scout ahead. He assigned men to ride along the front, flanks, and rear, thus guarding the moving camp in a box-like formation with himself traveling on horseback at the front of the company's main column. The company did very little trailblazing and was able to follow existing roads and trails for much of the journey. Young's group, in contrast to the Mormon companies that had struggled across Iowa the previous year, was disciplined and well-organized. Thus, the distance traveled averaged ten miles a day—more than three times the three-mile rate averaged the previous season. The company's daily routine involved reveille at 5:00 A.M. followed by morning prayer and breakfast, then departure at 7:30, one hour for lunch, camp at 6:30 P.M., circle wagons, supper, evening prayer at 8:30 P.M., and taps at 9:00 P.M. Near the end of each day's journey, Young would ride ahead to personally select the campsite for the night. Much of the fuel used for the campfires while on the Great Plains consisted of dry buffalo dung—"chips" or "meadow muffins" as they were known. The task of gathering, considered women's work, was left in the hands of the camp's three females, as was all the cooking, washing, sewing, and nursing.

The first portion of the journey took Young and his party from Winter Quarters to a point near present-day Kearney, Nebraska, where the Mormon Trail linked up with the well-traveled Oregon Trail. This initial phase took the Mormons across a flat plain along the broad and shallow Platt River.

Upon entering this frontier region beyond the established line of white settlement, Young urged his men to remain alert and vigilant: "Every man must carry his loaded gun or else have it in his wagon where he can seize it at a moment's notice"—advice that seemed appropriate when the company came in contact with a group of Pawnee Indians just two days after leaving Winter Quarters. The Pawnees, indigenous to Nebraska, stood in contrast to any Indians previously encountered. Nomadic, warlike, powerfully built, with body paint and unusual hairstyles, a number of Pawnees approached the pioneers and demanded a gift as a toll for allowing the Mormons to cross their lands. The Mormons gave them some tobacco and salt, but the Indians were dissatisfied and stole two of the party's horses.

While encamped in the Pawnees' midst, the Mormons maintained a close-armed vigil, with Young himself standing guard. Guns were of no use, however, against the Pawnees' most dangerous weapon—prairie fire. The disgruntled Indians utilized this weapon, setting fire to dry prairie grass ahead of the traveling pioneers in order "to injure us," noted Young. An awesome sight, prairie fire was a scourging wall of flame and when wind-driven could reach a height of twenty feet and could overtake a horse or slow moving ox train. But Young's company was lucky and did not suffer any ill effects either from the prairie fire or the Pawnees who set it.

Young and his followers undoubtedly wondered why the Pawnees exhibited such hostile feelings. The Pawnees, one of the smaller of the Plains tribes, were being pushed off their lands by larger tribes, particularly the Sioux, as white Americans expanded westward. The Mormon exodus itself caused particular hardship on this small Great Plains tribe and helped generate hostile relations between the Pawnees and Sioux.

Leaving the Pawnees, the Mormon pioneers continued to push westward to Kearney, Nebraska, which marked the beginning point of the second phase of the journey, and where the Mormon and Oregon Trails converged. Although the two trails covered the same route along the Platt River for several hundred miles, Young kept his followers north of the river and left the south side for Oregon-bound emigrants. Young did this to prevent possible conflict over grazing and camping rights along the river.

Soon the Mormons spotted buffalo for the first time and gave chase. The pioneers tasting buffalo flesh for the first time found "the meat . . . very sweet and [as] tender as veal." As the pioneers traveled westward they killed more and more buffalo, giving the camp an overabundance of meat which upset Young, particularly when he found some of the pioneers had thrown away good meat simply because "it was not hind quarter!" "God has given us a Commandment," he lectured, "that we should not waste meat, nor take life unless it is needed." Young's prudent approach stood in contrast to the behavior of many westerners who indiscriminately killed buffalo either for sport or as a tactic to deprive the Plains Indians of this necessary commodity and thus subdue them.

The pioneers continued westward, and by mid-May passed the 100th meridian, the point beyond which there is insufficient rainfall for nonirrigated farming. In late May, the company encountered a party of thirty-five Sioux Indians. The Sioux, largest of the Great Plains tribes, were unlike the Pawnees in that they were friendly and happy with their gifts. The pioneers were impressed with the Indians' clean appearance, describing the men as "noble looking fellows" and the women as "pretty brunettes." This amicable Mormon-Sioux encounter stood in stark contrast to the hostile relationship that would generally characterize Sioux interaction with white Americans over the next fifty years.

Young's party then moved into what is today western Nebraska, passing Chimney Rock, the most famous landmark on the Oregon Trail. This eroded tusk of volcanic ash, clay, and sandstone, jutted some 500 feet above the Platt River. Shortly past Chimney Rock, Young became upset with the pioneers because of what he deemed their offensive behavior. Free from family responsibilities, the male pioneers acted in a careless manner, spending their leisure time playing cards and dominoes. Distressed, Young called "the camp to repentance," condemning the pioneers for stooping "to dance as niggers" and for general behavior unbecoming to the elders of Israel. Young's tongue-lashing was effective and thereafter the pioneers behaved much more to his liking.

On June 2, the pioneers arrived at Ft. Laramie, an important way station on the Platt River. Here they were joined by seventeen members of the so-called Mississippi Company, a contingent of 275 Mormons who had migrated from the South the previous summer. The rest of this southern company was encamped at Pueblo on the Arkansas River awaiting direction from Young. Also at Ft. Laramie, Young received word that ex-Governor Lilburn Boggs of Missouri was traveling just ahead of the Mormons on the Oregon Trail. Boggs, who had directed the persecution of Mormons during the 1830s, planned to settle in California and secure an appointment to federal office when and if the United States acquired that region.

Young's pioneer company left Ft. Laramie on June 4, beginning the third and most challenging phase of its journey across present-day Wyoming to Ft. Bridger 350 miles away. It was more difficult to secure choice campsites and adequate grazing for their livestock since they were forced to travel on the south side of the Platt and thus placed in competition with emigrants bound for Oregon and California. The trail proved extremely rugged as the pioneers had to cross and recross the Platte three different times before leaving it for good. They also faced trials along the barren stretch between the Platte and Sweetwater Rivers—a region of bad campsites, bad water, and little green grass. The pioneers, moreover, confronted problems of thin air, cold nights, and hot days, created by the steady, gradual climb in elevation to 7,750 feet as the pioneers reached the continental divide at South Pass.

Besides these difficulties, Young received disheartening information concerning the Great Salt Lake Basin. Moses Harris, a seasoned mountain man who for many years had lived and trapped in the Oregon-California country, spoke unfavorably of the Salt Lake country for a settlement, describing the region as destitute of timber and vegetation. The following day, another negative report came from Jim Bridger. This famous mountain man, considered by some the greatest scout of all and the first white man to visit the Great Salt Lake, described the entire region as barren. He characterized the local Indians as bad and noted that the climate with its cold nights would prevent the growth of crops. He was so pessimistic concerning the region's agricultural potential that he offered to pay Young $1,000 for the first bushel of corn grown there. The pioneers questioned

Bridger's report, finding it at variance with John C. Fremont's optimistic descriptions and maps in which they had placed so much faith. But Bridger refuted Fremont's reports with the comment that Fremont knew nothing about the country.

Five days later, after crossing the Green River, Young received a third visitor, Samuel Brannan, the leader of the New York Saints, who had arrived in San Francisco the previous summer. Brannan also tried to discourage Young from settling in the Great Basin. He wanted Young to continue to the Pacific Coast extolling California as a place that produced barley "with no hull on it," and clover "as high as a horse's belly." Wild horses and game abounded, and salmon dominated the rivers. The climate was mild, with plenty of rain and a comfortable, dry season. A Mormon gathering to California, Brannan argued, would be logical since the 238 members of Brannan's contingent were already there and the 500-man Mormon Battalion had just arrived at Los Angeles after completing its long march from Fort Leavenworth. Despite Brannan's arguments, Young decided against California. He reasoned that if he led the Mormons there, they would not last five years because this desirable region would attract many non-Mormons, leading to renewed Mormon/non-Mormon conflict.

Thus, Samuel Brannan returned without Young to California, where he played a role in the drama surrounding the California gold rush. The initial gold discovery at Sutter's Mill in January of 1848 was made, interestingly enough, by recently discharged members of the Mormon Battalion, temporarily employed by John Sutter. Brannan publicized this discovery in his newspaper, the *California Star*, under the banner headlines "Gold! Gold! Gold from the American River!" helping to set off the California gold rush. Brannan himself became California's first millionaire through his investments in merchandising, hotels, real estate, and shipping. But Brannan did not remain a Mormon, for Brigham

Young in 1851 ordered his excommunication, because of Brannan's failure to pay tithing on his huge fortune and his central role in organizing the San Francisco Committee of Vigilance, which Young denounced as a lawless assembly organized to commit murder and other crimes.

Young resumed his push toward the Great Salt Lake Basin with the pioneers arriving at Fort Bridger on the Green River on July 7, 1847. Here they did some trading and repaired their wagons in preparation for the final phase of the journey. After departing Fort Bridger, the company left the Oregon trail for good and turned southwest. It picked up the Hastings Cutoff which had been followed by the Donner-Reed Party the previous year. This California-bound group had done some trailblazing through the rugged mountains, making the Mormons' final descent into the Salt Lake Valley easier. The Donner-Reed party itself became stranded in the snows of the Sierras during the winter of 1846–47 and only a few individuals survived by resorting to cannabalism.

While on the Hastings Cutoff, the Mormons met Miles Goodyear, another mountain man, who lived 50 miles north of the Mormons' final destination (near present-day Ogden, Utah). Much to the relief of Young and in contrast to Bridger and Harris, Goodyear gave a favorable account of the country. He affirmed its agricultural potential, describing his own "garden planted with all kinds of vegetables."

Armed with this knowledge, Young could now proceed with confidence. But the last twelve days of the journey were miserable, for Young was struck with Colorado tick fever. In great pain, he found it impossible to travel on horseback and was placed in the back of a carriage. By the time Young caught his first glimpse of the Great Salt Lake Valley from the mouth of Emigration Canyon on July 24, 1847, the worst symptoms of the illness had passed. Although weakened, Young managed to lift himself out of his carriage to view the semi-arid wilderness slated to be the Mormons' new desert home. What he saw stood in stark contrast to Nauvoo, Illinois. Whereas Nauvoo was set in a lush, green, wooded region aside the Mississippi River, the Salt Lake Valley was dry and desolate. The valley, 40 miles long from north to south and 25 miles wide, east to west, was surrounded on all sides by a semi-circle of purple, snow-capped mountains. To the far northwest was the turquoise expanse of the Great Salt Lake. Although a number of small creeks watered the valley from the east, the June grass had yellowed by this time.

Despite the valley's desolate appearance (or more properly because its barrenness would discourage all but Mormons from settling there) Young was satisfied, proclaiming "It is enough. This is the right place. Drive on." Thus, Brigham Young had found a new frontier sanctuary far from other regions of white, non-Mormon settlement. There Young could establish a new center for Mormonism and settle his followers throughout the Great Basin.

V

Establishing the Sanctuary

MIGRATING TO THE GREAT BASIN was one thing, but establishing this remote frontier region as a secure Mormon sanctuary was quite another. Not all the pioneers shared Young's enthusiasm for this region. His pioneer wife, Clara Decker, unimpressed with this desolate region, remarked that she would rather walk another thousand miles than remain. But Young was convinced he had selected the right place and proceeded to explore the valley. He designated a site for the building of a new temple and, using the temple site as a central survey point, he ordered the laying out of city streets in a perfect grid square, north and south, east and west. The streets were eight rods wide—wide by the standards of the time—to allow for the smooth flow of traffic. The intervening lots were laid out in ten-acre blocks.

Young selected a lot for himself and his family adjacent to the temple block. In distributing land, Young moved to prevent land speculation (which had contributed to Mormon difficulties back in Nauvoo) by announcing, "No man can buy land here, for no one has any land to sell." Each settler had land measured out to him by Church leaders and was told to cultivate it in order to retain it. He also decreed, "no private ownership of the streams that come out of the canyons, nor the timber that grows on the hills. These belong to the people; all the people."

Aware of their precarious situation in this frontier region, Young ordered the pioneers to establish their first homes

The Lion and Beehive Houses where Brigham Young resided
with the majority of his wives from 1854 until the time of his
death in 1877. The smaller structure in the center was Young's
office where he conducted official business as territorial governor
and Mormon Church President. (Courtesy of the LDS Church Library-Archives. Printed with permission.)

within a fort to protect themselves from Indian attacks.
Young utilized his long-dormant skills as a craftsman in building four small adobe houses for his family inside the fort.

Following completion of the fort, Young left Salt Lake in
August of 1847 to return east to Winter Quarters to supervise the migration of the rest of his family. Accompanying
Young were a hundred others, including Heber C. Kimball
and various church leaders. En route, Young found the
Mormon migration west to be proceeding more rapidly than
he had anticipated as he met ten companies of 1,553 Mormons headed for the valley. This alarmed Young, who had
given earlier instructions that only 400 should migrate that
first season because of the Great Basin's limited resources.

He met two of his wives, Eliza R. Snow and Margaret

Pierce, near South Pass in a joyful reunion, but in the midst of this, a raiding party of Crow Indians made off with fifty horses, including Young's own riding horse. Undaunted, Young called upon the brethren to walk with him to Winter Quarters. Further on, Young's company suffered the loss of more horses to the Sioux Indians. Young and Heber C. Kimball also had a close call when an angry grizzly bear chased them to the top of a rocky embankment near a creek. At Fort Laramie, Young met Commodore Robert Stockton who had returned east following his exploits in the California Bear Flag Revolt and Mexican War. Stockton traveled with Young's company a short distance until his route of travel diverged onto the main part of the Oregon Trail. The Mormons continued on to Winter Quarters.

Young occupied himself with two matters during the fall and winter of 1847–48. First, he strengthened his position as Church leader by having himself sustained as Church prophet, seer and revelator and reorganizing the church's First Presidency. Although Young had been acting as Church president in conjunction with his control over the Council of the Twelve since 1844, he did not formally assume the designation prophet, seer, and revelator, a title heretofore held only by the martyred Joseph Smith. Young had held back in deference to Smith's immediate family because of his desire to avoid conflict and hopefully to secure their allegiance. But three years had passed and Smith's family continued to refuse to join Young on his westward trek or acknowledge his authority as Mormon leader, choosing instead to remain in Nauvoo. In reconstituting the Church First Presidency, Young appointed his long-time friend Heber C. Kimball First Counselor, and his cousin Willard Richards Second Counselor.

The second matter that concerned Young was preparing his family for the spring migration west. Three of his wives had already arrived in Great Salt Lake Valley. But most of the others were still in Winter Quarters. Two other wives, Lucy and Mary Jane Bigelow, whom Young had married the previous spring, had left Winter Quarters for St. Louis to find employment, hoping to earn money to buy supplies for the trip west. They secured employment in a shirt factory, toiling ten hours a day, but found their earnings consumed by room and board. Young, upon hearing of their plight, remarked that he "would rather have given the last coat off his back" than to have had those women exist under such conditions and arranged for their immediate return to Winter Quarters.

By late May of 1848, Young completed preparations for the migration west. All his wives and dependents were present or accounted for except for three wives who chose not to accompany him. One of these, Mary Ann Clark Powers, became disillusioned, claiming that Young had not given her sufficient attention, and asked that her marriage be terminated, a request granted by Young. Young's family was part of a contingent of 1,229 individuals—ten times the size of the vanguard company Young had led west the previous summer. This large company, larger than originally anticipated, came about because of pressure from the federal government. Federal authorities, feeling that continuing Mormon presence on Indian lands in Nebraska posed a danger to peaceful relations, had ordered the abandonment of Winter Quarters. This placed Young in a dilemma concerning these displaced Mormons. On the one hand, he could move them back across the Missouri River to Iowa, an area open to the Saints but already overcrowded, or he could lead the displaced pioneers to the Great Basin that season and hope they could get by on limited provisions. Young chose the latter course despite his misgivings. The total of 1,848 migrants included Young's large group and the additional companies of Heber C. Kimball, and Willard Richards.

The actual journey from Winter Quarters to the Salt Lake Valley took 116 days, just five days longer than Young's earlier pioneering trek. This was remarkable in light of the group's size and diverse makeup, consisting of old as well as young women and children. In leading this vast multitude, Young traveled by carriage with Mary Ann, keeping track of both his large family and the company as a whole. Brigham Jr., then twelve years old, helped out by driving an ox team. Along the way, the Mormon leader's wife Louisa Beaman "was delivered . . . of 2 fine Boys which verry much delighted [him]." Another wife, Emily Partridge, assessed the journey as follows: "We were more comfortably fitted out than we had been at any time before." On September 20, 1848, Young arrived in the Salt Lake Valley, a return that signaled not just the completion of this particular journey but marked the last time that he would ever travel east of the Rocky Mountains.

Upon his return, Young found that the Salt Lake Valley had undergone change. For one thing, the Great Basin was no longer a part of Mexico but had been ceded to the United States in February, 1848, as provided in the Treaty of Guadalupe Hidalgo, ending the Mexican-American War. Thus, the Mormons' far western sanctuary was now a part of the expanding American frontier. A second change involved a dramatic increase in the number of Mormon settlers from the 300 pioneers Young had left in the valley the previous summer to 5,000 individuals! These settlers had moved out of the fort, building houses, shops, mills, bridges, and had brought 1,000 acres of land under cultivation.

There had also been problems during Young's absence. The winter of 1847–48 had been particularly difficult with more precipitation than expected. Assuming the Great Basin to be a semi-desert region, the pioneers at first constructed their houses with flat roofs. When snow came, it piled high on the roofs, melted, and then leaked into the dwellings.

The following summer, the pioneers, after planting their crops, faced disaster. Hordes of creeping, flying, giant crickets invaded the green fields, destroying every living thing in their path. At first the Mormons tried beating them to death with shovels and brooms. Then they flooded their fields, attempting to drown them. But there were just too many of them. Just as the pioneers were about to give up, a large number of seagulls came in from the Great Salt Lake and proceeded to sweep up and consume the crickets. According to one eyewitness, "it seems the hand of the Lord is in our favor." Although the crickets did considerable damage, a significant portion of the first year's crop was saved. Cricket and grasshopper plagues, however, would continue to be common terrors in the Great Basin for many years to come.

Young's return to the valley did not bring an end to the Mormons' problems. During the extremely harsh winter of 1848–49, many more recent emigrants were unable to construct adequate shelter, having to survive in wagonboxes or tents. Members of Young's own family found themselves in this situation. Also, food was in short supply due to the heavy immigration and short harvest. Thus, many Latter-day Saints were forced to survive on beef hides, wolves, dogs, and even skunks and dead cattle, with others following the dietary habits of the Indians by surviving on bitter sego lily roots. Young ordered the strict rationing of all available foodstuffs, attempting to stave off widespread starvation and death. He vigorously ferreted out individuals hoarding food for themselves or to sell at a profit. Thanks to Young's efforts, no one died of starvation that winter.

During the winter and spring of 1848–49, Young was also concerned about the California gold rush. He feared that the harsh weather and severe food shortages would cause many of his followers to defect and join the stampede to the gold fields. A few Mormons caught the gold fever despite Young's warnings. Young tried to play down the utilitarian value of gold, noting that "The true use of gold is for paving streets, covering houses and making culinary dishes." The overwhelming majority of Mormons heeded Young's advice and remained in the Great Basin.

Although Young discouraged his followers from direct involvement in the gold rush, the Mormons did benefit indirectly from it. Beginning in the late spring of 1849, hundreds of California-bound gold seekers began arriving in Salt Lake City in search of fresh supplies, wagon and harness repair, and help in lightening their loads. The Mormons provided the desired goods, receiving a favorable rate of exchange.

Young had mixed feelings concerning this trade. He realized that such trade would benefit his new Great Basin settlements, helping this region establish an economic foundation. But at the same time he did not want Mormon economic prosperity dependent on commerce with non-Mormons (or "Gentiles" as they were labeled by the Saints). Thus, Young urged his followers to make the best trade possible, charging whatever the traffic would bear. But at the same time, he encouraged them to move toward economic self-sufficiency in manufacturing and commerce. Young himself profited from the California trade, accumulating $17,000 from just one year's worth of trade. In overall terms, the California trade helped Mormonism to survive economically in the Great Basin during these precarious early years.

Besides economic matters, Young dealt with political affairs. Prior to the Mormon migration west, Young indicated to President Polk his desire for a Great Basin territorial government. But by early 1849, Young wished to bypass the territorial stage and immediately organize a state government. Statehood would give the Mormons a greater degree of autonomy and allow them to practice their religion without interference. A territorial government, by contrast, would mean the presence of outside federal officials who would monitor the Saints' every move. Looking toward statehood, Young established a provisional state government and asserted Mormon claims to a vast region that reached to Oregon on the north, the Rockies on the east, the Sierra Nevada Mountains to the west, the Pacific Ocean to the southwest, and Mexico on the south. This proposed Mormon site included what came to be known as Utah, along with northern Nevada and Arizona, much of Wyoming,

Colorado, and New Mexico, southern California, and portions of Oregon and Idaho—one-sixth of the total land mass of the continental United States! This Mormon state was dubbed Deseret—a *Book of Mormon* term that meant "honey bee," and that suggested industriousness. Young was chosen governor, and two delegates, John M. Bernhisel and Almon W. Babbitt, were dispatched to Washington, D.C., to petition Congress for immediate admission into the Union.

Mormon efforts to gain statehood came at a bad time politically. Bernhisel and Babbitt, upon arriving in Washington, D.C., found Mormon statehood caught up in the crisis over territorial slavery. This crisis was triggered by the acquisition of the Mexican Cession, which included the Mormon Great Basin. Extreme anti-slavery Northerners wanted to prohibit slavery in all parts of this region, thus affirming the spirit of the Wilmot Proviso. Pro-slavery Southerners, by contrast, wanted to leave the entire region open to slavery. Young and other Mormon leaders had anticipated the possibility of such a conflict when they drew up Deseret's proposed constitution. This document deliberately failed to mention slavery in order to convey the impression that this topic was of no concern to the Saints—a fallacious assumption. In reality, the Mormons had brought to the Great Basin 75 to 100 black slaves, a fact that Brigham Young tried to conceal from federal officials. Latter-day Saint spokesmen, moreover, maintained that the Great Basin was beyond the natural limits where slave labor could be profitably employed.

Despite these tactics, the Mormons found it difficult to secure statehood. Throughout 1849 and early 1850, Congress delayed action on the Mormon petition, debating instead the status of slavery in the entire Mexican Cession. In the meantime, President Zachary Taylor presented his own plan in which the California gold fields of the Far West would be combined with the Mormon-dominated Great Basin into a single state where slavery would be prohibited.

The immediate creation of such a free state, Taylor hoped, would settle once and for all the vexing issue of slavery in the Mexican Cession. The need to combine these two diverse settlements into a single state was prompted by Taylor's erroneous perception that each region alone did not have sufficient population to become a state, whereas together they did.

In promoting his proposal, Taylor dispatched a personal representative, General John Wilson, to confer with Brigham Young and leaders in California. After meeting Wilson, Young expressed support for Taylor's proposal, provided that the new state's constitution contained a provision allowing for dissolution of the combined state by 1857, whereby each region would become a "free sovereign and independent state without any further action of Congress." Although Young approved, California officials were of a different mind, rejecting Taylor's proposal as impractical, stating "you might as well connect Maine and Texas as California and Deseret." These officials instead pushed for their own state of California, which was formed in September of 1850.

All this time, Young continued to promote his first option of a separate Great Basin state. However, the Mormons encountered increased opposition abetted by rumors concerning Mormon "Sedition" and the practice of polygamy. These rumors, spread by William Smith and other dissenters, caught the notice of President Zachary Taylor who, accepting them at face value, suddenly and unexpectedly turned against the Mormons. He labeled the Mormons "a pack of outlaws . . . not fit for self-government," and pledged to veto any Mormon bill passed. Coupled with the belief by Washington politicians that the Great Basin lacked sufficient population, Taylor's opposition eliminated any chance for immediate Mormon statehood.

But in the end, the Mormons did secure a territorial government. This occurred only after the sudden death of Zachary Taylor in July of 1850, and elevation of Millard

Fillmore to the presidency. Fillmore was both more sympathetic to the Mormons and sensitive to the need to end the current slavery crisis. The new president supported the Compromise of 1850 as worked out by Henry Clay, Daniel Webster, and Stephen A. Douglas, a compromise which provided the Mormons a territory known as Utah—named for the dominant Ute Indian tribe in the region. (Federal officials rejected the name Deseret. They felt that it had an undesirable connotation, sounding too much like "desert.") The boundaries of this territory were considerably smaller than those proposed for the original state of Deseret— made up primarily of the present-day states of Utah and Nevada, with small portions of Wyoming and Colorado thrown in. The Compromise dealt with the slave issue through "popular sovereignty," that is, leaving it up to local residents to decide in the future when they applied for statehood whether to be a free or slave state. The Compromise of 1850 dealt with the rest of the Mexican Cession, according New Mexico the same status as Utah, a territorial government based on popular sovereignty, and admitted California as a free state. Other provisions included a stringent fugitive slave law, prohibition of the slave trade in the District of Columbia, and the settlement of Texas' debt and boundaries.

There was some initial Mormon apprehension over the imposition of a territorial government through which federal officials could monitor Church activities, thereby limiting the autonomy of their Great Basin sanctuary. But President Millard Fillmore, unlike his predecessor, manifested a "most liberal and friendly feeling towards" the Mormons, promising "not [to] appoint any man who was not friendly disposed towards" the Saints. Thus, Fillmore, in an extraordinary step, appointed Brigham Young Utah's first territorial governor and chose Mormons for several other official positions, including Associate Justice of the territorial supreme court, U.S. Marshal, and U.S. Attorney.

When Brigham Young received word of his appointment as territorial governor, he was busy expanding Mormonism's Great Basin sanctuary. In 1849, after settling the majority of Mormons migrating from Nauvoo and elsewhere in the eastern United States, he turned his attention to missionary activity abroad. Young appointed dozens of new missionaries, dispatching them throughout Europe to the Pacific Islands, Australia, South Africa, and to various parts of Asia and the West Indies. He sent members of the Quorum of Twelve abroad to supervise these missionaries and also organized a transportation company to assist in emigration of these converts to the Great Basin. Known as the Perpetual Emigrating Fund Company, this operation supplied ship passage to either New York or New Orleans, then rail or boat passage from there to the frontier, and finally teams and wagons as transportation across the plains.

When first established, the Perpetual Emigrating Fund Company needed an initial infusion of capital. With a touch of humor, Brigham Young admonished those Saints already in Utah for contributions: "Come on you tobacco chewers and put your 1,000 into [the] Poor fund and I will give you liberty to chew another year. . . ." Young himself put his money where his mouth was by contributing $1,000 to $2,000 a year to the fund. It was money well spent. The fund helped some 26,000 Mormons migrate from Europe to America in the period 1849–87—36% of the total European Mormon migration.

Once in the Great Basin, these migrants established settlements throughout the region. From 1849–52, Young authorized dozens of new settlements stretching three hundred miles along the west slope of the mountains both north and south of Salt Lake City. Young authorized purchase of a homestead belonging to Miles Goodyear, the non-Mormon mountain man located at Ogden to the north and shortly thereafter settlers moved into the region. Other settlements were established south of Salt Lake City at Provo (the future location of the university bearing his name), at Nephi, and at Manti. Young expected agriculture to be the Mormons' economic mainstay. But he also encouraged other economic activities designed to make the Mormons economically self-sufficient. Thus, Young ordered the establishment of a so-called "Iron Mission" settlement some 250 miles south of Salt Lake City near deposits of iron and other raw materials. An even more remote settlement was San Bernardino, in present-day Southern California, designed as a strategic way-station within the so-called Mormon corridor linking the Great Basin with the Pacific Coast.

Brigham Young maintained close contact with settlers throughout this far-flung frontier sanctuary. He would "call" the desired pioneers either in the privacy of his office or from the stand in a public meeting—a call that might be anticipated or come as a complete surprise. Some disgruntled Mormons considered such a call unreasonable in light of previous sacrifices and refused to go. But most pioneers responded positively, pulling up stakes and relocating in some new corner of Mormonism's frontier sanctuary.

Young paid attention to every detail of settlement, issuing instructions to the pioneers on how to conduct themselves relative to the construction of forts and other buildings, the cultivation of crops, and in dealing with the Indians. The first Mormon pioneers found the Great Salt Lake Valley free of Indian settlements. But in other parts of the Great Basin Mormon colonizers came in contact with various groups of Indians. The region's primary Indian tribes included the Utes to the south, the Shoshones to the north, and Gosiutes in the west. Young's overall approach toward the Indians could best be described as ambivalent. On the one hand, Young, like most frontier Americans, considered the Indians an impediment to settlement. Thus, Mormon-Indian conflicts (sometimes bloody) erupted as the Indians tried to halt Mormon encroachment on their lands. Young ordered the pioneers to secure themselves and their families from the dangers resulting from settling those regions inhabited by savage tribes. The settlers were to secure their settlements, guard and herd their stock, and keep their ammunition in order, ready for use.

But at the same time, Mormon dealings with the Indians had a humanitarian side. Young expressed a basic Mormon belief that the Indians were "our brothers" due to their descent from "Israel, through the loins of Joseph and Manassah." He urged the Mormons to "feed and clothe them . . . never turn them away hungry" and "teach them the art of husbandry" and otherwise civilize them. Young on occasion utilized personal diplomacy. He met with Chief Walker, a principal leader of the Utes in southern Utah in 1849, negotiating a treaty opening up that region to Mormon settlement. Generally, Young urged the Mormons to "be just and quiet, firm and mild, patient and benevolent, generous and watchful in" handling the Indians. This fit in with Young's common sense philosophy that "it was cheaper to feed the Indians than to fight them." His main object was to avoid, wherever possible, Mormon-Indian conflict.

In addition to handling general problems of settlement, Young had to provide for his own large family. He moved several of his wives and children from their cramped accommodations inside the fort into new quarters consisting of several small adobe houses built by himself just east of the Temple Block. He also constructed a larger facility, the so-called "log row" containing five good-sized bedrooms all with entrances opening to the outside where he housed some of his younger wives. He settled other wives as best he could, locating one wife in a second story room above the milk house near the log row and several others in wagon boxes until better lodgings could be built.

Mary Ann and her family were provided a temporary residence separate from other family members in a structure known as the Corn Crib. Soon thereafter, he built her a more commodious residence, dubbed "the White House," located to the west and somewhat distant from the Young family compound. The White House also served as Brigham Young's personal living quarters and official headquarters where Young carried out his duties as Church leader and territorial governor. Young also used it as a center to entertain visitors to the Great Basin.

Indeed, the continuing influx of such visitors, coupled with his visible role as territorial governor, made it increasingly difficult for Young to conceal Mormon polygamy. His own polygamous family continued to grow and by 1852 he had married a total of forty-four wives and had fathered thirty-two children by twelve of these women. In addition, other Mormon leaders had polygamous families. Thus, non-Mormon territorial officials, including Judges Perry G. Brocchus and Lemuel G. Brandebury, along with Secretary of State Broughton D. Harris, who arrived in Salt Lake in September, 1851, were appalled to find polygamy openly practiced by the Mormons.

Brocchus brought up the topic during an address he gave to a Salt Lake audience responding to a Mormon goodwill proposal to send a block of Utah marble east to aid in the construction of the Washington Monument. Brocchus rejected the Mormon offer, replying, "in order to make this presentation acceptable . . . you must become virtuous, and teach your daughters to become virtuous or your offering had better remain in the bosom of your native moutains." Brigham Young, who was present, was outraged and leaped to his feet verbally attacking Brocchus as an "illiterate ranter" and "corrupt . . . coward." He also noted: "I love the government and Constitution of the United States, but I do not love the damned rascals who administer the government." Thus, relations between Young and Brocchus were poisoned from the start. Within a few months, Brocchus had abandoned his post and, with Brandebury and Harris, left Utah for good.

The departure from Utah and return to Washington of

these three disgruntled officials, complicated the Mormons' situation. Brocchus confirmed what many Americans had long suspected, that the Mormons were openly practicing polygamy. In response to spreading criticism, Young decided to publicly acknowledge and defend plural marriage at a special Mormon conference held in the Tabernacle on the Temple Block on August 28, 1852. While Young addressed this gathering, he left the most important sermon defending polygamy to Apostle Orson Pratt, a member of the Council of Twelve. Young considered Pratt the most articulate theologian within Mormonism and thus best suited for this task. Bookish-looking, with a long, thin face, Pratt had received some formal training in bookkeeping, mathematics, geography, grammar, and surveying, but was largely self-educated. Although he practiced polygamy with six wives of his own, Pratt had been initially reluctant to embrace plural marriage back in Nauvoo. This reluctance had led to Pratt's brief excommunication before he publicly recanted and was restored to full fellowship.

Now in 1852 Young enlisted Pratt as a leading spokesman for the practice he had once despised. In his sermon, "Celestial Marriage," Pratt outlined several different arguments justifying polygamy. First, he defended it on hereditary grounds as an essential practice for procreation. Polygamy would facilitate the peopling of this world by producing numerous posterity through a righteous chosen [Mormon] lineage. Pratt also presented a Biblical argument, defending polygamy as divinely sanctioned by the Old Testament as evidenced in its earlier practice by Abraham, Isaac, and Jacob. Pratt also upheld polygamy on the less lofty grounds, namely, "man's nature" or basic sexual drive. Men (but not women) were polygamous by inclination as a result of their stronger sex drives. Vigorous men must be allowed legitimate outlets for these sexual drives beyond the conventional monogamous relationship, or the alternative would be "whoredom, adultery and fornication."

Women, by contrast, were monogamic by nature with limited sexual drives, and thus could be "perfectly one" with just a single husband.

Apostle Pratt also responded to those who questioned the Mormons' legal right to practice polygamy in an American society where monogamy was the accepted norm. The First Amendment, he maintained, "gives the privilege to all the inhabitants of this country . . . the free exercise of their religious notions," which meant that the Mormons were protected by the "highest law in the land." Brigham Young was well aware that the Mormon admission of plural marriage would cause an outcry of indignation from many Victorian-minded Americans. But he felt that his followers could withstand such an assault now that they were located in their far western sanctuary.

This controversy came at a time when Young was already extremely busy discharging his duties as territorial governor. During his first year and a half in that post, Young supervised the enactment and enforcement of a series of laws passed by the territorial legislature, including authorizing the incorporation of towns, the building of roads, canals, and bridges, and legislation calling for the establishment of a territorial capitol, prison, and militia.

But the most intriguing territorial statute enacted at Young's request dealt with the vexing issue of slavery. Young asked for legislation legalizing black slavery throughout the territory! Young apparently wanted this legislation for several reasons. First, it appears that Young was responding to the interests of twelve prominent Mormons who brought sixty to seventy slaves into the Great Basin during the late 1840s. Young apparently also hoped to win converts among Southern slaveholders who had a great amount invested in slaves and who might be persuaded to migrate to Utah if their property in slaves was protected by territorial statute. But the most important explanation for Young's action involves his acceptance of certain racist beliefs. In particular, he felt blacks to be inherently inferior and therefore suited for involuntary servitude. The end result of Young's action was "An Act in Relation to Service" passed in February, 1852, which made Utah the only territory west of the Missouri River and north of the Missouri Compromise line of 36°30' to legalize slavery.

Although concerned with Utah's small slave population, Young was much more interested in another minority—the American Indian. Young's keen interest stemmed primarily from the fact that the Mormons were settling on lands formally held by the Indians. Also, Young's appointment as Superintendent of Indian Affairs, an office held in conjunction with that of territorial governor, further intensified this interest. In this post, Young assumed overall responsibility for establishing policies designed to maintain peace between various Utah Indian tribes and Mormon settlers.

Young pursued a policy of peace, maintaining his basic philosophy that it was cheaper to feed the Indians than fight them. In this spirit, he promoted the education of Indians in the art of husbandry. His Indian farm concept, as it came to be known, called for the employment of a few farmers among the Indians, as well as the establishment of schools. In this way, the Indians would be pacified and not revert to their "wild propensities."

Young also encouraged participation at the Fort Laramie meeting of 1851. Here, Indians and whites from throughout the Northern Plains tried to define tribal boundaries, pledged peace between whites and Indians, and secured approval for the construction of roads through the Indian country.

Despite his apparent desire for peaceful coexistence with the Indians, Young considered this merely a temporary expedient. Ultimately, he hoped for the removal of all Indians from Great Basin lands as Mormonism's sanctuary was expanded. Thus, he pushed for federal government action to extinguish Indian title to all Great Basin lands and to remove all Indians to a reservation.

Despite Young's efforts at peaceful Indian relations, the Mormons found themselves on the verge of open warfare in the spring of 1853. Chief Walker, the main southern Ute leader, prepared to attack Mormon settlements to the south. Walker and his followers were angry due to the continuing Mormon encroachment onto their lands. To make matters worse, Young refused to compensate the Indians, claiming Mormon stewardship over the land. He maintained that the land did not belong to man but to God, and that the Mormons were entrusted to plow and plant it—arguments that did not make much sense to Walker, in light of the fact that other frontier Indians were receiving compensation for their lands.

The Indians were further angered when the Utah territorial legislature passed an ordinance prohibiting trade to the Indians in arms, ammunition, and alcoholic beverages. Also, Young refused to assist Walker in recovering a bunch of Ute horses stolen by the Shoshones—arch foes who lived on lands north of the Utes. Young was anxious to prevent a full-scale conflict between the Utes and Shoshones, believing that such a conflict could spread to Mormon settlements, thus causing Young to appear ineffective as an Indian superintendent.

The final break between Walker and Young came when the Mormons tried to stop the Indian slave trade. In this lucrative enterprise, Walker and his fellow Utes would sell large numbers of Indian children captured from rival tribes to Mexican slave traders, who would then transport them to Mexico to be used as slaves. Young, out of humanitarian considerations and because he believed that Mexican slave traders were stirring up the Indians against the Mormons, sought to preempt the slave trade. He had the Utah territorial legislature enact a statute in 1852 that legalized Indian slavery as a form of indenture. This allowed the Mormons to purchase Indian children to prevent them from falling into the hands of Mexican slave traders.

The statute allowed Indian children to be reared under

the civilizing influences of Mormonism and be provided with adequate food, clothing, and schooling. At the end of twenty years, the Indian would be released from his or her apprenticeship. Although several hundred Indian children were protected under this statute, it did not stop the continuing invasion of Mexican slaving parties into the territory. Thus, in April of 1853, Governor Young issued a proclamation prohibiting all Indian slave traffic throughout Utah.

This prohibition incensed Walker and led to the Walker War. Starting in July, Walker's Ute band launched a number of raids against Mormon settlements in central Utah. During the hostilities, twelve Mormon settlers were killed and four hundred head of cattle lost. Young instructed his followers to maintain an armed vigilance, but at the same time he made overtures of peace. In a letter accompanied by some tobacco, Young admonished Walker "You are a fool for fighting your best friends [the Mormons] . . . the only friends that you have in the world." Young offered to meet personally with Walker. Although Young hoped to settle these difficulties peacefully, he took no chances and placed the entire territory under martial law. He sought to prevent Walker's rebellion from spreading to other tribes. In a circular addressed to all the chiefs of various tribes throughout the territory, he expressed his desire for peace, announcing that he, along with "all the Mormons, over whom I am the Big Chief, are friendly to you all [and do not] intend to hurt any Indians."

Despite his efforts, Young could not prevent Indian hostilities from spreading. In late October, 1853, eight members of a U.S. Army Topographical Survey team were slain by Indians near the Sevier River in Central Utah. This team, under Lieutenant John W. Gunnison, was surveying a possible route for the transcontinental railroad. Walker or the Utes were not responsible; another tribe, the Pauvan Indians, killed the whites in retaliation for the killing of one of their own by a party of non-Mormon emigrants. Young quickly condemned the Gunnison Massacre. But this did not stop rumors from circulating in the East accusing Young and the Mormons of this atrocity. Young wrote a strong letter of denial to Secretary of War Jefferson Davis condemning these "various false Malicious and Slanderous reports" as the product of "wicked and designing men."

Meanwhile, Young continued his efforts to restore peace. In May, 1854, he arranged a peace conference with Walker and Kanosh, leader of the Pauvans. He traveled south to personally attend this meeting, and upon his arrival found Walker very sick. Walker asked Young "to lay hands on him" to cure him through "faith healing," which Young did. He also presented Walker with "a wagon load of flour and wheat, a quantity of tobacco, and other presents." Then the pipe of peace was passed around and smoked by Young, Walker, Kanosh, and other Indian and Mormon leaders, ending the Walker War.

Following the Walker War, Young looked for ways to prevent future Mormon-Indian hostilities. He expanded his Indian farm concept into a full-scale Indian mission program and ordered the Mormon establishment of settlements in Indian-dominated areas. Here he dispatched experienced Mormon frontiersmen to help the Indians: "learn their language . . . feed them, clothe them and teach them." Young's effort followed in the tradition of earlier Spanish and American Indian missionary efforts of pacifying the Indians by civilizing them. The first Mormon missionaries arrived at Harmony in southwestern Utah in early May of 1854. The most famous missionary in this group was Jacob Hamblin, who developed a close rapport with the Indians and over the next several years worked closely with Indians throughout southern Utah. He became known as the Mormon "Apostle to the Indians." Other Indian missions were established at Elk Mountain (in southeastern Utah), in the White Mountains (near the present-day Utah-Nevada border), at Fort Supply (northeast of Salt Lake City on the Overland Trail), on the site of present-day Las Vegas, and at Ft. Lemhi, on the Salmon River.

Through his Indian policy, Brigham Young was fairly successful in maintaining peaceful Mormon-Indian relations over the next decade, although there were scattered acts of violence. This accomplishment was remarkable in light of the continuing heavy influx of Mormon migrants into Utah and their continuing encroachment onto Indian lands. According to Young, Utah had fewer Indian difficulties than the neighboring territories of Oregon and Washington.

However, Young soon discovered that federal officials did not like his handling of Indian affairs. On August 31, 1854, Lieutenant Colonel Edward J. Steptoe, dispatched by President Franklin Pierce, arrived in Salt Lake City with 175 soldiers and 180 civilian personnel to investigate the Gunnison Massacre. Steptoe also had orders to assume the post of Utah Territorial Governor, replacing Brigham Young whose four-year term was due to expire the following spring. There were initial tensions. Young did not want to see Salt Lake converted by Steptoe's men into a frontier military outpost with its attendant problems and vices. Also, he did not relish giving up his position as territorial governor to an outsider. He had indicated his desire to be reappointed, noting that his continuing service would spare Utah the usual type of federal appointees, namely, "dirty sneaking, rotten, heathen, pot house politicians."

Young's worst fears concerning Steptoe and his military contingent did not materialize. There were isolated instances of rowdyism and several Mormon girls were the victims of seduction, but overall Steptoe and his officers were courteous, and he was able to control his men. The troops were also helpful in protecting Mormon settlements from Indian aggression. Young, in return, cooperated with Steptoe in investigating the Gunnison Massacre throughout the fall and winter of 1854. In the spring, several Indians implicated in the massacre were captured, tried, and convicted by territorial authorities of murder in the second degree, sentenced to three years imprisonment, and fined $500 each.

For their part, Steptoe and his men developed positive feelings toward the Mormons. Steptoe decided not to assume the post of Utah territorial governor and instead addressed a petition to President Pierce recommending the reappointment of Brigham Young for another four-year term. Pierce reappointed Young and Steptoe and his men moved on to California the following spring. It had been a close call, but Young, through his astute diplomacy, saved his position as territorial governor and convinced an occupying force of U.S. Army troops that it could move on and leave the Mormons alone.

During the early 1850s the number of Great Basin Latter-day Saints increased from 10,000 to 60,000—a sixfold increase in just five years! These emigrants came from the eastern United States and abroad, with Great Britain alone accounting for 15,000 of the total. Many of these individuals arrived destitute, with little more than the clothes on their backs. Remembering the hardships of his own unsettled youth, Brigham Young was sensitive to the needs of these people. But he did not believe in charity, subscribing instead to the dignity of labor. Thus, Mormon officials organized a public works program calling for the building of roads, bridges, and canals, which provided employment for these individuals. Young, moreover, hired many new arrivals to make improvements on his own property.

After the emigrants became acclimated to the area, they were either dispatched to established communities or assigned to help found new communities. Thirty-two such settlements were established during the years 1852–57, bringing to ninety-six the total number of communities established since the arrival of the first pioneers. In setting up these colonies, Young took a common sense approach, realizing that newly arrived emigrants could not do the job themselves. Thus, he included both new and experienced frontiersmen along with a mix of industrial and agricultural workers.

Young assumed overall direction of Mormonism's expanding Great Basin sanctuary. But he delegated significant responsibilities for day-to-day affairs to his subordinates. He assigned members of the Council of Twelve responsibility for particular geographic regions. Thus, Apostle George A. Smith, a portly cousin of the slain Joseph Smith, oversaw settlements in southern Utah. Apostle Lorenzo Snow, a younger brother of Eliza R. Snow (Young's plural wife), took charge of a settlement at Brigham City, in northern Utah. Orson Hyde, president of the Council of Twelve, supervised the settlement of Fort Supply, an outpost on the Overland Trail east of Salt Lake City. Later, Hyde was reassigned to a Mormon settlement in Carson Valley (in present-day Nevada). Two other apostles, Amasa M. Lyman and Charles C. Rich, oversaw affairs at San Bernardino, California, a Mormon settlement they had earlier founded in 1851. This California outpost attracted many Mormons and by the mid-1850s boasted a population of 3,000, making it Mormonism's second largest settlement.

Young also delegated authority on a local level, assigning primary responsibilities to local church officials known as bishops. Bishops assumed responsibility for the religious well-being of individuals within their ward (or parish). They were also assigned secular responsibilities, looking after local economic and political problems such as water rights, maintenance of roads and bridges, property rights, Indian affairs, etc.

Although Young delegated direct day-to-day responsibility for Mormon settlements to his apostles, bishops, and other subordinates, he did maintain a high degree of personal contact with his followers by visiting various settlements. At first, Young's visits were limited to settlements near Salt Lake City—areas that could be easily visited over a weekend. He would meet with local leaders, conduct a two-day meeting, and then return to Salt Lake City. But as the Mormon sanctuary was expanded, Young's visits grew into regional tours, taking anywhere from two weeks to a month.

His first regional tour in 1853 took him south to Provo,

then Sanpete, and finally as far south as Manti, one hundred miles south of Salt Lake City. He visited Mormon settlements along the way and also took time to confer with local Indian leaders. A second regional tour the following year took him again south. This time, however, he traveled beyond Ceder City to Fort Harmony, three hundred miles south of Salt Lake City. The following year Young first traveled north and then went south to Fillmore, the Territorial capitol, to convene the territorial legislature.

These tours consumed a great deal of Young's time and energy. But it was time well spent because the tours gave him the opportunity to observe first hand conditions in distant settlements. Plus they allowed him to give his followers counsel, usually a sermon that focused on practical matters such as improving homes, fields, or herds, or building fortifications to protect themselves from the Indians.

Another aim involved strengthening the settlers' commitment to Mormonism. Young's visits conveyed an important message to the settlers that their leader cared enough to travel many miles to see them. These settlers were thus more likely to remain loyal to Mormonism. Finally, Young's tours provided settlers a respite from the pattern of daily toil. These visits lifted local spirits and provided opportunities for social interaction.

Young also exercised his powers as a strong leader through his effective sermons. But Young's effectiveness as a public speaker was not always evident to visiting outsiders. To many, he seemed unimpressive as he mounted the speaker's podium in the Old Tabernacle and started to speak slowly with his opening phrases barely audible. This initial reticence apparently reflected Young's own fear of public speaking. His delivery, moreover, betrayed mispronounced words or grammatical errors. Thus, impetus became im-PEET-us and there were provincialisms such as "leetle," "beyond," "disremember," "aint't you," and "they was." To outsiders Young's sermons seemed rambling and disorganized. This disjointed characteristic reflected Young's lack of formal training and the frontier setting. Although he thought in advance about what he would say, Young's oratory was not polished and he seemed to speak in an informal, impromptu fashion. In addition, Young's remarks seemed filthy and profane to refined Easterners or Europeans. His language was sometimes crude when he talked of sending enemies "to hell across lots."

Young's followers, however, saw him in a somewhat different light. In their eyes, he was an effective speaker. His physical appearance alone commanded respect. He stood five feet ten—taller than most men of his time—with penetrating, ice-blue eyes, and lips that according to one observer "came together like the jaws of a bear trap." While he started his sermons in a slow, low tone, he used his resonant bass voice to its fullest as he got going. Although rough, his language merely reflected his audience. He understood public speaking's most basic rule—know your audience and speak to their level. Although disorganized, Young's sermons were direct, to the point, and in a style understandable to the most unsophisticated listener. Young frequently scolded his followers for their shortcomings and failings. But he also took care to temper such "thunder from the pulpit" with statements betraying his own feelings of genuine concern for their welfare. He came across as a gruff but loving father, alternately scolding but befriending his listeners.

Young's sermons were also effective in that they usually dealt with practical matters such as thrift, frugality, and hard work. When he did deal with doctrinal matters, his sermons were usually upbeat and liberal. Young, through his preaching, strengthened the bonds of identification that existed between himself and his followers, thereby maintaining the loyalty of most Mormons through bad times as well as good.

Young worked to strengthen bonds within his own large family as it continued to grow. He took on more wives during the early 1850s, bringing to forty-three the total number of women he had married since 1842. He fathered sixteen children by nine different wives—bringing to forty-four his total offspring. To accommodate his large family, Young supervised the construction of two new residences in Salt Lake City. The first, the Beehive House, a large, two-story structure, was completed in 1854. Constructed of adobe and painted a pale yellow with green shutters, it contained fourteen rooms. Young designed the house with the assistance of his brother-in-law, Truman O. Angell, the older brother of his wife Mary Ann.

Indeed, Mary Ann was the first and, until 1860, the only wife to live there. The Beehive House replaced the White House as Young's own official residence. His sleeping quarters were located on the first floor. Next to this room were his offices, convenient for work at any hour. Here, he transacted most of his business activities as Church leader and governor. One of the rooms served as Young's private office where he met with counselors and other advisers. The second, larger office, housed Young's clerical staff and provided for the storage of church and territorial records. Two or three secretaries or clerks aided Young in the dictation of letters of instruction dispatched to Mormon bishops or church leaders in distant settlements. The whole operation revealed an order and neatness that reflected the character of Brigham Young himself.

The Beehive House also served as a place to entertain guests. It contained two spacious parlors, one upstairs and the other down. Young would generally take his breakfast in the downstairs parlor. Behind the parlor were a buttery, kitchen, a small bedroom, and a large dining room for Young's hired help and workmen. Finally, on the extreme north end of the house was the "family store" where staples, notions, drugs, dried fruit, and vegetables, and calicoes were kept and distributed to Young's various wives.

The majority of those wives lived in a second new residence, the Lion House, next door to the Beehive House.

This structure took its name from a carved stone lion which rested over the main entrance and symbolized Brigham Young, known as the "Lion of the Lord." This residence, a rectangular, three-story structure, was finished in cream plaster with white woodwork and green shutters. The upper floor contained twenty bedrooms where the childless wives and older boys and girls slept. The middle floor held the apartments of the wives with small children along with the parlor or "prayer room," as it was known. The basement floor included a buttery, kitchen, laundry, and most important, a large dining room which accommodated about fifty people. Here Young generally joined other family members for the evening meal. Following the meal, Young would gather the family together in the Lion House parlor, discuss topics of the day, and finally kneel down in prayer.

This system of communal polygamy appeared to work reasonably well. In carrying out certain domestic tasks a division of labor prevailed. For example, Lucy Decker, Young's first plural wife, took charge of the Lion House kitchen. A second wife, Zina D. Huntington, trained in obstetrics, served as the family midwife and nurse, delivering the numerous babies and caring for sick family members. Harriet Cook taught Young's school-aged children, first in the Lion House and later in a separate building. Other specialized tasks, too strenuous for the wives, were performed by hired men. Gardeners cared for the family garden and orchard, and, at harvest time, the wives and children did their share in packing and processing the fruits and vegetables. Young also hired individuals to oversee the family's own carpenter shop, shoeshop, blacksmith shop, flour mill, and family store.

Not all household tasks fell under this communal arrangement. Each wife did her own laundry, ironing, sewing, and weaving, and assumed direct responsibility for her own children. Young did not experiment with communal childrearing and made no effort to detach children from their mothers after birth.

While Young left most responsibility for childrearing in the hands of his wives, he did exercise some influence. He taught his children with a firmness "that neither humiliated the child nor lowered his own self-respect." In contrast to his own harsh, authoritarian upbringing, Young disciplined his children "not by the whip or rod" but by "setting a good example before them." He believed in making his authority felt by "superior intelligence." He sought to be not "a tyrannical ruler, but . . . an indulgent and affectionate father."

When conditions warranted, he exhibited a practical knowledge of child psychology. On one occasion, a wife confronted him with a misbehaving toddler son who when fed would knock his dish and spoon to the floor. Young did not inflict corporal punishment in handling this matter as some parents might have done. But he advised the mother that "the next time he knocks the dish from your hand . . . lean him against the chair, do not say one word to him [and] go to your work." The mother did this. At first the child stood by the chair looking at his mother and at the objects on the floor. But presently he crawled over to the spoon and dish and returned them to the table. The child never knocked the dish out of his mother's hand again.

But if conditions warranted, Young would use stronger force in correcting a misbehaving child. One evening during family prayer, a noisy child "was running about squealing with laughter." Young stopped his prayer, grabbed the child, spanked her and laid her sobbing in her mother's arms and then quietly concluded the prayer. Such occurrences, however, were rare, and a far cry from the physical punishment of his own youth.

While Young's basic views concerning the place of his children were fairly straightforward, his overall attitudes relative to his various plural wives were less clear cut. They appeared paradoxical. On the one hand, he defended polygamy itself as absolutely essential for complete salvation. But at the same time he admitted "there are probably but few men in the world who care about the private society of women less than I do." With such mixed feelings, Young grappled with the problem of keeping all of his wives content and his family together. This was a crucial undertaking since his household symbolized the total institution of Mormon polygamy. If polygamy did not work in his household, where would it work? The ideal polygamous arrangement was one in which all wives were treated impartially and equally.

However, this ideal went unfulfilled. Young himself suggested the need to treat certain wives different than others. He admonished fellow polygamists that the first "wife of our youths who dwelt in our bosoms" prior to polygamy should be shown some preference because of her unique situation. Thus, Young provided Mary Ann a separate residence in the Beehive House apart from his other wives. Young also exhibited a preference for two or three other wives. One of these, Emmeline Free, was a favorite because of her beauty, elegant manners, and quick wit and tact. Possibly reflecting her favored position, she bore Young more children (ten in all) than any of the rest. Another favorite was Clara Decker, a sweet, charming personality and the pioneer wife who had first accompanied Young to the Great Basin.

The time that Young took to establish a positive relationship with certain favorite wives meant less time to spend with other wives whom he found less appealing. Reacting to Young's inattention, some wives found contentment in their children or other domestic activities. Others, such as Eliza R. Snow and Zina B. Huntington, involved themselves in Church work and civic activities. The case of Eliza R. Snow is particularly interesting. Young continued to rely on the advice of this bright, articulate woman relative to various church matters. Other wives developed close bonds of friendship with one another.

Although harmonious relationships tended to prevail within the Young household, things did not always go smoothly and occasionally pent-up feelings or frustration broke into the open. In extreme cases, divorce or separation was the only answer. Sensitive to his own situation as well as that of other polygamous Mormons, Young allowed the liberal granting of divorces to women (but not men) dissatisfied with polygamy. Within Young's own household, seven wives had left him through divorce, separation, or annulment by 1857. Most of these women departed quietly. But one, Sarah Malin, publicized her discontent through a series of newspaper articles published in the *New York Times*.

Young encountered the wrath of other dissatisfied wives. Emily Dow Partridge, the wife who had faced so much hardship during her trek across the Plains, decided by 1853 she had had enough. She wrote Young, "I feel more lonely and more unreconciled to my lot than ever." She continued, "[since] I am not essential to your comfort or your convenience, I desire that you will give me to some other good man who has less cares." Although Emily did not leave Young, her feelings of alienation were not unique. Another dissatisfied wife was Susan Snively, a German by birth and labeled by one observer as the plainest of the wives. She developed a reputation as a whiner in addition to being selfish and self-centered.

A third wife, Harriet Cook, manifested frustrations through her outrageous behavior. Cook, one of Young's first plural wives, had remained in Nauvoo following her husband's departure but later rejoined the family in Salt Lake City. Tall, fair, and blue-eyed, with a sharp nose which bespoke her temper, she enjoyed shocking people with her rough words and vulgar references. On one occasion when workmen were repainting the Lion House, and asked what color she wanted her apartment, she retorted, "I want my room painted in a color between piss-brindle and shit brown." The startled workmen turned to Young, who was standing behind her, and he replied, "Brethren, do just exactly as she says." Thus, Harriet's apartment was the ugliest place in the entire Lion House! On another occasion she barged into

Young's private office and despite finding him busy meeting with his counselors, she proceeded to complain about her aches and pains "dwelling especially upon the condition of her female organs." She then asked Young about taking a new patent medicine to relieve these pains. Young replied, "Take it, Sister Harriet, take it, Hell fire and brimestone wouldn't hurt you." Young avoided intimate contact with this irascible woman and fathered only one child by her.

Outside of his family, Young faced greater problems. During the summer of 1855, the Great Basin experienced drought, followed by a severe grasshopper plague. The following autumn the Mormons had a poor fall harvest, resulting in an acute food shortage that rekindled painful memories of the first Great Basin winters. This situation was exacerbated by a huge influx in 1855 of European Mormon emigrants. These immigrants arrived in Utah in record numbers, completely dependent on resident Mormons for provisions. Compounding this situation, the winter of 1855–56 was one of the worst on record.

By late January of 1856, the situation became critical with food supplies running low and cattle dying. Young attempted to boost morale by telling them, "for until we ate up the last mule from the tip of the ear to the end of the fly whipper, I am not afraid of starving to death." Young's actions matched his words as he ordered all Great Basin Saints to ration their meager food supplies. In this spirit, each member of his own large family was put on a half-pound of breadstuff per day. Thus, the Mormons made it through this difficult time in reasonably good shape.

Facing these difficulties, Young concluded that more than bad weather was to blame. Perhaps the Lord was manifesting displeasure because his followers had failed to store provisions out of early abundant harvests. "My soul has been grieved to bleeding," noted Young, "to see the waste, and the prodigal feeling of this people in the use of their bountiful blessings." "You are suffering," he continued, "because you have neglected yourselves." He advised the Saints to "never . . . be without three to five years' provisions on hand."

Young chastised his followers in the spirit of the Mormon Reformation, a movement calling for a renewed emphasis on religious piety. The Mormon Reformation drew much of its force from the personality of one man—Jedediah M. Grant. Grant had been selected by Young as Second Councilor in the Church First Presidency, replacing Willard Richards, who died in 1854. Tall, grim-looking, with a thin face somewhat resembling "Andrew Jackson with a broken nose," Grant was a man of proven executive ability. He served as a Speaker of the Territorial Legislature, Superintendent of Public Works, and Major General of the Territorial Militia and had a reputation as a fiery exhorter, earning him the nickname "Brigham's Sledgehammer." His sermons were filled with hell-fire and damnation in which he harangued his listeners as "abominable characters," "old hardened sinners . . . little better in appearance and in their habits than a little black boy." These misbehaving Mormons, continued Grant, "live in filth and nastiness, they eat it and drink it and they are filthy all over." He called upon them to repent and be "baptized and washed clean from your sins" and was for letting the "wrath of the Almighty" fall on those who failed to repent. Grant's preaching was effective, stirring whole congregations to a recognition of their sins, real and imagined, thus generating strong desire to repent. Grant presided over this process through the rebaptism of those who confessed.

Brigham Young viewed these revivalistic activities with mixed feelings. On the one hand, Grant's fiery sermonizing undoubtedly reminded him of the emotional camp meetings that had adversely affected him earlier as a youth on the New York frontier. Young himself tended to avoid such emotionalism in his own preaching. But he approved of what the Mormon Reformation was trying to do in revitalizing Mormon spiritual awareness. He encouraged the Reformation as "essential" to awaken the people "from a drowsy stupor & lethargy" and get them "to live their religion and do right."

In upholding the spirit of the Reformation, moreover, Young appointed two or more home missionaries from each ward to go from house-to-house and examine the individuals within, relative to their religious beliefs and practices. They presented a catechism of thirteen questions prepared by Young and Jedediah Grant, which touched on such major things as the shedding of innocent blood, stealing, drunkenness, lying, and, of course, adultery. But they also probed some seemingly minor areas: "Have you labored faithfully for your wages? Have you coveted that which belongs to another? Have you contracted debts without prospect of paying?" and "Do you preside in your family as a servant of God?" Young got into the spirit of this process through his role as chief Church inquisitor. At a special meeting of Mormon men, Young exhorted the crowd by asking all those who had committed adultery to stand up. Much to his surprise, three-fourths of the men got to their feet! Many of those standing had probably committed adultery only in their hearts and not in fact. But the excitement and fervor of the Mormon Reformation caused these guilt-ridden Mormons to confess.

The Mormon Reformation also provided Young an opportunity to publicize a couple of new, controversial beliefs. One of these was the Adam-God concept first articulated in 1852, which maintained that Adam had existed in a premortal state before coming into this world. In this state, Adam had helped to "make and organize this world" and was "our Father and our God, and the only God with whom we have to do." This unusual belief raised eyebrows outside of Mormonism, and was a point of disagreement within the Mormon Church hierarchy, causing friction between Young and Orson Pratt. In the long run, the Adam-God concept received only limited publicity and did not become essential Mormon doctrine.

A second controversial belief was the "doctrine of blood atonement" drawn from the Old Testament admonition that "who so sheddeth man's blood, by man shall his blood be shed." Certain grave sins by an individual could receive Divine forgiveness only through the voluntary shedding of the sinner's own blood. Young articulated this concept in announcing that "there are sins that men commit for which they cannot receive forgiveness in this world, or in that which is to come, and if they could see their true condition, they would be perfectly willing to have their blood spilt upon the ground, that the smoke thereof might ascend to heaven as an offering for their sins; and the smoking incense would atone for their sins." Young's words seemed to justify ritualistic murder. But this was not the case because Young also taught that blood atonement could be averted through "sincere repentance." There was, moreover, no rash of killings in Utah despite the forbodings of certain anti-Mormon detractors. Indeed, the level of violence in Mormonism's frontier sanctuary was much lower than in other western regions.

The Mormon Reformation itself suffered a mortal blow with the loss of Jedediah Grant. In December, 1856, the thirty-nine-year-old Mormon counselor died of a combination of typhoid fever and double pneumonia—the latter complicated by the long hours he spent in the water rebaptizing repentant sinners. He left behind three wives, nine children, and a Mormon Reformation that had pretty well run its course. It had accomplished its main goal by regenerating a renewed sense of religious purpose.

In the fall and winter of 1856, Young was primarily preoccupied with building up Mormonism's Great Basin sanctuary. It appeared that the migration of pioneers needed for this process might be disrupted due to complications resulting from the extremely severe winter of 1855–56. Most of the Church cattle used on the incoming emigrant wagons had starved or frozen to death. Also, the wagons and equipment were almost worn out and Church funds depleted. In response, Young developed a plan to make handcarts and let the emigrants "foot it" across the Plains. He did not invent this method of pioneer travel, which had been previously used by goldrushers to California. Handcarts, Young felt, would work for the Mormons since most emigrants in wagon companies walked most of the distance anyhow, utilizing wagons only for carrying supplies. The use of handcarts would, moreover, be much less expensive. When news of the handcart scheme reached Europe, Church headquarters in Liverpool was flooded with applicants, as a huge backlog of poorer Mormons who could not afford to emigrate heretofore looked forward to migrating.

This response encouraged Young to push ahead with the handcart plan during the spring and summer of 1856. He placed Franklin D. Richards in charge of dispatching the emigrants from England. A second apostle, John Taylor, assumed responsibility for the emigrants from the East Coast to the Plains of Iowa. At Iowa City, the migrating Mormons would secure their handcarts—already built by skilled Mormon carpenters and blacksmiths previously sent from Utah.

At first, the handcart migration went smoothly as the first three companies left Iowa in early June and arrived in Salt Lake City by late September of 1856. But two later handcart companies ran into unforeseen difficulties. Their handcarts were not as well constructed, the lumber being green, making the carts heavier and harder to push. The green lumber, moreover, caused the boards to shrink and iron rims to fall off the wheels, causing further delays. Their provisions ran out and winter storms hit earlier than expected, just as they reached the Wyoming Mountains.

Young soon received word of the two handcart companies' stranded condition. He dispatched teamsters with supplies for the marooned pioneers. By late November Young became aware of the full extent of the handcart tragedy with the completion of rescue efforts. Almost 200 of the 900 pioneers perished. He was appalled by the tragic loss of life and condition of the survivors, whom he visited upon their arrival in Salt Lake. Meeting this group with their tattered clothing and frostbitten limbs moved the Mormon leader to tears. Who was at fault? Some critics blamed Young. But Young placed the blame elsewhere. He reprimanded Franklin D. Richards in a public sermon: "If there had only been someone, even a little bird, who might have whispered to Brother Franklin that it was too late in the year to send men, women, and children onto the plains and into the mountains." He also lashed out at John Taylor for supplying improperly seasoned wood and other materials, characterizing him as "not fit to handle means no more than a child." Young then warned that in the future immigration across the Plains after a given time would not be allowed and that anyone doing so would be severed from the Church. Young, however, reserved his harshest attacks for the critics who blamed him or his counselors for this tragedy. "If any man or woman complains of me or my counselors . . . let the curse of God be on them and blast their substance with mildew and destruction, until their names are forgotten from the earth." This reaction betrayed Young's extreme sensitivity to personal criticism and the lengths he would go to protect his reputation as an effective colonizer of Mormonism's frontier sanctuary.

However, in the long run, Young need not have worried for his successes far outweighed his failures. In particular, his handcart scheme was a qualified success for over 3,000 Mormons traveled to the Great Basin in this way without incident. In a larger sense, Young had succeeded, for by 1856 he had founded settlements throughout the length and breadth of the Great Basin, thus establishing Mormonism's frontier sanctuary on a solid foundation. But over the next ten years the very existence of that sanctuary would be threatened by direct conflict with an increasingly hostile federal government that would culminate in the dispatch of army troops to Utah.

V I

Conflict with the Federal Government

As EARLY AS 1854, Brigham Young faced the problem of deteriorating relations with the federal government. Basically, Young had little respect for the majority of non-Mormon federal officeholders in Utah, characterizing them in general "a gambling, drinking, whoring set." Clearly fitting into this category was William W. Drummond, a Utah territorial judge. Drummond had deserted his wife and family in Illinois, but through his political influence had secured a Utah judgeship in 1854. Soon after his arrival in Utah, he upset the Mormons by his outspoken opposition to polygamy, on which he admonished the Mormons from the bench. He further outraged the Mormons by allowing his mistress, a prostitute whom he had picked up in Washington, D.C., to sit beside him on the bench. Drummond, according to Young, "demeaned himself very much like a dog or wolf" and was as "ignorant as a jack-ass."

Ultimately, Drummond's tenure as Utah judge came to an end because of a personal feud with a Salt Lake Jewish merchant whom Drummond tried unsuccessfully to murder. When news of his bungled effort surfaced, Drummond left the territory quickly but not quietly. Upon his return East, he wrote a vitriolic letter attacking Brigham Young, accusing him of destroying federal court records and of keeping his people in abject bondage. He characterized Young and his

134

followers as disloyal, accusing the Mormons of plotting to break away from the United States and set up their own independent western empire with Brigham Young as emperor.

Drummond's accusations came at a time then the Mormons were coming under increased attack in the national political arena. Leading these attacks was the newly-formed Republican party, which had emerged in opposition to the Kansas-Nebraska Act and slavery expansion westward. The Republicans lashed out against the Mormons and polygamy, placing it in the same category as slavery. Prominent Republicans, including Charles Sumner of Massachusetts, Schuyler Colfax from Indiana, and Brigham Young's old New York neighbor William H. Seward, all attacked Mormon polygamy. In 1856, the Republican party issued its strongest statement against the Mormons at its first national convention in Philadelphia when it gathered to nominate John C. Fremont for president. The Republican platform declared it "the imperative duty of Congress to prohibit in the Territories those twin relics of barbarism—Polygamy and Slavery."

This Republican assault contrasted with the position of the Democratic party, which endorsed a policy of noninterference with the Mormons and polygamy. The Democrats

---

Left: Brigham Young and twenty-one of the fifty-five women he married during his lifetime. *Top row:* Emmeline Free Young; Mary Ann Angell Young; Mary Van Cott Young; Augusta Adams Young; and Martha Bowker Young. *Second row from top:* Miriam Works Young; Eliza Burgess Young; Naamah Kendell Jenkins Carter Young; and Clara Chase Ross Young. *Third row from top:* Lucy Decker Young; Zina Diantha Huntington Young; Margaret Pierce Young; and Clara Decker Young. *Fourth row from top:* Harriett Cook Campbell Young; Lucy Bigelow Young; Harriet Barney Young; Emily Dow Partridge Young; and Susan Snively Young. *Bottom row:* Ann Eliza Webb Young; Harriet Amelia Folsom Young; and Eliza Roxy Snow Young. (Courtesy of the LDS Church Library-Archives. Printed with permission.)

chose to allow citizens on the local level to regulate their domestic institutions, whether slavery or polygamy, an approach in harmony with Stephen A. Douglas' concept of popular sovereignty. In contrast to John C. Fremont, the Democratic presidential candidate, James Buchanan ran on a platform calling for "non-interference by Congress with slavery" and by implication polygamy. Not surprisingly, Young favored Buchanan over John C. Fremont and was relieved to see Buchanan elected in November, 1856.

Young expressed his personal belief that as president Buchanan would "be a friend to the good" as had Fillmore and Pierce before him. This, however, was not to be. Buchanan adopted a hostile approach toward the Mormons, ordering the mobilization of 2,500 U.S. Army troops in May of 1857, and secretly dispatching them to Utah to remove Brigham Young as territorial governor. Buchanan wanted to replace Young with his own appointee, Alfred Cumming of Georgia. There appears to be several possible motives behind Buchanan's sudden assault on the Mormons. To some extent, Buchanan was apparently reacting to Republican attacks made during and after the 1856 presidential campaign that he and his fellow Democrats were too pro-Mormon. One Republican newspaper had characterized the Democrats as follows: "What a tricolor for freemen, for Americans, for religion, for progress, to contemplate—Democracy—Slavery—Polygamy!"

Despite Buchanan's own election, the Republicans increased their numerical strength in Congress and began to push for the enactment of anti-polygamy legislation. Buchanan also faced pressure from within the Democratic party. Illinois Senator Stephen A. Douglas, who had presidential aspirations of his own and was Buchanan's intraparty archrival, unleashed his own diatribe against the Mormons in early 1857. He characterized Mormonism as a "pestiferous disgusting cancer ... gnawing into the very vitals of the [American] body politic [which] must be cut out by the roots." Douglas attacked Young in particular as a tyrant who maintained absolute control through "horrid oaths and penalties." Douglas called for the repeal of Utah's territorial charter, the region's partition, and its annexation to surrounding states and territories. These drastic suggestions ran counter to Douglas' own cherished concept of popular sovereignty and against his previous pro-Mormon stance. But the Illinois Senator justified his position by characterizing the Mormons "alien enemies and outlaws unfit to be citizens of a territory."

Other individuals close to the president called upon him to take action against the Mormons. Two close associates from Buchanan's home state of Pennsylvania, the Reverend Henry Slicer and United States Senator William Bigler, called upon the president to heed the "honest indignation in the country against the conduct of the Mormons." There was also pressure for action within Buchanan's own Cabinet. Secretary of War John B. Floyd apparently had a personal economic interest in outfitting and dispatching a large armed force to Utah. Floyd received huge kickbacks from Army supply contractors, a fact when later disclosed led to his resignation as Secretary of War. Buchanan may have also viewed an assault on the polygamous Saints as a way to reunite a Democratic party deeply divided over the controversy surrounding the *Dred Scott* decision. This decision, which allowed black slaves to be taken into any American territory regardless of prevailing local opinion, pleased James Buchanan and pro-Southern Democrats but dismayed Stephen A. Douglas and moderate Democrats who supported popular sovereignty. Also, strong federal action against the Mormons—a group universally detested—would divert public attention away from the increasingly vexing question of slavery in the territories and unite the entire country.

Whatever his motives, James Buchanan's action in sending federal armed forces to Utah caused Brigham Young his greatest crisis since the death of Joseph Smith, and the Mormon exodus west a decade earlier. When he received word of Buchanan's action in July of 1857, Young angrily lashed out at the president, characterizing him "a stink in the nostrils of every honorable person throughout the nation." The specter of an armed force advancing toward Utah created widespread Mormon apprehension, reviving bitter memories of the Missouri state militia, Governor Lilburn Boggs, and his infamous "extermination order" of 1838. According to Young, the federal government was sending an army to Utah "to simply hold us still until a mob can come and butcher us as has been done before."

In response to this critical situation, Young took action, ordering the abandonment of all outlying Mormon settlements, including San Bernardino in California, Las Vegas, Carson Valley, Fort Lemhi in Idaho, and both Fort Bridger and Fort Supply along the Overland Trail. Young wanted all his followers close to him during this time of crisis. There was the possibility of moving the Mormons from the Great Basin to some new location, which would be consistent with what the Mormons had previously done in responding to armed anti-Mormon assaults. But then came the related question: Where would the Latter-day Saints move?

Young looked into a number of possible locations, including the Colorado River area, the Mojave Desert, and the valleys of the Sierra Nevada Mountains. Young seriously considered sending an advance company of five hundred families to the desert region of western Utah territory (present-day Nevada) to raise crops for other Mormons who would follow later. Young was also presented with the option of moving outside the United States. Possible locations included British Canada, Russian Alaska, Sonora, Mexico, or Central America. In fact, two representatives from Nicaragua traveled to Salt Lake City with an offer to have the Mormons purchase land there. These men apparently represented the infamous American adventurer and filibusterer, William Walker, who, at different times during the 1850s, seized control of Sonora, Mexico, and Nicaragua.

Although Young considered a Mormon exodus, he soon realized that he lacked the time to carry it out, due to the rapid speed at which the federal force was advancing. Nor did he find an enticing place to migrate. Thus, Young decided that the Mormons would stand their ground and resist the federal troops. In a speech to his followers, Young declared: "I wish to avoid hostilities . . . but before I'll see this people suffer . . . I will draw my sword in the name of Great God and say to my Brethren let our Swords fall upon our enemies." Despite his inflexible opposition to the entry of armed forces, Young promised to allow Alfred Cumming and other civilian officials entry.

The Mormon leader moved to back up his words with action. The territorial militia known as the Nauvoo Legion assumed responsibility for defending the Mormons. This force was under the direct command of Daniel H. Wells, a craggy, full-maned Lincolnesque figure with jutting chin and a cast eye. Wells had been a non-Mormon resident of Nauvoo prior to the Mormon arrival. Wells befriended the Mormons following their arrival, but did not join the Church immediately because of his wife's opposition. But by 1846 Wells changed his mind and became a Mormon. He quickly moved up in the ranks of the Church hierarchy, serving as Young's aide-de-camp during the migration west. Once in Salt Lake, Wells assumed positions of increasing responsibility, including Superintendent of Public Works, Commander of the Nauvoo Legion, and finally in 1857 Second Counselor in the Church First Presidency, replacing Jedediah M. Grant. In contrast to the zealous, almost fanatical Grant, Wells was known as a statesman and conciliator. But at the same time, he was not afraid to utilize the armed forces under his command to protect Mormon interests.

Young pressed the Nauvoo Legion quickly into action in August of 1857. A few select Legion members undertook a scouting expedition to determine the exact location of the advancing federal force. The advance elements of this force were surprisingly close, near South Pass. Next, the Nauvoo Legion built defensive fortifications, or breast-works, at the mouth of Little Emigration Canyon and along Echo Canyon—the two main routes into the Great Salt Lake Valley.

Meanwhile, the commander of the federal force, Colonel E. B. Alexander, made known his desire to avoid a direct conflict with the Mormons by dispatching his assistant quar-termaster, Captain Stewart Van Vliet, to Salt Lake City to meet with Brigham Young. Van Vliet sought to convey the troops' peaceful intent and secure a place for them to en-camp. Young responded to Van Vliet with a combination of deference and firmness. Young noted that the Mormons were law-abiding citizens who "love [the] Constitution and respect the law of the United States." Young also sought to refute Drummond's charges that he had burned United States court records. But he expressed strong opposition to the federal troops, warning Van Vliet: "If the government persists in sending an army to destroy us, in the name of the Lord we shall conquer them." Young also suggested possible Indian harassment: "I shall not hold the Indians by the wrist any longer: they shall go ahead and do as they please." Young also told Van Vliet that his army could not count on the Mormons for supplies. Finally, he warned if the army "succeeds in penetrating this Valley [all] they will find here [will be] a charred and barren waste."

Young managed to impress Van Vliet of Mormon deter-mination and resolve and convinced him that the Mormons had been unjustly maligned in the Eastern press and by national politicians. Van Vliet concluded that the Mormons had "been lied about the worse of any people I ever saw." He promised Young that he would do what he could to prevent an armed confrontation and return to Wyoming to convince E. B. Alexander to halt the army's advance. Van

Vliet also promised to continue east to Washington, D.C., and meet with President Buchanan and urge him to send an investigating committee to Utah before pressing ahead against the Mormons.

Brigham Young considered Van Vliet a "gentleman" who "understood our position" and endorsed his efforts. But Young had no illusions that Van Vliet could easily accomplish his honorable intentions and thus continued preparations for a possible armed conflict. On September 15, Young, by his authority as territorial governor, placed Utah under martial law. His official proclamation: "forbid all armed forces of any description from coming into this Territory under any pretence whatsoever." The Nauvoo Legion was ordered to hold itself in "readiness to march at a moment's notice to repel any and all such invasion."

Young then sent a letter of warning to "The officer commanding the forces now invading Utah Territory" accompanied by his "proclamation." But Young's letter was ignored by the Army Commander who continued to push his troops toward the Great Basin. Young then ordered direct action, by 100 so-called "Mormon Raiders", directing them to do what was necessary to slow the advance of federal troops short of actual conflict. This force undertook a campaign of harassment, starting with the burning of two forts along the Overland Trail in western Wyoming to prevent their capture by federal troops. Mormon forces also imitated the practices of the Plains Indians by setting grass fires, driving off stock, and burning government supply wagons.

These Mormon actions delayed the army sufficiently that heavy November snows caught them still in the mountains east of Salt Lake City, forcing them to postpone plans to enter the Salt Lake Valley that fall. The army established a winter camp near the charred remains of what had once been Fort Bridger and a new commander, Colonel Albert Sydney Johnston of Kentucky, took over. A West Point graduate with a reputation as a capable soldier, Johnston faced the thankless task of providing for the comfort of his troops, already on short rations following the Mormon destruction of their supply trains. Johnston found the winter weather intensely cold as his men camped without adequate shelter at an elevation between six and seven thousand feet. No longer did his soldiers brag about "scalping Old Brigham" or helping themselves to "extra" Mormon wives as during the previous summer. They merely concentrated on survival until the following spring.

When Young heard of the army's plight, particularly its shortage of salt, he donated eight hundred pounds of the scarce commodity as a goodwill gesture. But Johnston rejected the Mormon gift by stating that he would "accept no favors from traitors and rebels"—a statement which would prove ironic in light of Johnston's own later behavior. As the winter of 1857–58 closed in around Johnston's forces, it was clear that Young had won the first round in his conflict with the federal government.

However, Brigham Young was much less successful in handling another group of outsiders, a company of emigrants from Missouri and Arkansas who entered Utah during that tense fall of 1857 as Young grappled with the "Utah War." These emigrants traveling south from Salt Lake City toward southern California made known their intense dislike for the Mormons as they were passing through. Certain individuals bragged of participation in the hostilities against the Mormons in Missouri years before. The more impudent boasted of having helped "shoot the guts out of Joe and Hyrum Smith at Carthage."

Further aggravating this situation was the news of the murder of Apostle Parley P. Pratt earlier that year in Arkansas, the home state of the majority of these emigrants. The emigrants also stirred up local Indians by killing their livestock and poisoning their wells as they moved south. Thus, when the emigrants reached Cedar City, their relations with both local Mormons and Indians had reached the flash point, particularly after Cedar City residents refused to sell the emigrants food. The angry travelers then took retribution, destroying Mormon property and threatening to return with a western army as federal troops attacked from the east wiping "every damn Mormon off the earth."

This threat caused Cedar City officials to wonder what to do about both the emigrants and the increasingly restive Indians—anxious to deal on their own with the obnoxious travelers. Southern Utah leaders sent a messenger to Salt Lake City to seek advice from Brigham Young. When the rider arrived, Young was busy meeting with Captain Van Vliet over the approaching federal forces, but he took time to quickly pen a letter to Isaac Haight, the presiding Church officer at Cedar City, advising him: "You must not meddle with [the emigrants] . . . let them go in peace." As for the restive Indians, Young added: "The Indians we expect will do as they please, but you should try to preserve good feeling with them." The messenger was ordered by Young to immediately return south with his written instructions, but he did not arrive in time. Local residents had already taken matters into their own hands. Two days earlier, fifty Cedar City Mormon militiamen, in cooperation with two hundred local Indians, had surrounded and killed virtually all of the members of the Missouri-Arkansas emigrant company—nearly one hundred individuals, including men, women, and children—at a place called Mountain Meadows, a short distance from Cedar City. The only individuals spared were eighteen small children.

The Mormon leader of this massacre was John D. Lee, a respected community leader who had served as a local Church agent among the Indians. By late September Young received the first reports on what became known as the "Mountain Meadows Massacre." Lee claimed that Indians alone were responsible for the massacre. According to the later recollections of one observer, Young "wept like a child

[and] wrung his hands in bitter anguish." Young apparently did not believe (or did not want to believe) that Lee and other Mormons were directly involved. If he suspected Mormon involvement, the approaching army gave him neither the time nor the desire to follow up his suspicions. This was unfortunate. For in subsequent years, the whole awful truth would become public knowledge and reflect negatively not just on Lee and those directly involved but on Brigham Young and the entire Mormon movement.

During the winter of 1857–58, Brigham Young's primary concern was not the Mountain Meadows Massacre but over what direction the Utah War would take the following spring. President Buchanan, despite the reverses suffered thus far, remained determined to force the issue. In his annual message to Congress in December of 1857, he lashed out at the Mormons in general and Brigham Young in particular, proclaiming Mormon religious practices "deplorable . . . and revolting to the moral and religious sentiments of all Christendom," and accusing Brigham Young of committing acts of hostility against the United States bordering on open rebellion. Buchanan further charged Young with exciting the hostile feelings of the Indians against the United States.

In the face of Buchanan's charges, Young worried anew about Johnston's army poised and ready to resume its offensive in the spring. On the one hand, Young hoped to avoid actual bloodshed, but at the same time he prepared for the worst. Mormon militia forces "secreted here and there," were prepared to "waste away our enemies." At the same time, Young was ready to destroy everything the Mormons had built "if driven to that extremity . . . our enemies shall find nothing but heaps of ashes and ruins."

As Young considered these drastic actions, there was a dramatic shift in Eastern public opinion. Initially, leading newspapers and politicians had been supportive of President James Buchanan's policies. But by late 1857, with disclosure of the sorry condition of Johnston's army, public opinion began to turn against the president. The *New York Times* observed: "The whole Utah business has been mismanaged in the most extraordinary manner from the beginning," while the *New York Herald* labeled the whole affair "a needlessly desperate service," with all the makings of a "disgraceful catastrophe." Horace Greeley, a leading politician and editor of the *New York Tribune,* also attacked Buchanan for his "shameful mismanagement." Senator Sam Houston of Texas expressed grudging admiration for Brigham Young from the floor of the United States Senate, declaring the time had come "to make peace with Brigham Young."

Indeed, officials within Buchanan's own administration came to the same conclusion. Captain Van Vliet, following his arrival in Washington, D.C., met with federal officials and informed them of Brigham Young's steadfast determination to resist federal troops. At this point, Thomas L. Kane, Young's politically influential non-Mormon friend, approached President Buchanan offering to act as a mediator. Buchanan agreed to let Kane represent him in a quasi-official capacity and Kane, despite his own frail health, immediately departed Washington, D.C., traveling incognito to avoid publicity. Journeying by way of Panama and Southern California, because of the heavy mountain snows, overland, Kane arrived in Salt Lake City in late February, 1858. Young, upon meeting the sick and weary traveler, expressed his extreme pleasure: "Friend Thomas, the Lord sent you here and he will not let you die . . . till your work is done." Young conveyed his willingness to allow Alfred Cumming to enter the Salt Lake Valley if he came peacefully and without the troops. He would also allow a two-man peace commission established by President Buchanan to enter and investigate allegations against the Mormons. Kane then left Salt Lake and traveled east to western Wyoming and the snow-bound army. Here he met with Alfred Cumming and together they returned back to Salt Lake City.

Meanwhile, Brigham Young continued to prepare for the worse despite his trust in Thomas Kane. Anticipating the possibility that Johnston's army, with the coming of spring, would resume its march, Young ordered all the Mormons living in northern Utah, including Salt Lake City, to completely abandon their homes and move south. This move was to be followed by even more drastic action, namely, the complete Mormon abandonment of the territory and destruction of all improvements should Johnston's forces enter. Young moved his own large family fifty miles south of Salt Lake City to Provo.

In the midst of this evacuation, Thomas Kane and Alfred Cumming arrived back in Salt Lake City in mid-April of 1858. Young met them and was undoubtedly relieved to find the new governor an open-minded, easy-going individual. Young treated Cumming with courteous civility and attempted to present the Mormons' version of the current difficulties and counter the charges of Mormon disloyalty. Young expressed his willingness to accept Cumming as his successor but remained firm in his refusal to allow entry of the federal army.

But Young backed off from his earlier threat of direct open warfare with the troops. Instead, the Mormon response would be a mass Mormon exodus and a scorched-earth policy involving the destruction of all man-made improvements throughout the territory. Thus, Cumming faced the bizarre prospect of governing a territory of charred ruins completely devoid of people.

Acutely aware of the Mormon position, Cumming left the Salt Lake Valley for Camp Scott to confer with Johnston and the two federal peace commissioners. Johnston pushed for a direct military assault against the Mormons. But the two peace commissioners, Lazarus W. Powell, the former Governor of Kentucky, and Major Ben McCullough, along with

Cumming favored an approach that would lead to a peaceful accord. The basis for their negotiations was "A Proclamation to the People of Utah" from President Buchanan, which was presented to Young upon their return to Salt Lake City. On first examination, this proclamation seemed a poor basis to restore peace, for it contained a total of forty-two separate charges against Young and his followers. It accused the Mormons of levying war against the United States and of treason. But the proclamation offered the Mormons a free pardon if they would accept the new governor.

Buchanan's proclamation, however, did not directly address the critical problem of Johnston's army still encamped at Camp Scott. The commissioners asked Young to let the army in to protect the inhabitants. Two of Young's close advisors scoffed at this absurd request and the negotiations appeared on the verge of collapse. At this point, Young expressed his belief that Buchanan was sincere in his quest for a peaceful solution. The public negotiations were then adjourned and Young met in private with the commissioners and worked out a compromise settlement in which he accepted James Buchanan's amnesty. Young also agreed to allow troops to come into the territory but stipulated that they must not be allowed to encamp in or near Salt Lake City. He warned the commissioners that if these terms were violated, he would order the implementation of his scorched-earth policy and the commencement of protracted guerrilla warfare against the army.

The commissioners departed Salt Lake City to convey Young's terms to Albert Sydney Johnston as the Mormon leader continued to direct the evacuation south. When Johnston's forces reached Salt Lake City in late June, they found it completely deserted except for a handful of non-Mormon residents who had remained behind. Also present were members of the Nauvoo Legion stationed at strategic points throughout the city, including Young's now-deserted residence, the Beehive House. Here, straw had been piled high in each room and Young had issued orders to set it on fire should Johnston's forces attempt to occupy it. Young's forces were prepared to destroy the entire city on a moment's notice should Johnston attempt to quarter his troops in Salt Lake City. But Johnston, despite his strong dislike of the Mormons, was also a Southern gentleman, and as good as his word ordered his army's continued march and established a permament headquarters in the Cedar Valley, an uninhabited region fifty miles southwest of Salt Lake City. The name chosen was Camp Floyd, in honor of John B. Floyd, the Secretary of War who had helped engineer the Utah Expedition. When Young received confirmation of this development, he allowed his displaced followers, including his own family, to return to their homes. Shortly thereafter, in July of 1858, he proclaimed the war over.

Although the Utah War had ended, Brigham Young did not feel comfortable with the presence of 2,500 federal troops commanded by Colonel Johnston, who made no secret of his personal dislike for Young and the Mormons. Remembering the death of Joseph Smith by the armed mob at Carthage, with the complicity of local militia troops, Young worried about the possibility of arrest, attack, or even assassination. Such anxieties bothered him even while sleeping. He related a dream in which a man came into his room and tried unsuccessfully to kill him. In an effort to prevent this, Young ordered all the gates into his estate locked and stationed a bodyguard at the main entrance. He also urged his followers to curtail their public activities and maintain a low profile. He did not want to give Johnston any excuse for unleashing his armed forces against the Mormons.

Young drastically curtailed his own public activities and remained secluded in the Beehive House. Although he was no longer territorial governor, he remained active and maintained communications with his successor, Alfred Cumming, with whom he developed a good working relationship. He also attended to his various business interests. Young's business philosophy revolved around the stewardship principle, in which he maintained that God appointed Young steward over his personal wealth. This stewardship principle was like that endorsed by such nineteenth century entrepreneurs as Andrew Carnegie and John D. Rockefeller. Young demonstrated his ability as a capable, shrewd businessman with his personal wealth from various business dealings estimated at between $200,000 to $250,000 by the late 1850s.

Brigham Young was involved in three broad categories of business enterprises. The first included those deals in which Young was in partnership with the Mormon Church. A second involved enterprises in which the Mormon leader established partnerships with other businessmen. Finally, Young had business ventures in which he was the sole investor. Young's construction and operation of a toll road into City Creek Canyon northeast of his property was an example of the latter type. This toll road, built at a cost of $30,000, provided access to the timber stands in the canyon. Although the timber was part of the public domain, Young charged a toll of one-third of the timber taken out to cover the cost and upkeep of the road. The acquisition of this lumber led to the establishment of an enterprise of the second type, the Big Cottonwood Lumber Company, operated by Young in partnership with several other businessmen. This company operated three mills and provided lodging for its workers. Also in partnership with others, Young owned a tannery located near Salt Lake City.

An example of a third type of business enterprise, one in partnership with the Mormon Church, was the building of a ferryboat, *The Timely Gull,* and its operation on the Great Salt Lake. Launched in June of 1854, the ferry was used to transport Church livestock to and from grazing pastures on two islands in the middle of the lake. Aside from these enterprises, Young's greatest personal wealth was acquired in real estate. Over the years he obtained numerous plots of land in Salt Lake City, built on many of them, and collected rents. Much of this came into his possession due to his standing offer to purchase the holdings of any dissatisfied Mormon who left the Church territory—a tactic intended to prevent land from falling into the hands of non-Mormons.

But Young was less than successful in other businesses. The Brigham Young Express and Carrying Company was one such venture. This company tried to carry out several functions, including a four-year contract acquired by Young to carry the U.S. mail between Independence, Missouri, and Salt Lake City. This company was also to establish and operate way stations between Independence and Salt Lake City at fifty-mile intervals to provide passenger service for Mormon immigrants, thereby, Young hoped, preventing a repetition of the earlier handcart disaster. Finally, the company planned to haul freight into the valley, thus freeing the Saints from dependence on local non-Mormon merchants. But all of Young's plans came to naught when the federal government cancelled Young's mail contract because of the Utah War, and Young and other investors sustained heavy losses.

Another enterprise of mixed success was the whiskey trade. Young established a distillery in the mid-1850s when there was no whiskey available. But just as Young started production, Johnston's army arrived, bringing great quantities of whiskey and thereby undermining the Mormon leader's enterprise. Young eventually rented his distillery to the Salt Lake City Corporation, which used it for producing its own liquor. A few years later, Young, in partnership with Daniel H. Wells, purchased a larger distillery that produced liquor sold to the Salt Lake City Corporation.

Although the Utah War adversely affected his express company and whiskey enterprises, Young and other Mormons did benefit economically from the presence of Johnston's army by selling lumber, sheep, horses, cattle, and wagons.

In contrast to contemporary entrepreneurs, Young maintained that the major goal behind his business activity was not individual enrichment but was furthering the best interests of the Mormon community as a whole. Thus, Young promoted several businesses designed to promote Mormon self-sufficiency, thereby reducing economic dependence on outsiders. This had been the primary purpose behind the earlier Iron County Mission. Young continued this quest throughout the 1850s as he established a pottery plant, attempted to promote wool manufacturing, and moved toward the manufacture of sugar from beets. But most of these enterprises were of limited success. The iron mission never lived up to its initial expectations and finally failed, the pottery plant was abandoned at a substantial loss in 1853, and efforts to produce sugar failed and were abandoned in 1856. Young's cherished goal of economic self-sufficiency remained as elusive as ever.

Despite his numerous business activities, Brigham Young still managed to find time to grant interviews to outsiders who made their way to Utah throughout the 1850s and early 1860s. Young considered these interviews valuable as a means of removing prejudices. One of the most famous interviews involved Horace Greeley, editor of the *New York Tribune* and a leading anti-slavery spokesman. Greeley had first attacked but then later defended the Mormons during the course of the Utah War. Greeley's interview covered a wide range of topics. He probed Young's wealth and extensive business interests. Young admitted, "I am called rich and consider myself worth two hundred and fifty thousand dollars; but no dollar of it was ever paid me by the church, nor for any service as a minister." Young pointed to the complete absence of a paid Mormon clergy. "No one is ever paid for any service pertaining to the ministry . . . a man who cannot make his living aside from the ministry of Christ [is] unsuited for that office."

On another sensitive topic, Greeley asked Young his position on slavery. Young replied frankly, "We consider it of divine institution and not to be abolished until the curse pronounced on Ham shall have been removed from his descendants." Greeley assessed Young's pervasive political influence, noting that he "carries the territory in his breeches pocket without a shadow of opposition." By contrast, Greeley labeled the federal judiciary, the territorial governor, and the federal army stationed at Camp Floyd as "three transparent shams—three egregious farces; . . . costing the [federal] treasury very large sums to no purpose." Greeley recommended in the spirit of popular sovereignty that Young be reinstated as territorial governor and that all non-Mormon federal office-holders and federal troops be withdrawn.

A year later, in August, 1860, Brigham Young entertained a second important visitor, Richard Burton, a world-famous British writer and traveler. Burton visited Utah to observe Mormon polygamy firsthand. Burton's interest stemmed from his studies of the sexual customs of peoples throughout the world. Meeting Young for the first time, he was favorably impressed. The British visitor found Young "remarkably well preserved looking more like forty five years of age than his actual age of fifty nine."

Burton found Young's powers of observation intuitively strong and found a "total absence of pretention in his manner." On the topic of polygamy, Burton found some surprises. Contrary to the sensationalized accounts appearing in the Eastern press, Mormon polygamy did not involve permissive sex designed to gratify licentiousness, but instead was a closely regulated institution, almost Puritan-like. Burton noted, "All sensuality in the married state is strictly forbidden beyond the requisite for ensuring progeny. . . . During the gestation and nursing of the children, the strictest countenance on the part of the mother is required. . . ."

A third, even more famous visitor, Mark Twain, arrived in Salt Lake in 1861 en route to the mining camps of Nevada and California with his older brother. Then a young, aspiring writer, Twain was on the whole favorably impressed with the Mormon leader, describing him as a "quiet, kindly, easy mannered, dignified, self-possessed old gentleman of fifty-five or sixty," with "a gentle craft in his eye that probably belonged there." Young's ability to converse, Twain wrote, "flowed on as sweetly and peacefully and musically as any summer brook." But Twain also found the Mormon leader guarded in the topics he chose to discuss, noting that when he tried to " 'draw him out' on Federal politics and his high handed attitude toward Congress," Young ignored him, conversing with other guests until the writer "subsided into an indignant silence." Twain did note Young's wry, somewhat condescending sense of humor as reflected in the Mormon leader's behavior at the end of the interview. When Twain got up to leave with his brother, Young, according to the author, "put his hand on my head, beamed down at me in an admiring way and said to my brother, 'Ah—your child, I presume? Boy or girl?' "

The presence of federal troops and the related growth of Utah's non-Mormon population tended to undermine the isolation of Mormonism's Great Basin sanctuary. By late 1858, Utah's non-Mormon population had grown large enough to support a newspaper, the Salt Lake *Valley Tan*, named for a poor grade of Utah whiskey. Although the *Valley Tan* hurled sharp barbs at the Latter-day Saints, Young publicly ignored its attacks and in private denounced it as a "filthy, miserable little sheet."

A year later, the isolation of Mormonism's Great Basin sanctuary was further undermined by the discovery of rich silver deposits in the Comstock Lode in the eastern Utah territory. The large non-Mormon population that settled there wished for their own territory separate from Utah. This was accomplished with the creation of Nevada. That same year a second mining rush occurred at Pikes Peak immediately to the east of the Great Basin. These two mining rushes meant a drastic reduction in Utah's territorial boundaries as Nevada was carved out to the west and Colorado to the east.

Brigham Young tried to put the best face on those developments, noting that the reduction relieved the Mormons "of much annoyance especially from our . . . neighbors and leaves our territory a very convenient shape." The "Pikes Peak gold [and] Carson Valley silver" rushes, he continued, exercised a "direct and highly ameliorating influence upon our moral atmosphere" by causing most transients to conclude that "Utah is a poor region for them and their desires, designs, and practices."

Indeed, Brigham Young looked optimistically to the future. By 1859, he assumed a more visible public profile. His preachings in the Old Tabernacle became more frequent. That same year he resumed his visits to outlying settlements, the first of these taking him to Cache Valley, some one hundred miles north of Salt Lake. Such visits would take place on a regular basis throughout the early 1860s. The willingness of Young to venture forth and thus break his self-imposed exile resulted, at least in part, from a reduction of army troops within the territory. In the spring of 1860, the federal government recalled to the East a large part of its Utah-based contingent—a removal necessitated by the worsening sectional crisis over slavery in the East.

The Mormons watched with keen interest the deterioration of North-South relations. Young labeled John Brown's Harpers Ferry raid "a lamentable affair" and alluded to this event's millennialistic-apocalyptic implications. Throughout 1860, Young kept on top of the critical political situation in Washington, D.C., through Utah's territorial delegate, William H. Hooper. "President-making," Young noted with sarcasm, "seems to be the order of the day, to the almost entire exclusion of Congressional business." With amusement, he indicated his incomplete knowledge concerning the "big fight" in the Democratic convention at Baltimore between the Douglas Democrats and Southern Democrats, asking "whether the 'fight' was with words, fists, or some potent weapons." Douglas emerged with the Northern Democratic nomination but did not have Southern support, which severely crippled his election chances. When Douglas did lose to Abraham Lincoln, Young considered this just vindication for his sudden anti-Mormon attacks during the Utah War. Young sarcastically observed, "Democrats within our borders are very much chopfallen at Lincoln's election."

But the Mormon leader might have added that he did not look forward to Republican control of the national government. The Republicans, long hostile towards the Mormons, pushed for a congressional bill in 1860 outlawing polygamy. Young was also less than impressed with Lincoln's personal qualities due to his past political conduct. Lincoln "was no friend" Young felt, because "he had never raised his voice in our favor when we were being persecuted" in Illinois, even though he knew Joseph and Hyrum Smith, and like them was a master freemason.

Young reserved his harshest criticism for outgoing president James Buchanan. He expressed dismay over Buchanan's failure to deal forcefully with the secession crisis in the wake of Abraham Lincoln's election and found the president's inaction ironic in light of his earlier hostile actions against the Mormons. His actions were doubly ironic since the bachelor president, according to Young, practiced his own form of polygamy through mistresses by whom he had fathered a number of illegitimate children. Further assailing Buchanan, Young wryly compared South Carolina to a dissatisfied, rebellious wife and Buchanan to her weak, indecisive husband who says, "I charge you not to go out, but if you do go I can't call you back, I charge you not to go but you can."

Despite their difficulties with the federal government and Utah's earlier recognition of black slavery as a legal institution, the Mormons did not join the Confederacy. Southern emissaries were sent to Utah and offered Utah statehood "with all the rights and privileges thereof, and with the question of polygamy untouched." But the Mormon leader held back, basing his decision on the realities of Utah's northern geographic position—closer to Unionist centers of military strength than to those of the Confederacy.

Also, despite the handful of Mormon slaveholders, most Utah Mormons came from outside the slaveholding South. Young and his followers, like other Northerners, manifested a definite anti-Southern, anti-slavery bias. Mormon anti-Southern animosity stemmed in part from earlier experiences in the slave state of Missouri. Also, according to Young, "The South in the time of our persecution had written letters to the General Government [offering] to furnish men to use up the Mormons." The Mormon leader considered black slavery itself to be "the ruin of the South. . . . The South has a beautiful climate and rich soil, but slavery ruins any soil."

Thus, Brigham Young and the Mormons affirmed loyalty to the federal government. Moreover, Young renewed his application for Utah statehood. This effort stood in sharp contrast to the actions of slave states in the lower South— namely, Florida, Georgia, Alabama, Mississippi, Louisiana, and Texas, which followed South Carolina's lead and seceded in February, 1861. Two months later, four more states—North Carolina, Virginia, Tennessee, and Arkansas—followed suit. In Young's words, "we [will] show our loyalty by trying to get in while others are trying to get out."

Brigham Young also viewed the cataclysmic events of Southern secession in an apocalyptic light. Events such as South Carolina's capture of Fort Sumter and subsequent North-South hostilities, starting with the Battle of Bull Run (which Young cuttingly labeled "Booby Run") represented the literal fulfillment of a "Revelation and Prophecy on War" received by Joseph Smith some twenty-eight years earlier. According to this oft-quoted revelation, "wars . . . will shortly come to pass, beginning at the rebellion of South Carolina, which will eventually terminate in the death and misery of many souls." It further stated "the Southern States shall be divided against the Northern States" and the South would "call on other nations" especially Great Britain, for aid, predicting that the "slaves shall rise up against their masters" and that the Indians would inflict a "sore vexation" upon white, non-Mormon Americans. Ultimately, war, famine, plague, earthquakes, and other natural disasters would bring about the end of all nations.

The Mormon leader saw the first parts of this prophecy being literally fulfilled and looked forward to the fulfillment of the rest with all of its millennialistic consequences. There was nothing that any man could do to thwart the prophetic will of God. Young hammered away at this basic theme in sermon after sermon. He declared, "There is no more a United States . . . It will not be patched up—it never can come together again—in a short time it will be like water spilled on the ground, and like chaff upon the summer threshing floor, until those wicked stewards are cut off." Young predicted growing disorder culminating in anarchy: "Mobs will not decrease, but will increase until the whole Government becomes a mob, and eventually it will be state against state, city against city, neighborhood against neighborhood. . . ." The fighting of the war itself would go on indefinitely, taking "years and years, and will never cease until the work is accomplished," that is to "empty the earth" of the wicked and "cleanse the land" in preparation for the establishment of the Kingdom of God.

The Mormons were not unique in viewing the critical events of this period as a prelude to the impending millennium. Many other Americans within various religious denominations saw the commencement of the Civil War as the beginning of the end; the setting off of a train of apocalyptic events culminating in the Second Coming and the establishment of the Kingdom of God.

Despite the national crisis of Civil War, Young continued to busy himself with the promotion of the migration and settlement of Mormonism's Great Basin sanctuary. Starting in 1860, the Mormon leader devised a more efficient means of transporting emigrants, replacing the handcarts with Church teams. The Church would provide ox teams and wagons and would dispatch these teams with teamsters to the Missouri Valley to pick up the emigrants and bring them to the Salt Lake Valley—a 2,200-mile round trip that could be made in six months. The use of Church teams turned out to be most efficient, enabling thousands of Mormons to migrate west.

Mormon colonization to outlying settlements also continued swiftly after a short hiatus during the Utah War. One hundred and twenty-four new settlements were founded during the years 1858–65, eclipsing the ninety-six established during the previous ten years. In May of 1861, Young visited some of these new settlements, traveling as far south as St. George. Here he promoted the extensive cultivation of cotton in an attempt to replace interrupted supplies of this commodity from the seceded South. Young also looked for other ways to make the Great Basin economically self-sufficient, thus eliminating dependence on outside markets during this time of national crisis.

The crisis enabled the Mormons to regain a degree of independence. It appeared that the federal government with which Young had been involved in direct conflict since the mid-1850s would at last leave the Mormons alone and allow them to develop their frontier sanctuary unimpeded. In May of 1861, Governor Alfred Cumming left Utah and returned to Georgia where he cast his lot with the Confederacy. Although Frank Wootton became acting governor, actual territorial control rested in the hands of Brigham Young. Two months later, the last of the federal troops under the command of Albert S. Johnston departed Camp Floyd for the East.

This departure must have seemed ironic to Brigham Young, particularly in light of the subsequent conduct of both General Johnston and Secretary of War James B. Floyd, who back in 1857 had berated the Mormons as traitors. Both of these men supported the Southern Confederacy! Johnston took up arms against the Union and served as one of the South's most prominent generals up to the time of his death at the Battle of Shiloh. The departure of Johnston's army was also ironic in an economic sense. As the army left Utah, federal officials auctioned off an estimated $4,000,000 of property. Young purchased about forty percent, or $1.6 million worth, for a mere $40,000. Thus, a federal army sent west to subdue the Mormons and overthrow Young contributed substantially to the economic prosperity of the Latter-day Saints.

Young could keep in close touch with the drama unfolding in the East thanks to improved communications. In April of 1860, the Pony Express was established between St. Joseph, Missouri, and Sacramento, California. Small, lightweight men rode big horses (not ponies) in relays along the way. One of these stops included Salt Lake City. Thus, news about events in the East that had previously taken weeks to reach Utah now arrived within days. Young praised the Pony Express but at the same time he proclaimed it too expensive for everyday use.

Also during the early 1860s, work was well along on a transcontinental telegraph line. Brigham Young gained a contract to construct the final link of this line, a thousand miles in length, from Fort Laramie through Salt Lake City and on to California. He had a voice in the control of the stations in Utah and received $175 for each mile in wire and poles that he completed for the Pacific and Overland Telegraph Companies. Young established the Deseret Telegraph Company, which eventually connected every major Mormon settlement to Young's own office in the Beehive House. Work on the telegraph line was completed in October of 1861, and Young marked this occasion by relaying a telegraphic message to J. H. Wade, president of the Pacific Telegraph Company, declaring that Utah had "not seceded but is firm for the Constitution!"

It was easy for the Mormons to profess loyalty and support

for the Union as long as they were left alone. But after December, 1861, that loyalty was severely tested as conflict between the Mormons and federal officials resumed anew. In that month, John W. Dawson, an Indiana lawyer and former newspaper editor, became Utah's new territorial governor and arrived in Salt Lake City. Brigham Young hoped to establish a good working relationship with the new governor, despite failing to secure the governorship for himself following an extensive Mormon lobbying effort. However, relations between Dawson and local residents got off on a bad foot almost immediately.

Dawson, in a message to the territorial legislature, urged the immediate payment of $26,982 in federal taxes that he claimed territorial residents owed. He also urged the recruitment of Utah soldiers to fight in the Civil War. Shortly thereafter, Dawson added insult to injury by vetoing a Mormon-sponsored legislative bill calling for a constitutional convention to promote Utah statehood.

John Dawson also created controversy by making indecent proposals to the widow of a prominent Mormon merchant. She refused his advances but he persisted and then tried to bribe her into silence. News of the whole affair leaked out and Dawson, fearing retribution, quickly left Salt Lake City. Just a short distance from the city, a gang of rowdies set upon the hapless governor and beat and robbed him. Dawson managed to make his way to Fort Bridger where he wrote President Lincoln that a secret vigilante force under Brigham Young's direction had assaulted him. Worried about the possible negative effects of the Dawson affair on the Mormon's quest for statehood, Brigham Young presented his own version of the incident to President Lincoln through Utah's congressional representative, John M. Bernhisel, denying any knowledge of the attack and condemning those involved as "scum . . . in the shape of thieves and vagabonds." Although this incident loomed large in Brigham Young's eyes, Lincoln and other government officials found it to be a minor incident in the environment of wartime Washington.

Actually, officials in the Lincoln administration sought cooperation rather than conflict with the Mormons during the spring of 1862. Indians, emboldened by national preoccupation with the war in the East and perhaps by the withdrawal of federal troops from Utah, destroyed several mail stations along the Overland Trail, burning coaches, stealing stock, and killing several stage drivers. In response, Lincoln's army adjutant, General Lorenzo Thomas, wrote Brigham Young and authorized him "to raise, arm, and equip one company of cavalry for ninety days' service" to deal with the Indians and keep the Overland Trail open. In writing directly to Brigham Young rather than territorial officials (which was normal procedure), federal officials gave tacit recognition to the Mormon leader's role as the primary power in Utah.

Young responded immediately to this federal appeal and raised the requested militia force within three days. He addressed the militia just prior to its departure east, admonishing its members to remember "their allegiance and loyalty to our government and also not forgetting that they are [Mormons by] never indulging in intoxicants of any kind, and never associating with bad men or lewd women."

Young viewed the militia's departure with some personal apprehension, for it included one of his own sons, 17-year-old John Willard. Much to the Mormon leader's relief, the militia force did no real fighting and only a little chasing of Indians. But their presence along the Overland Trail helped keep the stage route open. This expedition represented the only direct military operation by the Mormons or Utah troops during the Civil War and was unique in that it was the only body of troops sponsored by a particular religious denomination.

Thus, cooperation replaced conflict with the federal government, albeit temporarily. But Brigham Young faced conflict on another front—within Mormonism itself. This revolved around the schismatic activities of Joseph Morris. An enigmatic figure and Englishman by birth, Morris converted to Mormonism and migrated to Utah in 1853. Upon his arrival, he began teaching his own unique version of Mormon beliefs presented through over 300 divine revelations received during the period 1857–62. These revelations attempted to predict the exact time for the Second Coming of Christ, questioned the practice of Mormon polygamy, and, most importantly, challenged the authority of Brigham Young himself.

At first, Young dismissed Morris as a "crazy man," labeling his teachings "twaddle" and "bosh." But as the charismatic Morris attracted his own following and ignored Young's counsel, the Mormon leader took direct action and excommunicated him. Undaunted, Morris established his own schismatic Mormon Church headquartered on the bottomlands of the Weber River, forty miles north of Salt Lake City. Morris managed to convert over 500 individuals, all drawn from Young's movement. Morris prophesied the imminent coming of the millennium by predicting the exact day and thus managed to persuade his followers to consecrate all their property into his keeping.

Morris, however, ran into difficulty when his announced date of millennial upheaval came and passed uneventfully. A number of his disillusioned followers demanded the immediate return of their property and when Morris refused, asked for assistance from federal authorities in Salt Lake City. In response, Chief Justice John F. Kinney, a non-Mormon but a close and influential friend of Brigham Young, issued a writ calling for Morris' arrest, which Morris promptly disregarded. Kinney then acted with the authorization of Acting Territorial Governor Frank Fuller and tacit approval of Brigham Young, activating a posse force of 250 men.

The posse grew in strength as it traveled north, attracting over 700 additional volunteers and numbered 1000 by the time it reached Morris' camp. Here a violent clash took place in which five individuals were killed, including Joseph Morris. Deprived of its principal leader, the Morrisite movement quickly collapsed and Brigham Young was relieved of a rival who was more of an embarrassment than a threat.

The major threat to Brigham Young and his followers during 1862 came not from within the Mormon movement but from renewed conflict with the federal government. The rejection of Utah's bid for statehood in early 1862 by the U.S. House of Representatives Committee on Territories signaled a deterioration of Mormon-federal government relations. Utah Territorial Delegate John M. Bernhisel wrote Young that the small size of Utah's population was the alleged reason for the rejection, but more important was the prejudice against Mormon polygamy and against the Mormons as a people. The Mormons appeared to many federal officials as unworthy of the privilege to govern themselves.

Adding insult to injury, federal officials in April of 1861 detached a considerable portion of western Utah, annexing it to neighboring Nevada. Worse still, late that same month Congress passed the Morrill Anti-Bigamy Bill signed into law three months later. The Morrill Anti-Bigamy Act provided that anyone practicing polygamy should be adjudged guilty of bigamy and upon conviction could be fined up to $500 and imprisoned for five years. Secondly, the act nullified all legislation passed by the Utah Territorial Legislature relative to polygamy. Finally, this measure ruled that no corporation or association organized for religious or charitable purposes could hold more than $50,000 in real estate in any territory— a provision aimed directly at the Mormon Church.

Brigham Young circumvented the latter provision by transferring title to most Church property into his own name. Thus, from 1862 on, Young treated all his business dealings, whether as trustee-in-trust for the Church or on a personal level, as exclusively private transactions. The Church, therefore, was able to work around the $50,000 limitation.

Despite these problems, Young hoped for improved Mormon-federal government relations with the arrival in July of 1862 of Utah's new territorial governor, Stephen S. Harding of Indiana. He arrived in Utah highly recommended. He also had previous contact with the Mormons, having met Joseph Smith some years before. In his first speech to a gathering of Utah citizens, Harding seemed anxious for good relations. He praised the Mormons as a "wonderful people!" who had made "wonderful progress!" in making "the desert . . . blossom as the rose" and indicated that he would not interfere with Mormon polygamy, declaring his belief in the "sacred right . . . that the Constitution of the United States secures to every citizen the right to worship God according to the dictates of his own conscience."

Such conciliatory statements were illusionary. Mormon-federal relations deteriorated markedly with the arrival in Utah of a regiment of 850 troops from California during the summer of 1862. The stated official purpose of this force, known as the California Volunteers, was to replace the Mormon militia in guarding the Overland mail route from Indian attack. But Brigham Young saw a more sinister purpose for the dispatch of these troops: the destruction of Mormonism. Despite Young's perception of Lincoln as a "sagacious . . . but wicked" man who intended "destruction upon" the Mormons, other individuals were primarily responsible for the dispatch of the troops. The most important was General George Wright, Commander of all Union troops on the West Coast. He felt that the Mormons needed to be closely watched, a perception that stemmed from his basic dislike of the Mormons, plus his belief that Brigham Young harbored pro-secessionist views or was on the verge of declaring Utah an independent republic. Rumors to this effect had found wide circulation in newspapers throughout the country.

Strongly backing Wright was Stephen S. Harding, who by late August of 1862 abandoned his initial pro-Mormon position. Harding wrote Secretary of State William H. Seward, complaining about alleged Mormon disloyalty. He quoted Young's millennialistic statements, which anticipated the complete exhaustion of both sides in the Civil War, and the Mormon leader's alleged eagerness to step in and take possession of the lands and all that would be left of the ruined cities. Harding asked Seward to dispatch a military force to Utah to "make [such] treason dumb."

Also supporting General Wright was Colonel Patrick Edward Connor, the actual commander of the force. Connor, a strong-willed, suspicious individual, developed an intense, almost pathological hatred of Brigham Young and the Mormons from the moment of his arrival in Salt Lake City. Connor refused to quarter his troops at Camp Floyd, away from Salt Lake City as Albert Sydney Johnston had done earlier. Instead, he made a dramatic show of force by marching his troops through downtown Salt Lake City past the Lion and Beehive Houses and then establishing his camp just east of the city in the foothills of the Wasatch Mountains. He named his headquarters, with seeming appropriateness, Camp Douglas, in honor of the recently deceased Illinois senator and arch-foe of the Mormons.

Connor's regular communications to army headquarters in San Francisco reflected an almost vitriolic anti-Mormon tone in which he characterized the Mormons as a "community of traitors, murderers, fanatics and whores," noting that "Brigham Young rules with despotic sway, and death by assassination is the penalty of disobedience to his commands."

The Mormon leader returned such feelings in kind. He considered the presence of Connor and his army insulting and was mortified at Connor's insistence that Mormon merchants take an oath of allegiance before selling anything to the army. He suggested that Connor could "go to hell for [his] potatoes" and other provisions and had even harsher words for Governor Harding, who became increasingly strident in his anti-Mormon attacks. Young characterized Harding as follows: "And that thing that is here that calls himself Governor . . . If you were to fill a sack with cow shit, it would be the best thing you could do for an imitation and that would be just as good as he is."

Tensions remained high between the Mormons and federal officials throughout the fall and winter of 1862–63. Connor and Harding continued to accuse Brigham Young and his followers of treasonist behavior.

There was, however, some respite in the ongoing Mormon-federal conflict as the attention of Connor's army was temporarily diverted away from the Mormons to the Shoshone Indians. These Indians, located in northern Utah, had caused serious disturbances along the Overland route, destroying property, stealing horses and cattle, and, on occasion, killing travelers. The Indians, who became increasingly aggressive during 1862, also posed a threat to scattered Mormon settlements in northern Utah. Thus, in January of 1863, Colonel Connor gathered together a force of 137 armed troops to march north and deal with the Indians in a brutal winter campaign fought in the snow on the Bear River. An estimated 224 to 300 Indians were killed, including women and children. By contrast, only fourteen soldiers lost their lives.

Connor's surprise attack brought a halt, at least temporarily, to Indian deprivations in this northern region. Young was undoubtedly disturbed by the loss of life. But there was little love lost between the Mormons and the marauding Shoshone whom the *Deseret News* labeled "that bastard class of humans who play with the lives of . . . peaceable and law abiding citizens." Thus the Mormons accorded Connor and his men grudging respect for making their northern settlements safe from Indian attacks.

Despite the Bear River Campaign, conflict between the Mormons and federal officials resumed anew and indeed intensified during the late winter and early spring of 1863. Patrick Edward Connor and Governor Harding resumed their verbal attacks on Brigham Young and the Mormons. Harding wrote General Wright in San Francisco, accusing the Mormons of conspiring with the Indians. Connor pointed to the Mormons' flagrant violations of the law through their crime of bigamy, which "mocks and insults the nation."

To deal with this Mormon menace, Connor and Harding suggested drastic measures. First, Connor called for the abolition of Utah as a territory through its division into four parts and the annexation of these parts to four adjoining territories. He also wanted to declare martial law and increase his military force to 3,000, which would enable him to end the institution of polygamy and give Young no alternative but to obey the Morrill Anti-Bigamy Law. Harding concurred in Connor's suggestions, even calling for some additional measures. These included having all jurors serving on federal territorial courts selected by the U.S. marshal rather than local officials, and having all officers in the territorial militia named by the governor.

These proposals, combined with anti-Mormon pronouncements, infuriated Brigham Young, who lashed out in an address delivered to a mass meeting of Latter-day Saints in Salt Lake City on March 3, 1863. He labeled Governor Harding "a man or a thing, which ever term you prefer" and announced that the people of Utah would not allow Harding and others to set up a military despotism. This Mormon gathering adopted a resolution calling for Governor Harding and two Utah federal judges who supported the governor's policies to resign or, if necessary, be removed from their positions by the president of the United States.

Thus, by March of 1863, Mormon-federal government relations had reached a critical juncture. Young was determined to force the removal of Governor Harding and other federal officers along with General Connor's armed force. But at the same time, Harding and Connor were determined to make Young and other Mormons respect the power of federal authorities through enforcement of the Morrill Anti-Bigamy Law. In March, 1863, Young responded to rumors that Connor planned to arrest him on charges of violating this law by mobilizing one to two thousand well-armed Mormon militiamen and stationing them near the Beehive House. Here, scaffolding was hastily erected inside the high walls so that the Mormon militia would be able to fire down on any attacking force. In addition, cannons were brought in and a telescope installed to watch all troop movements at Camp Douglas.

Mormon fears were exaggerated. But Brigham Young took no chances and avoided arrest through a shrewd legal maneuver engineered by Utah's Chief Justice John F. Kinney. On March 10, Kinney issued a writ charging Young with violating the Morrill Anti-Bigamy Act and calling for the Mormon leader's arrest. Alerted to this move, Young immediately appeared before Kinney and posted bail. Kinney then ordered Young's case bound over to the next term of court, but the case never came to trial. Kinney's action had the effect of precluding Young's arrest by Connor and trial before a hostile federal judge. In describing this move to his son, Brigham Jr., then on a mission in England, Young noted that "Harding, Connor, & Co. are at present quite crestfallen and apparently at a loss what to try next."

This affair represented the climax of Mormon-federal government conflict during the Civil War. But Lincoln and other federal officials preferred conciliation to conflict and thus moved to ease this tense situation. In June of 1863, he removed Stephen S. Harding as territorial governor and replaced him with J. Duane Doty, Superintendent of Indian Affairs for the territory—a move that pleased Brigham Young. Doty, in his age and background, was remarkably similar to the Mormon leader. At 65, two years older than Young, Doty was a native of upstate New York and as a young man had migrated to the Midwest, settling first in

Michigan and then Wisconsin, where he practiced law and became involved in politics. His service as Utah Indian Superintendent gave him a reputation as a conciliator who could steer a middle course. He was respected by the Mormons, federal officials, the army, and the Indians.

Doty's appointment brought a welcome respite in Mormon-federal conflict. Lincoln tried to allay Mormon anxieties in other ways. He met with Mormon representatives who called upon him at the White House and outlined his overall policy toward the Mormons, stating simply: "I propose to let them alone." He than went on to illustrate his statement with a personal story, comparing the Mormons to a knotty hemlock log that he had found on his farm. The log had been too hard to split, too wet to burn, and too heavy to move, so he "plowed around it." Lincoln concluded, "That's what I intend to do with the Mormons. You go back and tell Brigham Young that if he will let me alone I will let him alone."

Although Lincoln was anxious to improve relations with the Mormons, he refused to order the withdrawal of Patrick Edward Connor or his troops from Camp Douglas. The president felt that Connor's forces should remain to deal with continuing Indian unrest. Although Connor concentrated on local Indian problems, he continued to manifest an obsessive, paranoid concern about the Mormons. He insisted that four-fifths of all Mormons were disloyal to the federal government and bent on the destruction of the Union.

In September of 1863, Connor came up with a plan of his own to annihilate Mormonism. This involved the development of possible mineral wealth in Utah. This course would encourage a large influx of non-Mormons into the territory to dilute the influence of the dominant Mormon population. Connor was encouraged by the recent discoveries during the early 1860s of gold and silver in eastern Nevada, Idaho, and Montana. Even within Utah itself, a deposit of silver ore was discovered in Bingham Canyon in mid-1863. Connor en-

couraged the men under his command to spend their spare
time searching for further mineral deposits. He also authorized the publication of a newspaper, the *Union Vedette*, to
further play up Utah's mining potential.

Brigham Young initially reacted to Connor's efforts with
dismay. He feared that Connor's actions would flood the
region with a non-Mormon population and destroy the iden-
tity of the Mormon community. But by early 1864, when
Connor's men failed to uncover any significant mineral deposits, Young's anxieties lessened somewhat. By the fall of
1864, even the *Union Vedette* admitted that gold had been
found only in limited quantities throughout the territory.

In the face of his limited success in mining, Connor
turned once more to direct military confrontation. In July of
1864 he found a pretext to move against Brigham Young by
accusing him of refusing to recognize treasury notes, or
greenbacks, as legal tender, but instead showing a preference for gold. Young's preference for gold-based currency,
according to Connor, drove up greenback prices for goods,
which in turn created hardship for Connor's troops, who
were paid in greenbacks. The general ordered a provost
guard of federal troops stationed in downtown Salt Lake
City near Young's residence. Connor wrote Major General
Irwin McDowell, the new commander of West Coast federal
forces, a long letter justifying his actions and outlining the
Mormon leader's alleged misdeeds.

Young was not actually in Salt Lake City when he received
word of the posting of the provost guard but was visiting in
Provo. When Young left Provo for his return home, he did
not have to worry about Connor's guard because he was
accompanied by a 200-man armed escort that grew to an
estimated 5,000 individuals by the time he reached Salt Lake
City. This crisis was short-lived due to direct orders Connor
received from General McDowell to immediately remove the
provost guard. McDowell, in contrast to his predecessor,
General Wright, sought to avoid rather than promote conflict. The prudent McDowell, who had no ax to grind with

the Mormons, told Connor that his Pacific Department was in no condition to wage war with the Mormons, and that any such war would be exploited by their domestic enemies. McDowell ordered Connor to concentrate his efforts on protecting the Overland route, the major purpose for which the federal force had been dispatched to Utah. Although with some resistance, Connor finally complied with McDowell's orders.

Thereafter, relations between the Mormons and Connor's federal forces improved somewhat. Connor continued to encourage efforts to find minerals within the territory. Although disappointed by limited results, Connor's efforts would, in time, provide a foundation for later, substantial mining activity. Brigham Young and the Mormons, for their part, moved away from their millennialistic belief that the North and South were going to wipe each other out. This Mormon shift was encouraged by the obvious fact that the Confederacy was dying and a Union victory was inevitable. William Tecumseh Sherman's March to the Sea, Ulysses S. Grant's victories in the Wilderness and Cold Harbor campaigns, and Grant's unrelenting pressure on the Confederate railroad center at Petersburg underscored this fact. Thus, Brigham Young and his followers assumed an increasingly pro-Union stance.

On March 4, 1865, Young and the Mormons participated in a joint celebration with Connor's federal forces in marking the inauguration of Abraham Lincoln to a second term, only to share the grief over his assassination one month later. Brigham Young lowered the flag on his residence to half-mast and had his carriage covered with crepe. He also authorized a memorial service in the Tabernacle at which both a Mormon elder and the chaplain of Camp Douglas gave eulogies to the slain president.

Despite the lessening of Mormon-federal conflict, uncertainty remained concerning the future. This uncertainty was caused not just by the assassination of Abraham Lincoln and the end of the war, but also by the death two months later of Governor Duane Doty, a tolerant official whom Brigham Young had respected. Even before Doty's death, Young had expressed anxiety. He feared that now with the war over troops would no longer be needed in the East and would be sent west to stir up trouble.

Such anxieties plagued the Mormon leader as he approached his sixty-fourth birthday. But at least for the present, despite the continuing presence of Patrick Edward Connor and his federal forces, Mormon–federal government relations had entered a more peaceful phase and Young could thus turn to the more important task of building up and indeed preserving Mormonism's frontier sanctuary, an increasingly difficult undertaking.

VII

The Fading Mormon Frontier

BRIGHAM YOUNG'S WORRIES about future relations with the federal government were part of his larger concern about the security of Mormonism's frontier sanctuary. This sanctuary was much less remote than twenty years earlier when he first arrived in the Great Basin—a fact dramatized by the carving out of new states and territories to the west, east, and north. Nevada, originally part of Utah, had been admitted to the Union as a state in 1864. Colorado, to the east, containing territory once claimed by the Mormons, was also a growing, non-Mormon mining region pushing toward ultimate statehood. To the north, miners were pouring into a previously exclusive Mormon region eventually known as Idaho. Access to these mining regions was facilitated by improved communications, namely, wagon roads and ultimately railroad lines. It seemed clear to the aging Mormon leader that Mormonism's frontier sanctuary was rapidly fading. In response, Young redoubled his efforts to preserve what was left of his shrinking Mormon domain.

Seeking this end, the Mormon leader hoped for amicable Mormon-federal government relations despite the continuing presence of Patrick Edward Connor and his army at Camp Douglas. Conditions looked favorable. The new president, Andrew Johnson, subscribed to a states' rights philosophy. Young endorsed Johnson's Reconstruction policy, sympathizing with the president's difficult task, particularly on the question of extending suffrage to blacks. Young ob-

Two views of Salt Lake City showing the growth that took place from the early pioneer period up to the time of Brigham Young's death in 1877. The first is from a sketch made by Fredrick Piercy in 1853 shortly after the Mormon arrival, and the second is a photograph taken in the 1870s. (Both courtesy of the Utah State Historical Society.)

served, "I do not know that there is any President who could swallow all the niggers there are, without bolting." The Mormon leader, in turn, hoped Johnson would be fair with the Latter-day Saints. Johnson did assume a hands-off policy, and conservative Democrats in Congress upheld the Mormons' religious practices in the spirit of basic religious liberty under the Constitution. Southern Democratic Congressmen seemed particularly sympathetic. In response, Young tried to establish bonds of identification with the states of the former Confederacy, promoting Mormon missionary activity in that region. He hoped Southerners would be attracted by the prospect of migrating to Utah, away from "the domination of negroes and negro worshippers."

Despite such sympathies, the Mormons had to contend with rising anti-Mormon feelings from Radical Republicans, or those Republicans who supported a stringent Reconstruction policy in dealing with the former Confederate states. Many of these same Radicals sought punitive actions against the Mormons. Radical Republican newspapers appealed to the then prevailing Victorian morality and condemned polygamy as lecherous. Congressional Radical Republicans supported an antipolygamy measure submitted in 1866 by Senator Benjamin F. Wade of Ohio, who at the time stood a heartbeat away from the American presidency due to his position as president pro tempore of the Senate.

Although Wade's measure did not pass, it was the first of a series of antipolygamy measures promoted by Radical Republicans. In the forefront of these radical foes was Schuyler Colfax of Indiana, Speaker of the U.S. House of Representatives, whose antipolygamy views evolved following an 1866 visit to Utah. Young condemned Colfax and Wade for trying to deprive the Saints of their liberty and reduce them to a condition of political serfdom.

Young's frontier sanctuary faced assault on another front. Renewed Indian hostilities erupted into open warfare in 1865. Ute Indians were dissatisfied with an 1865 treaty through which they gave up claims to land in Mormon-settled areas and agreed to go onto a reservation in eastern Utah. While most Indians acquiesced, a young Ute leader named Black Hawk rejected it and led a group of two to three hundred warriors into open warfare against outlying Mormon settlements in southern Utah.

During the course of what became known as the Black Hawk War (not to be confused with an earlier Illinois conflict of the same name), Young sought to minimize the loss of life and restore peaceful relations. He also tried, unsuccessfully, to secure military aid from U.S. Army forces stationed in the territory. The Mormon militia, therefore, bore the brunt of the fighting. The Mormon leader mobilized his followers and issued elaborate instructions for self-defense to those settlers in danger. But he also urged that unhostile Indians not be made to expiate the wrongs of those who were hostile. This stood in contrast to the attitudes of many white frontier settlers who were anxious to punish any and all Indians whether or not they were involved in hostile acts.

Young offered the Indians food and clothing in exchange for the restoration of peaceful relations and professed friendship by concluding: "We have never spoken to them with two tongues, nor wore two faces. We have never wanted to shed their blood, and when driven to it, we have only done it in self-defense." He even tried to attribute the present difficulties to the misbehavior of his own followers. He characterized Indian attacks as light chastisement from the Lord on those Mormons who had become careless.

During the four years of the Black Hawk War, the Mormons lost over two thousand horses and cattle and were forced to abandon twenty-five settlements at an estimated cost of over one million dollars. More than seventy settlers lost their lives. Finally, in 1869, Black Hawk, bowing to superior white forces, gave up the fight in exchange for peace.

Black Hawk's capitulation further underscored the fact the Utah was becoming less of an isolated frontier sanctuary.

There were other indications of this fact. Gold and silver were discovered in eastern Nevada. And in the Sweetwater region of present-day Wyoming the non-Mormon mining frontier was even closer to the Mormon sanctuary. Young viewed this mining activity with mixed feelings. On the one hand, if gold were found in significant quantities, he feared that his followers might be lured into mining, anxious to find rich gold deposits.

But at the same time, this mining activity could be turned to the Mormons' advantage. Development of the Sweetwater district could stimulate business activity within the territory, enabling the Mormons to secure and improve their homesteads. Looking toward the expansion of mining activity, Young called for the introduction of college-level classes in mineralogy, geology, and chemistry so that Mormons could perform the labor in those mining regions.

Another sure sign of the fading Mormon frontier, and indeed of the larger American frontier, was the approach of the transcontinental railroad. As with mining, Young viewed this development with mixed feelings of hope and anxiety. On the one hand, he welcomed the railroad. As early as 1853, he had petitioned Congress for the construction of a transcontinental railroad to link the Great Basin with the East Coast, making it easier for East Coast-European Mormons to migrate west. Young was so anxious for a transcontinental railroad that he had paid the entire cost of the first two-year survey made by the Union Pacific Railroad prior to actual construction. And he attempted to influence the proposed route by recommending its construction along the North Platt, over the hills to the Sweetwater, to South Pass, and from that point to the Green River, and ultimately to Echo Canyon down the Weber River into the Great Basin.

In the end, Young's proposal was almost identical to the actual route followed by the Union Pacific. By 1868, as the railroad reached present-day Wyoming, Young secured a contract to grade, bridge, and tunnel for the Union Pacific and enlisted the services of several thousand Mormon workers. The Mormon leader viewed the contract a godsend for helping to pull the region out of a severe economic slump.

Young was bitterly disappointed when railroad officials decided to bypass Salt Lake City, in favor of a shorter route around the northern end of the Great Salt Lake fifty miles to the north. Despite his disappointment, he maintained close contact with railroad officials and in January of 1869 traveled north to confer with Thomas C. Durant, vice-president of the Union Pacific Railroad, and Leland Stanford of the Central Pacific Railroad. He talked these officials into establishing the major terminal point for their two railroads at Ogden, Utah, rather than at some more remote point.

Finally, on May 10, 1869, construction on the transcontinental railroad was completed and a ceremony held at Promontory Point, Utah. Here, Leland Stanford, Thomas C. Durant, and other railroad officials gathered to drive a golden spike to mark this historic occasion. Citizens in Salt Lake observed this event with their own celebration. The principal business places, stores, and factories were closed, work suspended, and a great celebration held in the new Mormon Tabernacle on Temple Square.

Brigham Young wasted little time utilizing the railroad for the benefit of himself and his followers. He organized his own enterprise, the Utah Central Railroad Company, which connected Salt Lake City with Ogden and the transcontinental route. Completion of this line in January, 1870, meant that the days of Mormon pioneer travel across the plains by wagon, horseback, or on foot were over forever. (Mormon emigrants who arrived in Salt Lake City after that time were dubbed "Pullman pioneers.") Young pointed with pride to the Utah Central Railroad, a line built entirely without government funds. Young also pushed the building of additional railroad lines, running both south of Salt Lake and north of Ogden, designed to establish closer transportation links throughout the territory.

Although the transcontinental railroad benefited the Mormons, Young worried about its negative effects. There was an increased influx of non-Mormons into the Great Basin, which forced the Mormons to confront more and more a non-Mormon population whose practices and beliefs that ran counter to their own. The railroad also contributed to increased dissension within the ranks of Mormonism itself.

One such source was the rival midwestern-based Reorganized Church of Jesus Christ of Latter Day Saints. Formed in 1860 in opposition to Brigham Young and the Utah Mormons, the Reorganized Church chose as its president Joseph Smith III, the eldest son of the slain Mormon prophet. Other Smith family members joined this new Mormon movement, including Emma, the prophet's widow, his surviving brother, William, and the prophet's other sons. The Reorganized Church, in contrast to the Utah Mormons, abhorred polygamy.

Joseph Smith III made a direct assault on Brigham Young by dispatching two of his younger brothers, Alexander Hale Smith and David Hyrum Smith, to Utah. The two held a public meeting in which they denied that their father had ever sanctioned polygamy, claiming that it originated instead with Brigham Young following Smith's death. Young scoffed at Alexander and David's naivete and characterized them as "weak babies" unworthy of their illustrious father. The two brothers were not very successful as missionaries and attracted just a handful of Utah Mormons to their ranks.

More serious dissension came from the Godbeites, a group of disaffected Mormons led by William S. Godbe, a wealthy Mormon merchant. The Godbeites felt that with the coming of the railroad, the Mormon Church should take the lead in developing Utah's mineral resources. The growth of Utah mining would allow the Great Basin to integrate itself into the larger American economy—a goal that ran counter to Brigham Young's quest for economic self-sufficiency.

The Godbeites also differed on Church doctrine. They

embraced spiritualism and claimed the ability to communicate with the dead. Spiritualism was not unique to the Godbeites but had first manifested itself in the "burned-over district" of New York during the 1840s. Here it had originated in the home of John D. Fox, where strange rappings were interpreted to be contacts from the spirit world. Promoted by Fox and others, spiritualism had spread from New York, eventually finding expression in a number of religious denominations, including Mormonism.

The Godbeites also objected to the authoritarian leadership of Brigham Young. They disliked the close relationship between Church and state mandated by Young and promoted instead greater individual freedom, particularly in economic affairs. Like many contemporary Americans, they embraced laissez-faire individualism, thus opposing the cooperative economic planning promoted by Brigham Young.

The Godbeites attracted a number of influential Mormon businessmen and intellectuals, including Amasa Lyman, a former Mormon apostle excommunicated some years before for his unorthodox beliefs. The Godbeites designated Lyman their spiritual leader and formed their own Church of Zion. They published a literary periodical, the *Utah Magazine,* and later a newspaper, the Salt Lake City *Daily Tribune.*

Brigham Young reacted by denouncing Godbeite doctrine as antagonistic to God. He countered Godbeite efforts at economic integration by pushing apace Mormon economic self-sufficiency and admonishing his followers to avoid trade with the Godbeites, as well as with non-Mormon merchants.

This boycott fit in with Young's larger program for Mormon economic self-sufficiency. He formed the Zion's Cooperative Mercantile Institution, or ZCMI, a Church-wide merchandising cooperative designed to bypass all trade with Utah non-Mormon merchants. ZCMI was chartered as a corporation and was operated under close Church supervision, with Young as president and principal stockholder. It had branches throughout the territory and tried to monopolize both the wholesale and retail sale of manufactured goods, and it brought virtually all Mormon merchants into its orbit. Various ZCMI branches operated their own factories and workshops, turning out boots, shoes, and clothing.

Young encouraged Mormon self-sufficiency in other ways. He promoted manufacturing in the home, in particular the knitting, weaving, and sewing of clothing by Mormon women. This would preclude the purchase of ready-made clothing manufactured outside of Utah. Homespun garments, Young felt, should be of a modest, uniform cut. He opposed the fashion trends of contemporary society and had no use for the popular hoop skirts, which he felt violated female modesty. "There is not a day [that] I go out but I see the women's legs, and if the wind blows, you see them up to their bodies." He also disliked the "Grecian bend," or bustle, and found its yards of wasted material an affront to his sense of economy. The wearer of the Grecian Bend, he jokingly remarked, could not be distinguished "from a camel" with her "great big—what is it you call it?" Young's own wives dressed plainly. In men's clothing, Young confessed a preference for homespun clothes. But he always appeared in public in fine, black broadcloth because he claimed that his wives and daughters insisted that he dress as becoming to his position as Church leader.

Brigham Young urged his followers to abstain from chewing and smoking tobacco. He claimed that $60,000 a year left the territory to keep local residents supplied with tobacco. Young's admonitions for abstinence were in keeping with traditional Mormon teachings, for Joseph Smith in 1833 had counseled against tobacco. Smith also had urged abstinence from wine, alcohol, and hot drinks—advice put forth in a revelation known as the Word of Wisdom. Initially, the Word of Wisdom was not strictly enforced, but in the 1860s it served as scriptural basis for Young's assault on tobacco consumption. He considered the use of tobacco a loathsome and dirty habit. Although he had used tobacco himself, even after becoming Church president, he gave up the habit by 1860 and urged all of his Mormon followers to do the same. But not all followed his advice.

In response, Young called for the local production of tobacco for those Mormons who insisted on its use, declaring that tobacco could be raised in Utah as well as in any other place. He also tried to control its use in public places, particularly in the Mormon Tabernacle, by berating tobacco chewers who spit tobacco juice on the floor. Such individuals "dirty the house, and if a lady happens to besmear the bottom of her dress, which can hardly be avoided, it is highly offensive."

Young also counseled abstinence from alcohol, coffee, and tea in the further promotion of Mormon self-sufficiency. He followed the Word of Wisdom in his own household, serving only milk and water at meals. But complete abstinence was not strictly enforced, and on occasion Young apparently enjoyed a glass of beer. Wine was used in the Mormon sacrament, a practice continued until the late nineteenth century. Short of complete abstinence, the Mormon leader tried to regulate alcohol's use by limiting consumption to that which was locally manufactured. But he continued to promote the ideal of complete abstinence, a virtue extolled in a Word of Wisdom song composed in honor of his own visit to an outlying settlement:

> Our father Adam and our mother Eve,
> Could not have been tempted to believe,
> That whisky was the med'cine to cure cough and cold,
>
> And tea to comfort them when old;
> They were not sickly, and it appears,
> They lived for more than nine hundred years.
>
> (CHORUS)
> Take away the whisky, the coffee, and the tea.
> Cold water is the drink for me.

After 1869, Young faced increased federal hostility that threatened anew Mormonism's frontier sanctuary. This resulted from Ulysses S. Grant's election to the presidency. Grant strongly opposed Mormon polygamy. His position was influenced by fellow Radical Republicans who, although busy with Reconstruction, were anxious to eradicate this other "relic of barbarism." Grant's vice-president, Schuyler Colfax, through his own anti-Mormon declarations, announced in December of 1869, "It is time to understand whether the authority of the nation or the authority of Brigham Young is the Supreme power in Utah." Also active was the Reverend Dr. J. P. Newman, chaplain of the United States Senate and a close friend of the Grant family. Newman had traveled to Utah to observe the Mormons firsthand and had debated Orson Pratt, Mormonism's leading theologian, on the question "Does the Bible sanction polygamy?"

Grant's antipolygamy policy involved the appointment of two avowed foes of the Mormons to federal positions in Utah—J. Wilson Shaffer as governor, and James B. McKean as chief justice. Shaffer, a former Southern "war governor," boasted: "Never after me shall it be said that Brigham Young is Governor of Utah." Judge McKean, the son of a Vermont minister and lawyer, had helped found the Republican party on the basis of opposition to slavery and polygamy.

In September, 1871, McKean impaneled a grand jury that indicted Brigham Young and other polygamous Mormon leaders on charges of violating a territorial statute prohibiting lewd and lascivious cohabitation. Young first responded with hesitation, pondering whether to appear in court. Some close advisers urged him to avoid arrest and flee, recalling the fate of Joseph Smith at Carthage under similar circumstances. There was also talk of armed resistance or a mass Mormon exodus to Mexico. But less militant individuals advised Young to give himself up and trust the legal system that they felt would exonerate him.

In the end, Young chose the latter course. Accompanied by four close advisers plus nine attorneys, Brigham Young appeared before Judge McKean and pleaded not guilty. Young was allowed to post a $5,000 bond and return home to await consideration of the case.

Young's next court appearance came on January 2, 1872. He had to answer not only the original charge of lascivious cohabitation but a more serious charge—murder. This resulted from the accusations of Bill Hickman, an embittered one-time Mormon and former bodyguard to Young who claimed that the Mormon leader had ordered him to murder a non-Mormon hunter and trader in retaliation for earlier hostile actions against the Mormons during the Utah War. This time McKean refused bail and ordered Young held prisoner in his own house under guard of a United States marshal until his case came to trial. In April of 1872 the United States Supreme Court in *Clinton v. Engelbrecht* ruled that the federal grand jury indicting Young had been drawn illegally. Thus, the indictment against Young was null and void and Young was set free along with all the other indicted polygamous Mormons. Nevertheless, these Mormon-federal government difficulties further dramatized the fact that Mormonism's frontier sanctuary was rapidly disappearing.

Changes within Young's own family further underscored this fact as the family grew and became more geographically diffuse. During the turbulent years from 1857 to 1865, Young had fathered twelve children by six different wives, bringing the total number of Young offspring to fifty-six. The family also grew with the addition of two new plural wives. The first, Amelia Folsom, was 24 when she married the 61-year-old Mormon leader in 1862. Tall, with a good figure, brown hair, and bluish-gray eyes, Amelia was an accomplished musician, elegant in her dress and manner. She had a penchant for "dainty petticoats" with crochet trimmings and wore "lovely-smelling bay rum and cologne." She

The shrinking boundries of Brigham Young's Great Basin sanctuary. Note the reductions from the proposed State of Deseret in 1849 to the final territory (and later state) boundries of Utah in 1868. (Courtesy of the Utah State Historical Society.)

captured Young's fancy and by 1865 became his favorite wife. Amelia could devote full time to pleasing Young for she did not (and apparently could not) have children. In 1865, the Mormon patriarch married the even younger 21-year-old Mary Van Cott, whose first husband had died, leaving her with a young daughter. She bore Young's fifty-seventh and last child in 1868.

There were other changes in the Young family. Young's senior wife, Mary Ann, was moved from the Beehive House back to the White House in 1860. Her advancing years and declining health apparently caused her to relinquish responsibilities as official hostess of the Beehive House to the younger Lucy Decker, Young's first plural wife. Young also established in 1862 a new rural homestead some three miles southeast of the Beehive and Lion Houses. Known as Forest Farm, this rural residence provided the growing Young household with produce and dairy products. It also served as a laboratory for experiments in scientific cattle breeding, sericulture, and sugar manufacturing. Another plural wife, Lucy Bigelow, was placed in charge of this estate. She soon found managing Forest Farm to be a very demanding and time-consuming job, so when she became pregnant in 1863, she gladly relinquished her responsibilities to Susan Snively. The departure of Snively gave Young and other family members temporary respite from this temperamental woman who was known as a whiner and complainer.

The fathering of twelve children and marriage to two youthful wives apparently reflected Young's desire to affirm what was left of his youthful vigor. He seemed to have succeeded, for outsiders continually commented on his youthful appearance. Young, however, was well aware of his advancing age. His older children had reached maturity, with his eldest daughters married with children of their own. His four eldest sons were also full-grown and had moved out on their own. The eldest, Joseph A. Young, followed in his father's footsteps, serving as a missionary to England during the mid-1850s. Following his return to the Great Basin, he served as Church leader in the Sevier District in Southern Utah. Brigham Jr. also performed missionary work in Great Britain and like his older brother presided over some outlying Mormon settlements located to the north in Cache Valley, Utah, and in Southern Idaho.

John W. Young moved to New York City where he commenced a long career in business. A shrewd individual, John cut a dashing figure with his natty clothes and handlebar mustache; he was considered by many to be Young's brightest son. When he first arrived in New York, he worked with his older brother, Joseph, in directing the continuing flow of Mormon emigrants from Europe to the Great Basin. A fourth son, Brigham Heber, like his older half-brothers, assisted with the emigration of Mormons to Utah. Young began to groom each of these four for future high positions of Church leadership. He apparently hoped that at least one of the four would one day succeed him as Church leader. In 1855, he had ordained John, then just an adolescent but considered a favorite, a Mormon apostle. Soon thereafter, he ordained Joseph, Brigham Jr., and Brigham Heber as apostles. By 1865, he had set apart the three older sons as counselors in the first presidency of the Church.

Several younger sons left the territory to further their education in the East. In a larger sense, the Mormons, like the Puritans before them, emphasized the value of education. Almost every Mormon community had its grammar school along with a chapel. The Mormons subscribed to a basic creed enshrined in Mormon scripture: "The Glory of God Is Intelligence." This belief extended to higher education. Young authorized establishment of the University of Deseret (later known as the University of Utah) at Salt Lake City, which commenced operations in 1868. This institution schooled twenty-four of Young's sons and daughters. Four of the sons, upon the completion of their studies, wanted to gain further training outside the Great Basin. Young supported the four but only after making strict provision that the knowledge gained would be used for the upbuilding of Mormonism's Great Basin sanctuary.

Willard, at nineteen, became the first Mormon to enter the United States Military Academy at West Point, New York. This came at a time when Brigham Young and the Mormons were coming under increasing attack from critics in the East. Among these was President Grant, who was extremely upset that the son of his Mormon antagonist had gained admission into his alma mater. Willard's entry came at the same time that Henry O. Flipper was admitted as that institution's first black. Willard's activities were closely monitored in the East, with New York newspapers carrying stories about "the Mor-

mon and the nigger at West Point." Some New Yorkers actually traveled up from the city to see the two curiosities. Not
all newspaper accounts were negative, however. The Chicago *Evening Post* described Willard's accomplishments, noting that West Point was becoming something more than just
an "asylum for dandies."

Willard graduated near the top of his class—fourth out
of forty-three—which qualified him for appointment to
the Army Corps of Engineers, considered the most presti-
gious branch. Willard's achievement countered the popular
anti-Mormon belief that the children of polygamous families were intellectually inferior to those of monogamous
parentage.

A second son, Alfales, also left Utah, enrolling at the
University of Michigan in 1875, where he studied law.
Brigham Young's response to Alfales' decision to become a
lawyer was ambivalent because of the Mormon leader's dislike of most lawyers. He advised Alfales of "Benjamin
Franklin's motto . . . that 'honesty is the best policy' " since
law more than any "other profession seems more open" to
dishonesty. Lawyers, he cautioned, were easily "led from
the direct path of honesty either through the desire to
make money fast, or . . . in the advocacy of a cause or the
defense of a client" regardless of the true justice involved.

Another son, Joseph Don Carlos, enrolled at Rensselaer
Polytechnic Institute at Troy, New York, to study architec-
ture, a more acceptable profession to his father and one that
he would eventually utilize in designing Church and public
buildings in the Great Basin. A fourth offspring, Feramorz
Little, entered the United States Naval Academy at Annapolis, Maryland.

But Feramorz, after two years, was not satisfied with the
schooling that he was receiving at Annapolis and wanted to
resign. He was, however, afraid that his resignation would
bring disgrace upon the Young family and Mormonism generally. He sought his father's counsel and after assurance

from Annapolis officials that he could resign honorably, he left. Feramorz then entered Rensselaer Polytechnic Institute and graduated with a degree in civil engineering.

Brigham Young also paid attention to his daughters as they grew and reached maturity. By the late 1860s and early 1870s, his eldest daughters had long since married and left home. But a younger group of ten daughters, all born of different wives about the same time during the late 1840s and early 1850s, had reached dating age. Young dealt with the continuous stream of suitors who called upon the "Big Ten," as these daughters were known. These gentlemen callers would be received in the parlor of the Lion House. On one occasion, when the girls and their beaux were in the parlor unchaperoned, someone suggested that "some semblance of privacy" could be obtained by turning down the brilliant lighted lamp in the center of the room and placing a barricade of books around it. This was done. Suddenly, the door to the parlor opened and there stood Brigham Young with a candle in his hand! Entering the room, he knocked down the book barricade and turned the lamp back up to its full brilliance. He then turned to the startled young group and said, "The girls will go upstairs to their rooms, and I will say good night to the young men."

The Mormon leader's family became increasingly diffuse in other ways. By the early 1870s, several of Young's wives moved out of the Lion House into residences of their own in and around Salt Lake City. Another wife, Eliza Burgess, was moved into a house of her own in Provo, which provided Young a place to stay while visiting that central Utah community.

Young himself spent more and more time away from Salt Lake City. He was drawn to St. George, located in the extreme southern part of Utah, where he established a residence to spend the winter months. And since the aging Mormon leader was increasingly bothered by rheumatism, an ailment aggravated by harsh winters in Salt Lake City, St.

George, with its more moderate climate, had a special appeal.

In 1870 he purchased a New England-style two-story house and moved one of his wives, Lucy Bigelow, into it. Lucy, accompanied by her three daughters, including Susa Amelia (who as a writer-author would eventually emerge as the Mormon leader's most famous and talented female offspring), acted as official hostess. During the winter months, Lucy looked after her husband and his entourage—his drivers, clerks, etc.—and entertained the numerous friends and visitors who called.

However, by 1873, Lucy Bigelow's health became uncertain because of her age and the strenuous load she bore as hostess. Thus, Young built a second house in St. George. As official hostess he selected Amelia Folsom, his childless wife. Lucy's feelings concerning this development were mixed. On the one hand she was undoubtedly glad to be relieved of overseeing her husband and his entourage and many visitors. But at the same time, in the words of Lucy's daughter: "mother's heart twisted with sorrow at the thought of her dear husband coming down to spend his winters in another wife's home. [After all] she was human—she was a woman."

One other important change took place within the family with Young's marriage to Ann Eliza Webb. Ann Eliza had previously been married to James L. Dee, a difficult individual who neglected and mistreated her. Two children resulted from this unhappy union before she divorced him in 1867. There is controversy concerning the circumstances leading to her marriage to Young in 1869. According to Young family sources, the 68-year-old Mormon leader was reluctant to take on the responsibilities of a 24-year-old divorcée with two small children. He protested "I am an old man, and I have all the wives and children I want. I am too old to be marrying again." But Ann Eliza persisted and, finally, under pressure from her and her parents, Young agreed to marry her in order to restore honor to her family.

Ann Eliza, however, had a different set of recollections. She maintained that Young, attracted by her youth and extraordinary beauty, vigorously sought her. At 24 she was tall and slender, had a face with regular soft features, dark blue eyes, and dark brown hair worn loosely, all of which made her reputedly the most attractive of all the wives. Ann Eliza claimed that she initially resisted the aging Mormon patriarch's advances, but finally gave in to his unrelenting pressure.

Whatever the circumstances, the marriage ran into problems almost from the start. Ann Eliza did not feel that the ever-busy Young gave her sufficient attention. She became jealous of the other wives, particularly Amelia Folsom. Unhappy while living in the Lion House, Ann Eliza became further estranged when Young sent her off to Forest Farm to replace the ailing Susan Snively. Still dissatisfied with her lot after two years at Forest Farm, she demanded and received from Young a house of her own in the center of Salt Lake City not far from the Lion House. After moving there, she proceeded to operate it as a boarding house, to supplement her income from Young. She associated more and more with non-Mormons to whom she related her marital difficulties. Finally, in July, 1873, she left Young for good, suing the Mormon leader for civil divorce, alleging "neglect, unkindness, cruel and inhuman treatment [and] absolute desertion." She asked for $1,000 a month until the granting of a final decree and a final settlement of $200,000 for her children and herself, plus $20,000 for attorney fees. This divorce case would occupy Young's attention as it dragged out over the next several years.

The Ann Eliza controversy helped focus attention on general Mormon attitudes toward women. Young, echoing the prevailing attitudes in American society, declared that "the man is the head of the woman." This harmonized with basic Christian tradition going back to the time of Paul. He went on:

The woman is the glory of man; what is the glory of the woman? It is her virginity until she gives it into the hands of the man who will be her Lord and Master to all eternity.

All "women of faith and knowledge" he claimed, would acknowledge this fact and proclaim: "It is a law that man shall rule over me; his word is my law, and I must obey him; he must rule over me; this is upon me and I will submit to it."

These convictions rested on Young's basic belief that women were inferior to men in a number of respects. Women, he said, were "weaker vessels." God gave men by virtue of "their superior ability" the "wisdom and ability to lead their wives into his presence." Women also possessed less intelligence than men. "A woman, be she ever so smart . . . cannot know more than her husband if he magnifies his priesthood . . . God never in the age of the world endowed women with knowledge above the man . . ." Female inferiority, moreover, stemmed from the curse of original sin, namely the temptation of Eve in the Garden of Eden. Thus, women are "more liable to be led astray and ruined."

The primary duty of the inferior sex was child bearing and child rearing. "The mothers are the machinery," Young declared, "that give zest to the whole man, and guide the destinies and lives of men upon the earth." This conformed with the basic nineteenth century American belief that motherhood was woman's one duty and function. Young warned that at the Resurrection the woman who in this life has sacrificed her duty as a wife and mother to pursue other interests would find that her whole life had been a failure.

While emphasizing woman's primary role as mother and wife, Young did leave the door open for other activities. During the late 1860s, the Relief Society, an official organization for Mormon females, was reinstituted. Under the overall direction of Young's wife, Eliza R. Snow, the Relief Society provided relief for the poor and promoted Mormon economic self-sufficiency. The Relief Society established its own cooperative and opened its own Woman's Commission Store.

Young also promoted vocational and professional education for women. He encouraged a division of labor between men and women that would enable the Mormon community to function more efficiently. He saw women better suited than men for certain trades. Telegraphy and clerking were two such occupations, because he thought that a woman could write and spell better than a man. He also encouraged women to pursue professions such as medicine and journalism. He declared with increasing emphasis during the late 1860s and early 1870s that a woman's sphere of activity could transcend the home and family in contributing to upbuilding of Mormonism's Great Basin sanctuary. In summary, he proclaimed:

> We believe that women are useful, not only to sweep houses, wash dishes, make beds, and raise babies, but that they should stand behind the counter, study law or physic, or become good book-keepers and be able to do the business in any counting house and all this to enlarge their sphere of usefulness for the benefit of society at large.

Young's primary concern during the late 1860s and early 1870s, however, was not with the role of women in his family or in Mormonism generally, but with preserving a rapidly fading Mormon frontier. One way of doing this was through the establishment of new settlements in Arizona and in the so-called "Four Corners" area where the boundaries of Utah, Colorado, New Mexico, and Arizona met. Young was encouraged in this move by the completion of railroad lines to this section of the country. Also, Young's non-Mormon friend, Thomas L. Kane, who visited Utah during the winter of 1872–73, suggested that settlements in Arizona could serve as a connecting link to the ultimate formation of a major Mormon center and gathering place in the Sonora Valley of Mexico. It was felt that the Mexican government would treat the Mormons with greater tolerance than the increasingly antagonistic American government.

Young promoted his Arizona colonization scheme, dispatching settlers first to the Little Colorado River, and later to the Gila River country. In all, twenty-five permanent Mormon settlements were established in Arizona. But the Mormons had difficulty with the Indians. Thus, in 1874, Young dispatched Jacob Hamblin to northern Arizona to prevent a threatened Navajo uprising against Mormon settlements. Arizona Mormons also had to reckon with the Apaches, a hostile tribe that harassed other white settlers. In response to Indian difficulties, the federal government established a military post in southern Utah, Ft. Cameron, and sent 181 troops to man it. Despite these difficulties, Young remained optimistic that the Mormons could influence the Indians to peace in accordance with President Grant's Indian policy.

Meanwhile, Ulysses S. Grant himself continued to assault the very frontier sanctuary that Young worked so hard to preserve. In his annual message to Congress in December of 1871, the president attacked the Mormons, characterizing their institution of polygamy "a remnant of barbarism, repugnant to civilization, to decency, and to the laws of the United States." A year later, in a second annual message, he attacked the Mormon-dominated territorial legislature for evading all responsibility to the government of the United States. Grant intensified his attacks in the wake of the unfavorable *Englebrecht* decision nullifying Judge McKean's method of selecting jurors. In a special message to Congress in February, 1873, he called for federal legislation to take the selection of jurors in antipolygamy cases away from local Mormon authorities. This would enable Utah federal district courts to secure impartial, non-Mormon jurors to administer justice in a more independent, efficient manner. In a third message in December of 1873, Grant once more called for greater non-Mormon control over Utah federal courts, along with curbs on all-powerful, Mormon-dominated probate courts.

Congress responded to Grant's repeated requests and in 1874 enacted the Poland Act. This measure, named for its chief sponsor, Representative Luke P. Poland of Vermont, revised the method of impaneling juries in an attempt to get around the *Englebrecht* decision. It also drastically curtailed the jurisdiction of the probate courts, limiting their jurisdiction to matters of estate settlement, guardianship, and divorce, and gave U.S. district courts exclusive civil and criminal jurisdiction. Encouraged by the Poland Act, President Grant pushed for additional antipolygamy legislation in his 1875 annual message. He compared polygamy to the importation of Chinese women into the United States for illegitimate purposes, and he called for federal legislation to punish this "licensed immorality."

The spectacle of President Ulysses S. Grant preaching decency and morality must have seemed ironic to Brigham Young, in light of the orgy of corruption that tainted Grant's administration; in particular, scandals involving three cabinet-level secretaries and the president's own private secretary, who protected a Whiskey Ring of corrupt Treasury Department inspectors. To Brigham Young and other Mormon leaders, all this official misbehavior was undermining the moral fabric of American society.

Reflecting this concern, Wilford Woodruff, one of Young's close advisors, related a dream in which the United States flag passed from north to south in the sky all tattered and torn, then the Constitution of the United States followed it but was all tied up with ropes to keep it from falling to pieces. Then followed a huge eagle with his talons in the head of President Grant, carrying him off. Anxious to see the latter part of this dream become reality, Young hoped to see Grant defeated for reelection in 1872 and thus favored Horace Greeley for president. Greeley, the eccentric editor of the *New York Tribune,* favored a hands-off approach toward the Mormons and polygamy. But Greeley was decisively defeated and the Mormons had to face four more years of Grant.

Following Grant's reelection, Young decided to test the constitutionality of federal antipolygamy statutes. In 1874, George Reynolds, the Mormon leader's secretary, an acknowledged polygamist with two wives, agreed to become a voluntary defendant in a test case involving the Morrill Anti-Bigamy Law of 1862. Reynolds argued that plural marriage was essential to the Church's social and religious life and should be left alone in conformity with the free exercise clause of the First Amendment. Reynolds also tried to refute the arguments of those foes who suggested that polygamy was intrinsically evil by maintaining that it could not be placed in the same category as "murder, theft, false swearing, and offenses affecting the rights of others."

The courts, however, rejected these arguments. They depicted polygamy an "odious practice" unacceptable in civilized societies and practiced almost exclusively by backward Asian and African civilizations. The courts went on to compare polygamy with the religious practice of human sacrifice in certain primitive societies. It was, therefore, the duty of civil governments to prevent such acts promoted in the name of religion. Thus, Reynolds was found guilty of bigamy, fined $200, and ordered to serve two years in prison. Reynolds subsequently appealed his case to the United States Supreme Court, which in 1879 upheld his conviction in the *United States* v. *Reynolds* decision.

Brigham Young faced more immediate legal difficulties. In 1875, Judge James B. McKean, Young's long-time antagonist, intervened in the Ann Eliza Webb divorce case, which was still tied up in the courts. Anxious to get Young, McKean ordered the Mormon leader to pay $500 per month alimony pending the outcome of the final settlement. At this point, the case took an ironic twist. By ordering Young to pay alimony, McKean gave implicit legal recognition to his polygamous marriage to Webb. In rebuttal, the Mormon leader maintained that he was not legally responsible for alimony because in the eyes of the law he had only one wife—Mary Ann Angell. Young maintained, moreover, that Webb had never been legally divorced from her first husband, James L. Dee. Young did concede a sacred obligation to Webb by virtue of his celestial marriage to her. But that was all, he maintained, and it did not legally obligate him to compensate her monetarily.

In response to Young's steadfast refusal to pay alimony, McKean found him guilty of contempt of court, fined him $25, and sentenced him to one day's imprisonment. On March 11, 1875, after passing sentence, McKean allowed Young to go home and say good-bye to his family. The 73-year-old leader then took bedding and other comforts, along with his second counselor, Daniel H. Wells, plus a servant, and returned to jail to serve out his sentence. He was at first placed in a cell already occupied by thirteen common criminals, but by nightfall was transferred to a smaller, more comfortable room next to the warden's office. Despite the short duration of his imprisonment, Young's followers were incensed. Through their official newspaper, the *Deseret News,* they condemned "the indignity [heaped] upon the head of the venerable and much respected gentleman." Outsiders also viewed Young's imprisonment in a negative light, with various Eastern newspapers condemning Judge McKean as a bigot. Federal authorities were also less than impressed and dismissed McKean from his judicial post.

James B. McKean's removal, however, did not end Young's legal difficulties. In June of 1875, McKean's replacement, Judge Jacob S. Boreman, upheld the deposed judge's original order that the Mormon leader pay alimony or be adjudged guilty of contempt. Boreman did not attempt to jail the aging Mormon leader, but instead ordered him held in the Beehive House under house arrest with his movements monitored by an ever-present United States marshal. Young endured this situation for five months, until November of 1875, when he was finally released from what he described as an unjust imprisonment.

But the Webb case dragged on. In October of 1876, Webb's lawyers tried once more, without success, to have Young held in contempt for nonpayment of alimony. Webb herself was far from Utah, busy traveling throughout the United States lecturing on the evils of Mormon polygamy, thereby making a living while generating support for pending antipolygamy legislation. In 1876 her reminiscences, *Wife No. 19, or the Story of a Life in Bondage,* were published and dedicated "to the Mormon wives of Utah."

Finally, in April of 1877, Judge Michael Schaeffer, chief justice of the Utah District Court, rendered a final judgment declaring that Ann Eliza Webb had never been legally married to Brigham Young and therefore was not entitled to alimony.

Meanwhile, an important, unexpected visitor arrived in Utah in October of 1875, none other than President Ulysses S. Grant, accompanied by his wife. Despite Grant's well-known animosity toward the Mormons, Young received the president with courtesy. The Mormon leader and a party of Church and territorial dignitaries traveled from Salt Lake to Ogden to meet the president's train. Young's chief advisor on this occasion was George Q. Cannon, a counselor in the Church first presidency, but also Utah's territorial delegate to Congress who had spent time in Washington, D.C. Young, after being introduced to Grant, extended his hand and said "this [is] the first time that I ever had the pleasure of seeing a President of the United States and of shaking hands with him."

Their meeting was apparently cordial enough. But the two men did not spend much time conversing with one another, for when the train resumed its journey from Ogden to Salt Lake, Grant retired to the observation car anxious to see the countryside, leaving the Mormon leader to carry on a conversation with the First Lady. Alluding to her husband's actions against the Mormons, Young bluntly stated, "Well, Madam, you will now have the opportunity of seeing this poor, despised, and hated people." Mrs. Grant told the Mormon leader that his followers were neither despised nor hated, that it was only the Mormon institution of polygamy that her husband objected to. Arriving in Salt Lake City, the party boarded carriages and traveled from the railroad station to downtown Salt Lake. Along the way, the visitors found "the street on either side [crowded] with rows of children . . . all singing songs of welcome and literally strewing the President's roadway with flowers." In retrospect, Young characterized Grant's visit as pleasant, even though the President maintained his hard line against the Mormons.

Brigham Young continued to look for ways to make the Mormons less dependent on the whims of federal officials like President Grant, and thus more self-sufficient. This quest assumed urgency following the Panic of 1873. Young noted that "one important lesson . . . taught us by the late financial panic [is] to avoid as much as possible, all entangling alliances." Young promoted a bold economic experiment known as the United Order, or the Order of Enoch, a system of economic cooperation that called upon selected Mormon communities to pool their equipment, their property, and their energy and work together. This plan was built upon the principles of the Zion Cooperative Mercantile Institution, established in 1869. The United Order was also inspired by a pilot experiment in economic cooperation undertaken by the Mormon residents of Brigham City (located some forty miles north of Salt Lake City) where local residents established a self-sufficient network of cooperatives, largely isolating themselves from the worst effects of the Panic of 1873.

The Mormon leader promoted the United Order, noting, "If we put our property into the hands of those capable of managing it, it will realize more; a united effort is more successful than individual effort." The United Order would lead to greater efficiency in performing basic household tasks, such as cooking. "Instead of having every woman getting up in the morning and fussing around a cook's stove or over the fire cooking a little food" for their immediate family, communal cooking and eating arrangements would prevail. After the meal, the dishes would "be piled together . . . and run back to the [individuals] who would wash them. We could have a few Chinamen to do that if we did not want to do it ourselves." This arrangement would free more women to "go to work making their bonets, hats, and clothing or [to work] in the factories." The "principle of oneness" in this communal arrangement would enable "a city of one thousand or a million people [to be] united into a perfect family, and they could work together as beautifully as the different parts of a carding machine work together." Young did not feel that the idea of consecrating all of one's worldly goods to the community would present a problem to faithful Latter-day Saints. According to Mormon belief, the bounty of the earth had merely been loaned by God to the people under the principle of stewardship.

Brigham Young put his plans into operation within selected communities throughout the Great Basin through the establishment of four basic variations on the United Order. One type common in larger Mormon communities required the least economic commitment and was likened to the earlier established cooperatives, such as the ZCMI. In this, each Mormon ward (or congregation) organized a particular type of manufacturing enterprise financed by its members. Thus, one ward might build a foundry-machine shop, and another a wood-working shop, and a third a dairy. A second type modeled after the Order established in Brigham City involved more economic commitment and provided for community ownership of manufacturing enterprises. There might be a general store with the profits derived therefrom used to establish cooperative sawmills, blacksmith shops, tanneries, etc. But each member of the Order retained private property.

A third variation, requiring even more commitment to community ownership and initially established in St. George, had its members pledge their time, energy, ability, and property and was under the direct supervision of an elected board of management. The members promoted cooperative manufacturing and promised to trade and sell only within the Order itself. Members, however, received different wages and dividends, depending on the amount of labor and property contributed. This became the most common type.

A fourth variety requiring the greatest economic commitment and first established at Orderville, a small community in southern Utah, involved an arrangement in which no private property was allowed. Instead, members shared equally in the community's production. In communities like Orderville, the members cooperatively built their apartment dwellings, shops, bakeries, barns, and other needed buildings. Everyone ate in a large community dining room, although each family had its own apartment. All members wore the same kind of clothes and no member could improve his or her situation unless all were likewise improved. This arrangement required a high degree of self-discipline and dedication. Young's eldest son, Joseph A., who directed an order of this type at Richfield in southern Utah, confessed that it was a trial to give up personal property for "the feeling of mine is the greatest feeling we have to combat."

The Mormons followed in the pattern of other Americans in promoting economic cooperation in response to the depressed economic conditions of the early 1870s. Midwestern farmers who belonged to the Patrons of Husbandry or Grange formed cooperatives for both consumer and producers, and the Knights of Labor organized producers' cooperatives. However, the cooperatives of these two groups were economic failures. Likewise, Mormon efforts were less than successful. The most extreme order—the Orderville type—failed due to a lack of investment capital. Wealthy and middle-class Mormons tended not to join, so the Order consisted primarily of poorer Mormons with little capital. Thus, a condition of persistent poverty prevailed in which the standard of living within the Order was lower than that in surrounding communities. This helped to undermine morale. Young people within the order compared their drab clothing and more limited material goods with more prosperous conditions in nearby non-Order towns.

There were also problems within other types of "United Orders." Those communities where members received different wages and dividends had difficulty determining the fair distribution of benefits, leading to dissension and discord and the ultimate breakup of these orders. Even those orders with the least economic commitment, that is, community ownership of manufacturing and agriculture enterprises, were forced to disband after undergoing attacks from hostile federal officials. These failures underscored anew the stark reality that Mormonism's frontier sanctuary was rapidly fading, a situation that the aging Mormon leader found increasingly difficult to deal with as he reached the final years of his life.

VIII

The Last Years and Young's Legacy

BY THE EARLY 1870s, the advancing years had begun to take their toll on Brigham Young. He had put on weight to the point where he was now described by visitors as stout. His auburn hair was touched with gray and rather thin. His chin whiskers, which he wore at a length of about six inches, were of a similar color and streaked with gray. Young's rheumatism bothered him more and more, particularly during the winter, which made spending the winter months in the temperate climate of St. George all the more important.

There were other health problems. During the winter of 1869–70 he had suffered from mumps. Although he quickly recovered, he quite possibly experienced "secondary sterility" as a complication, since he had fathered the last of his fifty-seven children in 1868, a year before contracting this disease. During the summer of 1872, he suffered from colds and fever, which left him confined for several days. Worse problems came during the fall of 1874 when he suffered from an enlargement of the prostate gland. This affliction incapacitated him for several weeks and gave rise to rumors that he was gravely ill. The prostate gland problem, his most serious illness in two decades, blocked urinary outflow from the bladder and necessitated catheterization. This mode of treatment was painful because it was still in its early stages of development as an accepted medical practice. A year later, in October of 1875, further complications arose

Brigham Young in 1873. (Courtesy of the LDS Church Library-Archives. Printed with permission.)

when the trauma of Young's self-catheterization led to local spasms and hemorrhaging. This problem was finally overcome with an improved soft, rubber catheter that made it easier for him to live with his urological disorder.

There were other reminders of his advancing years. Death became an increasingly frequent visitor. His old friend and close associate, Heber C. Kimball, whom he had known since his pre-Mormon days, passed away in 1868. Two years later his eldest brother John died. One of his daughters, Mary Eliza, died the following year, and a second daughter, Alice Clawson, in 1874. The following year a one-time favorite wife, Emmeline Free Young, died. Her later years had been difficult as she became addicted to morphine, the apparent result of her treatment for medical problems. The sight of his favorite becoming "a dope fiend" greatly upset the aging patriarch, according to his daughter. At Emmeline's funeral, Young reportedly told her children that he "wanted them to follow in his footsteps and not in the footsteps of their mother, who had refused to take his counsel and who had set a bad example to her children in many ways."

Two other deaths in 1875 caused Young further anguish. In August, just one month after Emmeline's death, 41-year-old Joseph Angell Young died suddenly and unexpectedly. The Mormon leader had been grooming Joseph as a possible successor. Already an ordained apostle, Joseph had assisted his father with correspondence and business affairs, and at the time of his death he had just established the United Order at Richfield, Utah. The following month, Young was confronted with the death of George A. Smith, his close associate and counselor to whom he had recently delegated additional responsibility as trustee-in-trust for the Church. The loss of Smith, whom Young eulogized as a devoted friend and lifelong companion, caused the Mormon leader to weep openly during the funeral.

These deaths and his own advancing years caused the Mormon patriarch to reflect with increasing frequency on the general topic of death and its meaning. Although death itself was a time for "solemn ritual," it was the forerunner of great benefits through eternal life. Spiritual resurrection, Young optimistically noted, would give him a new body that would not have the defects of his present one. He would get a "good set of new teeth" to replace his bad lower ones and dentures and have perfect vision enabling him to read "without using glasses." He would, moreover, be reunited with those relatives and friends who had passed on before him. Sacred temple ordinances through "sealing" assured him and other faithful Latter-day Saints that they would be with their families and relatives throughout all eternity.

Mormon optimism concerning the ultimate rewards of eternal life extended even to those who did not embrace Mormonism. The vast majority of mankind would be saved that is, receive some degree of eternal glory. Although concepts of hell and Satan existed in Mormon cosmology, only a handful of individuals would suffer eternal damnation or become what the Mormons labeled as sons of perdition. Thus, the Mormon view of eternity differed sharply from that found in much of contemporary Protestantism. Instead, they tended to be like the Universalists—a small, liberal offshoot of Puritanism.

Despite Mormon universalism, Young maintained that the *degree* of glory would vary in accordance with one's behavior in this life. Individuals who embraced Mormonism and followed all its principles would receive the greatest rewards and dwell the closest to God throughout eternity, but backsliders and nonbelievers would receive a lesser degree of eternal glory. Mormon teachings went one step further, suggesting that the most devout believers could ultimately become "Gods" and hold dominion over worlds of their own through a process known as "eternal progression." This belief was based on a basic Mormon maxim: As God is at present man may become.

Acutely aware of his own advancing years, Young continued

to groom his eldest sons as possible successors to lead the Mormons. But at the same time, he prepared for the possibility that his sons might be bypassed and succession determined by seniority within the Council of the Twelve Apostles. This was how Young himself as the senior apostle within the Quorum had claimed leadership back in 1844. But during the early 1870s, unlike 1844 when Young was clearly the senior apostle, there was confusion concerning Quorum seniority. This revolved around the status of Orson Hyde, the current Quorum president. Hyde had been an apostle since 1835, which gave him the longest tenure of any of the apostles. But he was an erratic and controversial individual, having been excommunicated in 1838–39 for turning against his Mormon co-religionists during the Missouri persecutions. Although he later repented and regained his apostleship, he continued on occasion to be unpredictable and controversial.

Thus, Hyde was an individual whom Young did not completely trust, and felt uneasy about as a potential successor. Therefore, Young, in 1875, after consulting with other Church leaders, decreed that seniority within the Twelve would be determined by *continuous,* unbroken service, which effectively eliminated Hyde from succession. This decision also eliminated Orson Pratt. Standing next to Hyde in seniority, Pratt, like Hyde, had been briefly excommunicated from the Church during the early 1840s due to his initial opposition to polygamy in Nauvoo. Pratt also frequently clashed with Young over points of Mormon doctrine and theology throughout the 1850s and 1860s. Young surely felt little regret in eliminating this brilliant but frequently misguided individual from future leadership.

The 1875 decision on apostolic seniority made John Taylor the senior apostle and potential successor. In contrast to Hyde, Taylor was generally low-keyed and noncontroversial; and unlike Pratt, he had not deviated from doctrines considered orthodox. An Englishman by birth, he had joined the Mormon faith in 1836 and within two years had shown sufficient dedication to be ordained a Mormon apostle. Unswerving in his devotion to Mormonism, he had been with Joseph Smith at Carthage, Illinois, when the Mormon prophet was murdered and just barely escaped death himself.

A committed polygamist with fifteen wives and thirty-five children, John Taylor vigorously defended the Church as an editor of several Church newspapers and the author of numerous Mormon tracts. He had also served as a missionary to his native Great Britain and to France. He had lived in New York for an extended period of time where, as editor of *The Mormon,* a Church newspaper, he had energetically countered anti-Mormon accounts that appeared in the Eastern press. Thus, Taylor was an individual whom Young could accept as a possible successor.

Brigham Young busied himself with other Church matters. He took on the office of trustee-in-trust for the Church following George A. Smith's death and also oversaw construction on Mormon temples in Salt Lake City and St. George. The latter structure was finished and dedicated in April of 1877. Young saw the erection of Mormon temples as essential in that they provided sacred space where important ordinances, known as endowments, could be performed. Young himself spent a great deal of his time performing these ordinances in the St. George Temple so that his deceased father and other departed relatives could be sealed to him. Young also authorized the start of construction on two more temples—one at Manti, in central Utah, and a second at Logan in northern Utah.

Young also undertook a sweeping reordering of basic Church organization, a task necessitated by the dramatic growth of population in Mormonism's Great Basin sanctuary from 12,000 in 1852 to over 100,000 by the 1870s. This growth rendered the existing structure of Church organization inadequate. Reorganization started with the Quorum of the Twelve. Up to this time, six of the members of this body, in addition to their general Churchwide administrative responsibilities, exercised direct supervision over local stakes (or dioceses) as stake presidents. Young felt that these men should concentrate their energies on churchwide duties and thus delegated their stake responsibilities to subordinates. Among the six apostles affected was Young's own son, Brigham Jr., who had heretofore served in northern Utah. Henceforth, all of the Twelve acted solely as general authorities for the Church as a whole.

There were other organizational changes on the stake level. Great Basin population growth necessitated increasing the total number of stakes from thirteen to twenty. The responsibilities of stake presidents were also increased by making them directly accountable for every person and program within their boundaries—an extensive responsibility since each stake contained from four to thirty-five wards.

There were also major changes on the ward level. The total number of Mormon wards was increased from 101 to 241. In addition, the structure and organization within each ward was tightened up, with the bishops held accountable for their ward members. There were also organizational changes within the Mormon priesthood. The lower orders of this priesthood, known as the Aaronic priesthood, were opened up to all young Mormon males. Previously, only a few select boys had been ordained to the offices of deacon, teacher, and priest within the Aaronic priesthood, with the vast majority of Aaronic priesthood holders being adult Mormon males. But by the 1870s, most adult males were advanced beyond the Aaronic into Melchizedek priesthood because membership in this higher order was a necessary prerequisite for participation in most sacred temple ordinances.

This practice depleted the ranks of the Aaronic priesthood. The logical solution was to ordain young adolescents not yet old enough to participate in the temple ordinances. These young priesthood holders as priests, teachers, and deacons could thus perform the essential functions of ward teaching (monthly visits to ward members) and caring for the meetinghouse. These changes made the Mormon priest-hood a lay organization consisting of virtually all Mormon males over eleven or twelve years of age (excepting blacks who continued to be excluded from all orders of the priest-hood—a ban in force until 1978). All of the Church orga-nizational changes completed in 1877 assured the aging leader that the basic stability of the Mormon Church that he had worked so hard to maintain throughout his tenure as Church president would be perpetuated.

Despite his advancing years, there was no let-up in the ef-forts of hostile federal authorities to undermine the prestige and authority of Brigham Young. In April, 1876, a federal grand jury investigated Young's business dealings with the city of Salt Lake. In its final report, it accused Young of unethical business dealings. It alleged that Young's private property was being assessed for tax purposes at only a frac-tion of its actual value and accused the Mormon leader of receiving rebates amounting to over $7,000 on liquor license fees for the Salt Lake House, an establishment he owned and operated. He was also charged with receiving from the city loans that were interest-free and acquiring from them a plot of land at an unreasonably low price. In response to these charges, the *Deseret News* came to Young's defense, characterizing the grand jury a political smear organization formed in a malevolent spirit and dismissed its report as twisted facts. It defended Young's property assessment as "fair" and maintained that the liquor license rebates were similar to those paid to other proprietors of bars in Salt Lake City.

In 1877, Young faced much more serious accusations stemming from the earlier Mountain Meadows Massacre. Al-most as soon as this event had occurred in 1857, rumors began to surface that the Indians did not act alone. In 1859 both a federal grand jury and Mormon Church officials con-ducted separate investigations that suggested the involvement of high Church officials in southern Utah. By 1866, affidavits were circulated connecting Young himself to this atrocity. In 1873, federal government officials indicated that one of their major purposes for establishing a military outpost at Fort Cameron close to the massacre site in southern Utah was to get to the bottom of this affair. The following year, John D. Lee was arrested and tried in federal court for his role in the massacre. The first trial in 1875 ended in a hung jury; but a second the following year resulted in Lee's conviction and a sentence of death imposed. In the meantime, Young ordered Lee's excommunication from the Church and gave Lee's nineteen wives permission to leave their condemned husband.

John D. Lee reacted to these developments with extreme outrage. While in jail awaiting execution, he dictated his autobiography, subsequently published under the title *Mormonism Unveiled*. In it, he accused Young of betraying him and, with some justification, of making him the sole scapegoat for the entire affair. "Young has sacrificed me," stated Lee, "through his lust for power, after all I have done for him and the Mormon Church." Lee maintained that Young knew the full details of Mormon involvement from the very beginning and had conspired to keep them covered up.

The story of Lee's trial and charges received wide publicity throughout the United States. In March of 1877, just prior to his execution, Lee dictated a confession to the New York *Herald* in which he intensified his attacks, accusing Young of not just a cover-up but of being directly responsible for the massacre itself through his teachings. On March 23, 1877, Lee was taken to the site of the massacre at Mountain Meadows and executed by a firing squad.

Brigham Young vigorously refuted Lee's charges through the New York *Herald*. He also sent a telegram directly to President Rutherford B. Hayes denying Lee's assertion that he was an accessory after the fact and by implication an accessory before the fact. Young maintained he had fully cooperated with federal officials in bringing to justice those responsible and called upon President Hayes to "appoint a commission fully authorized to investigate that inhumane slaughter with jurisdiction to try and punish the offenders thereof." Despite these actions, the specter of Mountain Meadows would continue to haunt Young and taint Mormonism for years to come.

The aging patriarch also faced problems within his own family involving his two eldest sons, Brigham Jr. and John W., whom he increasingly relied upon for help and advice. John W., who was frequently absent in the East attending to business affairs, ran into financial difficulties. He also had health problems apparently aggravated by anxiety over his finances. Thus, the Mormon leader was pleased when John W. settled his financial affairs and returned to Utah to accept appointment as first counselor in the Church in October, 1876.

Brigham Jr. also experienced health problems of his own worse than those of his younger brother. In May, 1877, he was very sick and so enfeebled that he could not travel with the rest of his family from St. George to Salt Lake City and had to be left behind. Thus, the old patriarch was concerned that his two eldest sons, like Joseph Angell, might precede him in death.

There were other family problems. Another son, Oscar Brigham, suffered from an occasional mental disorder due to severe injuries sustained while working as a blacksmith. Oscar also had marital difficulties ultimately ending in divorce. Another son, Phineas Howe, the Mormon leader's youngest, suffered from a severe case of typhoid fever in 1877 and required hospitalization. He was treated with morphine to help relieve the severe pain and became addicted to the drug.

Two of Young's daughters by his St. George wife, Lucy Bigelow, had poor marriages. The eldest, Eudora Lovina, fell in love with Morely Dunford, who, although a Mormon, had a weakness for alcohol. Despite Young's vigorous opposition to the match, the young couple eloped and were married by a Presbyterian minister, further adding to Young's distress. Lucy Bigelow's second daughter, Susa Amelia, unfortunately followed in her sister's footsteps and married a cousin of Eudora's husband, Alma Dunford, an erratic individual who also drank. Susa's marriage ultimately ended in divorce.

Such family problems bothered the elderly patriarch. He issued what Susa later recalled as an "awful indictment . . . against his family . . . he wondered, when he looked at the actions of some of his wives and children . . . if he would have to go into the Kingdom of Heaven wifeless and childless." He confessed that the communal arrangement of the Lion House might have been a mistake in raising his children, particularly the daughters. These daughters, he suggested, "would have been better raised . . . if each wife had had a home of her own and had brought up the girls in all the science of house-keeping arts and labors." However, it was too late, the mistake made.

But Young was not one to dwell on past mistakes. He remained very busy during the spring and summer of 1877 as he approached his seventy-sixth birthday, declaring: "I mean to live just as long as I can" and "I calculate to die in harness." Young traveled extensively, visiting settlements south of Salt Lake and later north in Logan. Generally he reported his health as excellent in contrast to that of his two ailing sons. During the summer of 1877, he discussed with Eliza R. Snow the possibility of sending a group of six Mormon women on a lecture tour throughout the United States to refute the prevalent anti-Mormon view that Latter-day Saint women were enslaved victims of polygamy. It was hoped that this tour would counter the growing antipolygamy crusade.

Young also kept up an active correspondence with his sons

living away from the Great Basin. He stayed in close contact with Willard, who had graduated from West Point and was on active duty with the Corps of Engineers. He was concerned when Willard's unit was mobilized during the summer of 1877 to help restore order during the wave of bloody railroad strikes that rocked the nation. Willard's unit was sent to Baltimore to relieve a regiment of Maryland militia forced to take refuge in a local armory after being stoned and fired upon. Although Willard escaped injury and order was eventually restored, Brigham Young viewed these events in an apocalyptic light as a signal of the near approach of the breakup of the present form of government.

The period 1876–77 was unsettling, not just for Young himself but for the nation at large. The controversy surrounding the disputed presidential election contest between Rutherford B. Hayes and Samuel Tilden, coupled with increasing mob violence directed against blacks in the South, and now the railroad strikes, gave Young little reason to look with optimism toward the future. In conformity with Mormon millennialism, Young expected an impending bloody revolution leading to "a common ruin for workingman and capitalist [alike]."

Despite his gloomy expectations, he continued through correspondence to instruct and encourage his sons in their activities. On August 23, 1877, he wrote Feramorz at Rensselaer Polytechnic Institute outlining his longstanding aversion to novels, advising him that the perusal of novels was not a wise means of increasing one's appetite to read. "Novel reading appears to me to be very much the same as swallowing poisonous herbs; it is a remedy that is worse than the complaint."

That very evening Brigham Young had his own reasons for complaint. He was "seazed with violent vomiting, purging [i.e. diarrhea] and cramping." His doctor diagnosed his illness as cholera morbus and the following day he was injected with a mild opiate to alleviate the intense pain. The ailing leader's condition appeared serious but not grave. Nevertheless, his physician, Dr. Seymour B. Young, his own nephew, called in three locally distinguised physicians to aid him in treating the case. By the third day, Young's condition worsened due to an inflammation of the bowels and swelling of the abdomen. He continued to receive small doses of opium and was fed every half hour a mixture of milk and brandy. By Monday, August 27, he had increasing symptoms of nervous prostration and sank into a semicomatose condition. The next day, the opiates were discontinued and the doctors commenced a new mode of treatment, "warm stimulating injections [enemas] . . . for the purposes of creating an action through the alimentary canal." But Young objected to this treatment and it was discontinued.

The patient was also administered to by the laying on of hands (faith healing). But his condition continued to worsen and by the seventh day of the illness, Wednesday, August 29, it was apparent that the end was near and family members were called in. He remained in a coma for much of the morning and his temperature began to rise, reaching 105°F by mid-afternoon. Several of the brethren once more administered to him by the laying on of hands and he roused briefly to respond in a clear voice, "Amen." He seemed to partially revive and opening his eyes he gazed upward exclaiming "Joseph! Joseph! Joseph!" But this was followed by a gasp and the rush of blood to his lips. Then "his countenance assumed the blanch palor of death, and all was quiet in the room save the sobs . . . of a grieved and bereft family and friends."

Almost immediately debate arose over the exact cause of Young's seemingly strange death. After all, he had been extraordinarily healthy for a man of seventy-six, active right up to the end. One theory held that the Morman leader died of a secondary kidney infection aggravated by his repeated self-catheterization in later years. A second theory maintained that Young died of acute arsenic poisoning administered by enemies anxious to do away with him. But the most likely cause of death appears to have been appendicitis, which was an unknown clinical entity in 1877. All of the symptoms point to this conclusion, including the nausea, vomiting, diarrhea, and pain in the abdominal area. Moreover, the administration of enemas made the condition worse.

The deceased Mormon leader left detailed instructions for his funeral and burial. He gave exact specifications for his coffin, reflecting the directions of the carpenter he had once been. It was to be "made of plump 1¼ inch [redwood] boards, not scrimped in length" or width so that "if I wanted to turn a little to the right or to the left, I should have plenty of room to do so." He urged frugality in mourning. He wished "all my family present that can be [gathered] conveniently" but ordered that "the male members wear no crepe on their hats or on their coats" and that the females to buy no black bonnets, dresses, or veils. The service was to be simple, in keeping with established Mormon practice: singing and a prayer and time allowed for a few words from friends. Internment was to be on Young's own estate in "the little burying ground which I have reserved on my lot east of the White House on the hill." All these instructions were carried out in accordance with Young's wishes.

Young's family was provided for in a will drawn up in 1873. It called for an equitable division of property among the sixteen wives and forty-four children who survived him. Not provided for were those nominal wives to whom he had been married in name only, his so-called spiritual wives. Also pointedly excluded was Ann Eliza Webb. In general, Young's wives were left with the homes in which they were living. Initially, the value of Young's total estate was estimated between $2–2.5 million.

Problems, however, developed over settlement of the estate. All of the properties of the estate could not be divided until the youngest child came of age, or until all of the wives died. To handle this problem, income from Young's undistributed property was placed into a trust fund to be divided among the various mothers for themselves and the support of their children effective until the children reached maturity and/or the mothers died. A second significant problem involved the question of which properties in Young's possession actually belonged to the Mormon Church and which were his personal acquisitions. This problem existed because much of the Church's property had been transferred into Young's name, as trustee-in-trust, for the Church to get around the Morrill Anti-Bigamy Law.

The job of settling these questions fell into the hands of George Q. Cannon, Albert Carrington, and Brigham Young, Jr., who were named executors for the estate. Also, a special Church committee was formed to audit Young's records as trustee-in-trust to calculate the precise value of Young's properties and determine which properties were Young's own and which actually belonged to the Church.

The committee found the actual value of the estate was only $1.6 million, considerably below the $2—$2.5 million figure originally estimated. It determined, moreover, that one million dollars of this belonged to the Mormon Church. Of the remaining $600,000, the committee found a considerable portion of this owed to pay outstanding indebtedness, executors' fees, and other deductions, leaving the Young family a mere $225,000!

While the smallness of Young's estate surprised his heirs, most accepted these figures. But in 1879, six of the deceased leader's children, one son and five daughters, filed suit against the executors and the Mormon Church accusing them of defrauding their father's estate of one million dollars. This suit was finally settled out of court and the plaintiffs paid a total of $75,000. But the Mormon Church had the last word, excommunicating the six for "joining together and making a complaint, entering prosecution . . . and refusing to make restitution."

Brigham Young's two eldest sons ran into problems of their own and did not live up to the hopes of their father.

Neither succeeded their father as Church leader. John W. Young was forced to resign as a counselor to the Twelve Apostles due to his financial difficulties and thus banished from the ruling councils of the Mormon Church. He was ruined financially and spent his latter years in obscurity in New York City supporting himself as an elevator operator. Brigham Young, Jr., was also passed over as a Church leader despite some speculation that he might succeed his father. Instead, John Taylor, as the senior member of the Council of the Twelve, became Church president in 1880.

Shortly before his death, Brigham Young, in a conversation with his daughter Susa Amelia, conceded that everything he had achieved he owed to his Latter-day Saint faith, pointing out, "but for Mormonism I would have [remained] a common carpenter in a country village." But Young might have added that he had given the Mormon movement a great deal in return.

In assuming leadership during the critical period following Joseph Smith's death, Brigham Young helped to save Mormonism, enabling it to become, in time, the largest indigenous religion in America. Young, moreover, contributed to the growth of the larger American frontier. In leading his followers west from Illinois to the Great Basin at the time of the Mexican War, he undoubtedly helped strengthen American claims to this region by making inevitable its ultimate annexation to the United States.

In pioneering hundreds of Mormon settlements throughout the Great Basin, Young established himself as one of the greatest colonizers in American history, placing him in the same category as John Winthrop, Captain John Smith, James Oglethorp, and William Penn. The Mormon leader helped to explode the popular myth that the Great Basin, along with other regions west of the hundredth meridian, was a "great American desert" unsuited for white habitation. Utilizing irrigation and other scientific agricultural techniques, Young proved this region could sustain a significant white population. In the wake of the Mormons' own success, the arid Great Plains were settled by utilizing similar farming techniques, to become a highly productive agricultural region.

In overall terms, Brigham Young personified the larger American frontier. His continuous westward migration into upstate New York, then to the midwest, and finally to the far west paralleled that of countless other uprooted Americans throughout the nineteenth century. In addition, the opportunity for Young to succeed along that frontier was similar to that available to other frontiersmen. Finally, the stark reality of Mormonism's shrinking frontier domain, so painfully evident by the time of Brigham Young's death in 1877 underscored the fact that the larger American frontier was rapidly coming to an end, a development officially acknowledged by the U.S. Department of the Census in 1890.

A Note on the Sources

THE SECONDARY WORK that comes closest to being the definitive biography of Brigham Young is Leonard J. Arrington's *Brigham Young: American Moses* (New York, 1985). Arrington, the foremost living scholar of Mormon history and former Church Historian and Director of the Library-Archives of the Church of Jesus Christ of Latter-day Saints, has utilized material from the most important manuscript collection of Brigham Young materials as contained in the Mormon Church Archives in Salt Lake City, Utah. In fact, Dr. Arrington supervised the identification and cataloging of the enormous mass of Brigham Young papers during the period 1973–1980. These materials include the Mormon leader's diaries and office journals, letterbooks, which includes twenty-one volumes of a thousand pages each containing copies of letters handwritten by Young or by his staff from 1844 through 1877. Also included are incoming correspondence containing twenty-eight archival boxes of about one thousand leaves per box, Young's telegram books, a collection of Young's speeches, minutes of meetings, letters, certificates, miscellaneous papers, and sermons. This collection also contains papers relative to Young's tenure as Utah territorial governor from 1851 to 1857 and as superintendent of Indian affairs. Utilizing these materials, Arrington presents the Mormon leader in a generally favorable light but at the same time provides candor in noting many of Young's difficulties and failures. However, Arrington avoids certain controversial topics, including divisions within Mormonism and tensions within Young's own large, diffuse family. Despite this, it stands as the most complete scholarly biography of the Mormon leader.

A number of earlier book-length studies on Brigham Young, while more limited in their research and/or conceptual organization, are still useful. Included in these is M. R. Werner's *Brigham Young* (New York, 1925), a well-written and generally objective work, but limited by its lack of a clear biographical focus in that it tends to be a hybrid combination of biography and general history of Mormonism. Werner, moreover, limited his sources to previously published Mormon and non-Mormon materials. Preston Nibley's *Brigham Young, the Man and His Work* (Salt Lake City, 1936), in contrast to Werner, made use of unpublished primary sources in the Mormon Church Archives, thus conveying a feeling for the actions and basic beliefs of Young. But at the same time, Nibley's work is highly sympathetic, avoiding various controversial topics, including polygamy and tensions within Mormonism. It thus tends to be more hagiographic than biographic. Ray B. West's *Kingdom of the Saints; The Story of Brigham Young and the Mormons* (New York, 1957), like Werner's earlier work, is a generally well-written, objective account conveying a sense of drama and tension. It handles controversial topics including polygamy, the Danites, and conflicts within Mormonism with balance and sensitivity. However, like Werner, West was limited in his use of source materials, and his biography tended to drift into a narrative history of Utah and the Mormons. Stanley P. Hirshson's *The Lion of the Lord: A Biography of Brigham Young* (New York, 1969) is written in a lively, readable style and tends to convey a portrait of the Mormon leader as he probably appeared to most contemporary non-Mormon Americans of his time. Therein lies the problem, for Hirshson presents Young as a liar and scoundrel, basing his research and writing on biased contemporary Eastern newspaper accounts, which generally viewed Young in a negative light. Hirshson thus ignored Young's accomplishments and, indeed, basic humanity. By contrast, Eugene England's *Brother Brigham* (Salt Lake City, 1980) did not suffer from this shortcoming. England conveys to the reader a feeling for the emotional qualities of the man himself, basing his conclusions on the use of the documentary materials on Young in the Mormon Church Archives. Although England's book is written in an absorbing, readable style, it lacks critical historical analysis and is disjointed in its basic organization. England, moreover, like Nibley before him, tends to present the Mormon leader in an overly idealistic light.

The problems of critical biographical writing faced by these writers and by others has been perceptively discussed in several scholarly articles. These include Donald R. Moorman, "Shadows of Brigham Young as Seen by His Biographers," *Utah Historical Quarterly*, 45 (Summer 1977): 252–264; P. A. M. Taylor, "The Life of Brigham Young: A Biography Which Will Not Be Written," *Dialogue: A Journal of Mormon Thought*, 1 (Autumn 1966), 101–110; and Ronald K. Esplin, "From the Rumors to the Records: Historians and the Sources for Young," *Brigham Young University Studies*, 18 (Spring 1978), 453–465. A brief, annotated bibliographical overview of the sources available for studying Young is Dean C. Jessee, "The Writings of Brigham Young," *Western Historical Quarterly*, 4 (July 1973), 273–294.

The most important location of primary materials on Brigham Young, as previously indicated, is the Library-Archives of the Mormon Church in Salt Lake City. But in recent years certain restrictions have limited the availability of these materials, thus forcing scholars to rely on other sources of information. I was fortunate to gain access to typescript copies of Brigham Young's papers in the Archives of Weber State College in Ogden, Utah. These transcripts were copied from the originals in the Mormon Church Library Archives by the late Donald R. Moorman, professor of history at Weber State. Other locations of primary source information on Young include the Utah Historical Society, the libraries of the University of Utah, Utah State University, and Brigham Young University. Outside of Utah important collections are found in the Henry E. Huntington Library, San Marino, California; Bancroft Library, University of California, Berkeley; and Beinecke Rare Books and Manuscript Library, Yale University, New Haven, Connecticut. An important published primary source is the *Journal of Disclosures,* 26 vols. (Liverpool, England 1854–86). This work contains complete texts of many of the sermons delivered by Brigham Young from the mid-1840s up to the time of his death in 1877. These sermons, which reveal much about the attitudes and character. of the Mormon leader, have been analyzed in a perceptive article by Ronald W. Walker and Ronald K. Esplin, "Brigham Himself: An Autobiographical Recollection," *Journal of Mormon History,* 4 (1977), 19–34.

Specific aspects of Brigham Young's life and activities have been examined in a large body of literature. The most useful work on Young's formative years is Richard F. Palmer and Karl D. Butler, *Brigham Young: The New York Years* (Provo, Utah, 1982). Also useful are S. Dilworth Young, *"Here is Brigham": Brigham Young—the Years to 1844* (Salt Lake City, 1964); Mary Van Sickle Wait, *Brigham Young in Cayuga County, 1813–1829* (Ithaca, New York, 1964); J. Sheldon Fisher, "Brigham Young as a Mendon Craftsman: A Study in Historical Archeology," *New York History* 51 (October 1980), 431–447; Rebecca Cornwall and Richard F. Palmer, "The Religious and Family Background of Brigham Young," *BYU Studies,* 18 (Spring 1978), 286–310; and James A. Little, "Biography of Lorenzo Dow Young," *Utah Historical Quarterly,* 14 (1946), 25–132.

For Brigham Young's activities during the years immediately following his conversion to Mormonism, an important primary source is "Manuscript History of Brigham Young," Elden Jay Watson, ed. (Salt Lake City, 1968). This autobiographical narrative originally published in 1863 in the *Millennial Star*, a church periodical, primarily covers Young's activities from 1832 to August 1844. James B. Allen and Malcolm R. Thorp's "The Mission of the Twelve to England 1840–41: Mormon Apostles and the Working Classes," [*BYU Studies*, 15 (Summer 1975), 499–526] is useful in discussing the activities of Young during his mission to England.

A number of works discuss Brigham Young and the Mormon leadership crisis following Joseph Smith's death in 1844. These include D. Michael Quinn, "The Mormon Succession Crisis of 1844," *BYU Studies*, 16 (Winter 1976), 187–233. Two works by Ronald K. Esplin that examine Young's consolidation of power during this crucial period are "Brigham Young and the Power of the Apostleship: Defending the Kingdom Through Prayer, 1844–1845," in *Sidney B. Sperry Symposium: A Sesquicentennial Look at Church History, January 26, 1980* (Provo, Utah, Church Educational System, 1980), 102–122, and "Joseph, Brigham and the Twelve: A Succession of Continuity," *BYU Studies*, 21 (Summer 1981), 301–341. Linda K. Newell and Valeen Tippetts Avery have examined the all-important relationship between Brigham Young and Joseph Smith's family, particularly with his widow Emma, in *Mormon Enigma: Emma Hale Smith* (New York, 1984). Also see their earlier article, "The Lion and the Lady: Brigham Young and Emma Smith," *Utah Historical Quarterly* 48 (Winter 1980), 81–97. For an informative overview of the various groups opposed to Brigham Young, see Dale L. Morgan, "A Bibliography of the Churches of the Dispersion," *Western Humanities Review* 7 (Winter, Spring, Summer, 1953).

Activities and relationships within Brigham Young's changing, complex family have been examined by a number of writers. Particularly valuable are three works by Dean Jessee. These include "Brigham Young's Family," *BYU Studies*, 18 (Spring 1978), 311–327; "Brigham Young's Family: The Wilderness Years," *BYU Studies*, 19 (Summer 1979), 474–499;

and *Letters of Brigham Young to His Sons* (Salt Lake City, 1974). The latter work contains complete typescript copies of all the letters Young wrote to his sons from 1854 until his death in 1877 and is thus a most valuable primary source. Also insightful are family recollections written by two daughters. These are Susa Young Gates, in collaboration with Leah D. Widtsoe, *The Life Story of Brigham Young* (New York, 1930), and Clarissa Young Spencer and Mabel Harmer, *Brigham Young at Home* (Salt Lake City, 1947). The highly favorable recollections of Gates and Spencer can be contrasted with the more critical account of Ann Eliza Webb, Young's dissident ex-wife, who wrote *Wife No. 19, or the Story of a Life in Bondage* (Hartford, Conn., 1875). Extremely valuable are the Susa Young Gates papers in the Utah State Historical Society, which provide revealing insights concerning relationships within the Young family not found elsewhere. Four useful secondary accounts focusing on four different wives are Susa Young Gates, "From Impulsive Girl to Patient Wife: Lucy Bigelow Young," *Utah Historical Quarterly* 45 (Summer 1977), 270–288; Mary Cable, "She Who Shall Be Nameless," *American Heritage*, 16 (February 1965), 50–55, which deals with Augusta Adams; Irving Wallace, *The Twenty Seventh Wife* (New York, 1961), focusing on Ann Eliza Webb; and Maureen Ursenbach Beecher, "The Eliza Enigma: The Life and Legend of Eliza R. Snow," in *Essays on the American West, 1974–75* (Charles Redd Monographs in Western History, Provo, Utah, 1976).

Young's attitudes toward and relationship with women in general is discussed in two articles by Jill Mulvey Derr, "Woman's Place in Brigham Young's World," *BYU Studies*, 18 (Spring 1978), 377–395, and "Eliza R. Snow and the Woman Question," *BYU Studies*, 16 (Winter 1976), 250–264. The Mormon practice of polygamy has been carefully examined by Lawrence Foster, *Religion and Sexuality: Three American Communal Experiments of the Nineteenth Century* (New York, 1981). Also see Kimball Young, *Isn't One Wife Enough?* (New York, 1954), and Louis J. Kern, *An Ordered*

Love: Sex Roles and Sexuality in Victorian Utopias—the Shakers, the Mormons, and Oneida Community (Chapel Hill, North Carolina, 1981).

Brigham Young's role in the migration to and settlement of the Great Basin is discussed in a number of works. Particularly informative is Ronald K. Esplin, "A Place Prepared: Joseph, Brigham and the Quest for Promised Refuge in the West," *Journal of Mormon History,* 9 (1982), 85–111. For the events surrounding the formation of the Mormon Battalion, see W. Ray Luce, "The Mormon Battalion: A Historical Accident?" *Utah Historical Quarterly,* 42 (Winter 1974), 27–38, and John F. Yurtinus, " 'Here is one Man Who Will Not Go, Dam um': Recruiting the Mormon Battalion in Iowa Territory," *BYU Studies,* 21 (Fall 1981), 475–487. The activities of Young's 1847 pilot pioneer company is vividly described in Hal Knight and Stanley B. Kimball's *111 Days to Zion* (Salt Lake City, 1978). The standard account on Mormon settlement in the Great Basin is Milton R. Hunter, *Brigham Young, the Colonizer* (Independence, Mo., 1940). Also see Eugene E. Campbell, "Brigham Young's Outer Cordon—A Reappraisal," *Utah Historical Quarterly* 41 (Summer 1973), 221–253; Herbert E. Bolton, "The Mormons and the Opening of the Great West," *Utah Genealogical and Historical Magazine,* 17 (1926), 40–72; and Richard L. Jensen, "Brigham Young and the Immigrants," lecture presented to the Sons of the Utah Pioneers, Salt Lake City, Utah, 1983 (unpublished paper).

Brigham Young's qualities as a leader and how he related to and influenced his followers is discussed in a number of works. See Gordon Irving "Encouraging the Saints: Brigham Young's Annual Tours of the Mormon Settlements," *Utah Historical Quarterly,* 45 (Summer 1977), 233–251; Leonard J. Arrington and Ronald K. Esplin, "Building a Commonwealth: The Secular Leadership of Brigham Young," *Utah Historical Quarterly,* 45 (Summer 1977), 216–232; Philip A. M. Taylor, "Early Mormon Loyalty and the Leadership of Brigham Young," *Utah Historical Quarterly,* 30 (1962), 103–

132; Ronald W. Walker, "Raining Pitchforks: Brigham Young as Preacher," *Sunstone*, 8 (May–June 1983), 4–9.

Several studies deal with Brigham Young's interaction with others in Mormonism's ruling elite. Recent biographies of four Mormon apostles are particularly enlightening. These are Leonard J. Arrington's *Charles C. Rich: Mormon General and Western Frontiersman* (Provo, Utah, 1974); Samuel W. Taylor, *The Kingdom or Nothing: The Life of John Taylor, Militant Mormon* (New York, 1976); Stanley B. Kimball, *Heber C. Kimball: Mormon Patriarch and Pioneer* (Urbana, Illinois, 1981); and Gene A. Sessions, *Mormon Thunder: A Documentary History of Jedediah Morgan Grant* (Urbana, Illinois, 1982). For the turbulent relationship between Young and a fifth apostle, Orson Pratt, see Gary James Bergera, "The Orson Pratt—Brigham Young Controversies: Conflict within the Quorums, 1853 to 1868," *Dialogue: A Journal of Mormon Thought* 8 (Summer 1980), 7–49. This can be contrasted with Stanley B. Kimball, "Brigham and Heber," *BYU Studies*, 18 (Spring 1978), 396–409, which deals with the much more positive relationship between the Mormon leader and Heber C. Kimball. Also important are two studies that examine Young's relationships with John D. Lee and Orrin Porter Rockwell, a rough frontier type who served as a marshall and deputy sheriff. See Juanita Brooks, *John D. Lee* (Glendale, California, 1972), and Harold Schindler, *Orrin Porter Rockwell: Man of God, Son of Thunder* (Salt Lake City, 1966). Young's dealings with Joseph Morris, a dissident Mormon who directly opposed him, are discussed in C. Le Roy Anderson, *For Christ Will Come Tomorrow: The Saga of the Morrisites* (Logan, Utah 1982). For Young's handling of another dissident Mormon group, the Godbeites, see Ronald W. Walker, "The Commencement of the Godbeite Protest: Another View," *Utah Historical Quarterly*, 42 (Summer, 1974), 216–244.

Brigham Young's relationship toward the American Indians is considered in a number of works. See Gustive O.

Larson, "Brigham Young and the Indians," in *The American West: An Appraisal* (Santa Fe, New Mexico, 1962), Robert G. Ferris, ed. Also see Lawrence G. Coates, "Brigham Young and Mormon Indian Policies: The Formative Years, 1836–1851," *BYU Studies*, 18 (Spring 1978), 428–452, and Floyd A. O'Neil and Stanford J. Layton, "Of Pride and Politics: Brigham Young as Indian Superintendent," *Utah Historical Quarterly*, 46 (Summer 1978), 236–250. Also useful are Howard A. Christy, "Open Hand and Mailed Fist: Mormon-Indian Relations in Utah, 1847–52," *Utah Historical Quarterly*, 46 (Summer 1978), 216–35; Juanita Brooks, "Indian Relations on the Mormon Frontier," *Utah Historical Quarterly*, 12 (January–April 1944), 1–48; Dale L. Morgan, "The Administration of Indian Affairs in Utah," *Pacific Historical Review*, 17 (November 1948), 383–409. Brigham Young's generally negative approach toward blacks is considered in Newell G. Bringhurst, "The Mormons and Slavery—A Closer Look," *Pacific Historical Review*, 50 (August 1981), 329–338, and *Saints, Slaves and Blacks: The Changing Place of Blacks Within Mormonism* (Westport, Conn., 1981).

Relations between Brigham Young's followers and non-Mormon outsiders, particularly the federal government, are examined in a large number of studies. Particularly useful are Gustive O. Larson, *The "Americanization" of Utah for Statehood* (San Marino, Calif., 1971); E. B. Long, *The Saints and the Union* (Urbana, Ill., 1981); and Norman E. Furnis, *The Mormon Conflict* (New Haven, 1960). Also see George U. Hubberd, "Abraham Lincoln as Seen by the Mormons," *Utah State Historical Quarterly*, 31 (Spring 1963), 91–108; Larry Schweikart, "The Mormon Connection: Lincoln, the Saints, and the Crisis of Equality," *Western Humanities Review*, 34 (Winter 1980), 1–22; and Thomas G. Alexander, "Federal Authority versus Polygamic Theocracy: James B. McKean and the Mormons, 1870–1875," *Dialogue: A Journal of Mormon Thought* 1 (Autumn 1966), 85–100. The most unfortunate Mormon incident involving non-Mormons, namely the

Mountain Meadows Massacre, has been carefully and incisively examined in Juanita Brooks, *The Mountain Meadows Massacre* (Norman, Okla., 1952).

Brigham Young's business-economic activities are discussed in David James Croft, "The Private Business Activities of Brigham Young 1847–1877," *Journal of the West*, 16 (October 1977), 36–51, and August C. Bolino, "Brigham Young as Entreprenuer," *American Journal of Economics and Sociology*, 18 (January 1959), 181–192. Also see Leonard J. Arrington, *Great Basin Kingdom: An Economic History of the Latter-day Saints* (Cambridge, Mass., 1958).

The ways in which Brigham Young came across to outsiders visiting the Great Basin have been examined in a number of works. These include Horace Greeley, *An Overland Journey from New York to San Francisco in the Summer 1859* (New York, 1863); Richard F. Burton, *The City of the Saints* (New York, 1862); Mark Twain, *Roughing It* (New York, 1872); Jules Remy and Julius Brenchley, *A Journey to Great Salt Lake City*, 2 vols. (London, 1861); William Chandless, *A Visit to Salt Lake City* (London, 1857); and James Bradley Thayer, *A Western Journey with Mr. Emerson* (New York, 1872). A secondary account that carefully analyzes the observations of Richard Burton is Fawn M. Brodie, "Sir Richard Burton: Exceptional Observer of the Mormon Scene," *Utah Historical Quarterly*, 38 (Fall 1970), 295–311.

Several enlightening articles deal with other aspects of Brigham Young's life and personality. These include Lester E. Bush, Jr., "Brigham Young in Life and Death," *Journal of Mormon History*, 5 (1978), 79–103, which traces the Mormon leader's health, varied illnesses, and circumstances surrounding his death. A related article is Linda P. Wilcox, "The Imperfect Science: Brigham Young on Medical Doctors," *Dialogue: A Journal of Mormon Thought*, 12 (Fall 1979), 26–36. Leonard J. Arrington "The Settlement of the Brigham Young Estate, 1877–1879," *Pacific Historical Review*, 21 (February 1952), 1–20] examines the events and controversy surrounding this event following the Mormon leader's death. Two essays examining Brigham Young's lasting legacy are Eugene Campbell, "Brigham Young: Paradoxical Prophet," paper presented at the 1980 Mormon History Association Meeting at Canandaigua, New York, in 1980 (unpublished paper), and Jan Shipps, "Brigham Young and His Times: A Continuing Force in Mormonism," *Journal of the West,* 23 (January 1984), 48–54.

In order to fully appreciate the motives and activities of Brigham Young, it is necessary to understand the Mormon religion that he was a part of and helped to mold. Particularly useful are Leonard J. Arrington and Davis Bitton, *The Mormon Experience: A History of the Latter-day Saints* (New York, 1979), and James B. Allen and Glen Leonard, *The Story of the Latter-day Saints* (Salt Lake City, 1976), which together and from different perspectives provide an excellent overview of Mormonism as it has developed over the past 150 years. Also enlightening are: Klaus J. Hansen, *Mormonism and the American Experience* (Chicago, 1981); Jan Shipps, *Mormonism: The Story of a New Religious Tradition* (Urbana, Illinois, 1985); Thomas F. O'Dea, *The Mormons* (Chicago, 1957); Nels Anderson, *Desert Saints: The Mormon Frontier in Utah* (Chicago, 1942); and Wallace Stegner, *The Gathering of Zion: The Story of the Mormon Trail* (New York, 1964). Two multi-volume studies written and/or compiled by Brigham H. Roberts, Mormonism's greatest historian, provide useful documentary information relative to Brigham Young and the Mormons. These include his *A Comprehensive History of the Church of Jesus Christ of Latter-day Saints: Century I,* 6 vols. (Salt Lake City, 1930), and his edited *History of the Church of Jesus Christ of Latter-day Saints,* 7 vols. (Salt Lake City, 1902–32). Finally, in order to fully appreciate Brigham Young and Mormonism generally, the elusive personality of Joseph Smith, Mormonism's founder, needs to be considered. Three varied works that examine Smith are: Fawn M. Brodie, *No Man Knows My History: The Life of Joseph Smith the*

Mormon Prophet (New York, 1945); Donna Hill, *Joseph Smith: The First Mormon* (New York, 1977); and Richard L. Bushman, *Joseph Smith and the Beginnings of Mormonism* (Urbana, Illinois, 1984). Any careful examination of Mormonism should also include a thorough reading of Latter-day Saint scriptural writings. These include the *Book of Mormon, Doctrine and Covenants,* and the *Pearl of Great Price,* compiled by Joseph Smith and which the Mormons accept as holy scripture on a par with the Bible.

A large body of literature exists that considers the larger American social-intellectual environment in which Mormonism developed. David Brion Davis ["The New England Origins of Mormonism," *New England Quarterly,* 27 (June 1953), 147–168] attempts to place Mormonism within the New England Puritan tradition. The seminal work on that larger tradition is Perry Miller, *The New England Mind: The Seventeenth Century* (New York, 1939). Also see Edwin Scott Guastad, *The Great Awakening in New England* (Chicago, 1968). Any study of the New York environment in which Mormonism actually emerged should start with the classic study of Whitney R. Cross, *The Burned-Over District: The Social and Intellectual History of Enthusiastic Religion in Western New York: 1800–1850* (New York, 1950). Also see Bernard A. Weisberger, *They Gathered at the River—The Story of the Great Revivalists and their Impact upon Religion in America* (Boston, 1958). Lorenzo Dow's *The Dealings of God, Man, and the Devil as Exemplified in the Life, Experience, and Travels of Lorenzo Dow* (Cincinnati, 1858) considers the Methodist itinerant who had an important influence on the Young family during their pre-Mormon years. Three general examinations of religion within American society at large during the nineteenth century are Sydney E. Ahlstrom, *A Religious History of the American People* vol. I (New Haven, Conn., 1972); Martin E. Marty, *A Nation of Behavers* (Chicago 1980); and Winthrop S. Hudson, *Religion in America* (New York, 1965).

Likewise, a large body of writings considers historical

trends within the American Western frontier environment where Mormonism flourished and expanded. Two monographs which consider Frederick Jackson Turner's so-called "Frontier Thesis" relative to the Mormon experience but that arrive at quite different conclusions are Alexander Evanoff, "The Turner Thesis and Mormon Beginnings in New York and Utah," *Utah Historical Quarterly*, 33 (Spring 1965), 157–173, and Davis Bitton, "A Re-Evaluation of the 'Turner Thesis and Mormon Beginnings. . .'" *Utah Historical Quarterly*, 34 (Fall, 1966), 326–333. An important work that carefully examines the Turner thesis relative to the total American frontier experience is Ray A. Billington, *American Frontier Heritage* (New York, 1967). Also see Henry Nash Smith, *Virgin Land: The American West as Symbol and Myth* (Cambridge, Mass., 1950). For a highly readable account of American migration westward during the mid-nineteenth century, see Bernard De Voto, *The Year of Decision 1846* (Boston, 1942). The forces of Manifest Destiny, which helped to encourage that migration, have been dealt with in Norman Graebner, *Empire on the Pacific: A Study in American Continental Expansion* (New York, 1955); Frederick Merk, *Manifest Destiny and Mission in American History: A Reinterpretation* (New York, 1963); and Albert Katz Weinberg, *Manifest Destiny: A Study of Nationalist Expansionism in American History* (Baltimore, 1935). An excellent treatment of migration along the overland trail is John D. Unruh, *The Plains Across: The Overland Emigrants and the Trans-Mississippi West, 1840–1860* (New York, 1981). Among the forces confronting the Mormons along with other western Americans were frontier violence and lawlessness, which are examined in W. Eugene Hollon, *Frontier Violence: Another Look* (New York, 1974). Also see David Grimsted, "Rioting in Its Jacksonian Setting," *American Historical Review*, 77 (April 1972), 361–397. Racist ideas and practices, which ingrained themselves into Mormonism itself and were a part of the larger frontier environment, are considered in Eugene H. Berwanger, *The Frontier Against Slavery: Western Anti-Negro Prejudice and the Slavery Extension Controversy* (Urbana, Ill., 1967). Particularly relevant to the Mormon experience is Klaus Hansen, "The Millennium, the West, and Race in the Antebellum Mind," *Western Historical Quarterly*, 3 (October 1972), 373–390. A good introduction to Indian-white relations along the shifting frontier is Wilcomb E. Washburn, *The Indian in America* (New York, 1975). The best interpretive study of the mining frontier that the Mormons confronted is Rodman W. Paul, *Mining Frontiers of the Far West, 1848–1880* (New York, 1963). For developments in transportation that greatly affected the Mormons, see Oscar O. Winther, *The Transportation Frontier: Trans-Misssissippi West 1865–1890* (New York, 1964). The classic study of the Great Plains where Mormon Great Basin success might have had an influence is Walter Prescott Webb, *The Great Plains* (Boston, 1931).

Finally, for an overview of the total frontier experience, three works are useful. The first is the classic standard work of Ray Allen Billington, *Westward Expansion: A History of the American Frontier*. First published in 1949, it is still in print and currently in its fifth edition (New York, 1982) with Martin Ridge as the coauthor. A second general history is Frederick Merk, *History of the Westward Movement* (New York, 1978), which, along with Robert V. Hine, *The American West: An Interpretive History* (Boston, 1973), examines the Western-frontier experience from two rather different perspectives.

Index